ASTAIRE & ROGERS

What so delicious as a just and firm encounter of two, in a thought, in a feeling? How beautiful, on their approach to this beating heart, the steps and forms of the gifted and the true!

Ralph Waldo Emerson, 'Friendship' (1841)

Astaire
&
Rogers

EDWARD GALLAFENT

COLUMBIA UNIVERSITY PRESS

NEW YORK

Columbia University Press
Publishers Since 1893
New York   Chichester, West Sussex

First published in North America in 2002 by Columbia University Press
in the Film and Culture series, edited by John Belton

Library of Congress Cataloging-in-Publication Data

Gallafent, Edward
    Astaire & Rogers / Edward Gallafent.
        p. cm.—(Film and Culture)
    Originally published: Moffat, Dumfriesshire, Scotland : Cameron & Hollis, 2000.
    Includes bibliographical references and index.
    ISBN 0-231-12626-3 (cloth : alk. paper)

    1. Astaire, Fred. 2. Rogers, Ginger, 1911- 3. Dancers—United States—Biography.
4. Dance—United States—History—20th Century. 5. Musical films—United States—
History and criticism. I. Title: Astaire and Rogers. II. Series.

GV1785.A3 G35 2002
792.8'028'092—dc21

                                                                        2001055262

                                        ∞

c 10 9 8 7 6 5 4 3 2 1

A Movie Book

First published in Britain in 2000 by
Cameron & Hollis
PO Box 1, Moffat,
Dumfriesshire DG10 9SU, Scotland

Edited by Ian Cameron and Jill Hollis

Designed by Ian Cameron

Stills reproduced by courtesy of
BFI Stills, Posters and Designs, Columbia
MGM, Paramount, RKO Radio, United Artists,
Universal-International

Printed and bound in Britain by
MPG Books Ltd, Bodmin

CONTENTS

INTRODUCTION
ASTAIRE & ROGERS, FRED & GINGER

Of all the images conveying the richness of the film world of the 1930s, that of Fred Astaire and Ginger Rogers dancing is one of the happiest. Endlessly represented in motion, whether they are embarking on a number, dancing through it or bringing it to its triumphant conclusion, this star couple seems to exude a sense of ease, or accessibility, even an intimacy – we can feel at home with them. It is perhaps not entirely a matter of chance that among the famous star couples of the 'thirties and 'forties, they are the only pair (still) popularly known by their first names. We can refer to them as Fred and Ginger where we cannot quite say Katherine (Hepburn) and Spencer (Tracy), possibly still less Humphrey (Bogart) and Lauren (Bacall).

I would not for the world deny that this deliciousness, this sense of the privilege of unimpeded access to such gifts and such beauty, is a vital element in our response. But it may have its cost. The brilliance of the couple's song and dance can dominate our way of thinking about them, which has perhaps encouraged a tendency to brush aside consideration of what takes place in the rest of each film. The paradox may be that the concentration of genius at work in the numbers – with music and lyrics by Irving Berlin, Dorothy Fields, George and Ira Gershwin, Jerome Kern and Cole Porter – creates a glow of such brilliance as to blind us to anything else. Take the case of Arlene Croce, a distinguished choreographer and author of *The Fred Astaire and Ginger Rogers Book* (Galahad Books, 1972), the pioneering account of the couple's ten films together. Writing about a famous and memorable duet, the song and dance to Cole Porter's 'Night and Day' in *The Gay Divorcée*, Croce calls it 'a movie in itself', and claims that, apart from the Astaire-Rogers dances, the rest of the film 'falls away in retrospect'. Elsewhere she writes of *Roberta* that it 'came as close to plotlessness as that ideal Astaire-Rogers musical we all like to think that they should have made' (Croce, p.83). But would such a thing be desirable or even tolerable? We might believe that this is what we want for as long as we are watching a dance sequence – we feel that we do not wish such dance to end, returning us to a greyer world. However, even dance compilations such as the MGM *That's Entertainment* series acknowledge the need not only for spaces between the numbers, but also for something to fill them: they include connecting material about the conditions in which the great musicals were made. This issue is contained in the Astaire and Rogers films themselves, and is answered in various ways, through the density of the relation between the dance and what provokes it (or what is prevented, interrupted, or superseded by it). One might say that the dance sequences answer questions raised elsewhere and raise other questions which it will be the business of the film to answer. For Astaire and Rogers, their dramatic and comedic scenes, and the context of their supporting players, play an inescapable role in defining what their dance can be – a way of avoiding or extending words, and what it cannot be – something that goes on forever.

There have been valuable studies (such as Rick Altman's *The American Film Musical*, Indiana University Press, 1987) that analyse the broader categories through which the genre of the musical can be understood, but much less attention has been paid to exploring the detail, and especially the non–musical detail, of these films. My aim in this book is to give an account of that detail and to examine how the Astaire and Rogers films, which were produced and originally viewed as a series, relate to one another. Other writers have dealt valuably with the context in which they were produced, whether this is understood as the Hollywood Studio System or the wider social and cultural history of the USA, and I do not claim to contribute to accounts of the musical as a genre. To those who frown here, I may say that I make no argument for the superiority of this (or any other) approach, but I hope it leads to an understanding of the films to which we might not otherwise have access and for which there is inevitably less space in contextual studies; doing justice to one perspective has to involve minimising another. I take some comfort in Henry James's words to William James: 'The whole of anything is never told; you can only take what groups together' (F.O. Matthiessen, *The James Family*, Knopf, 1947, pp.318-319).

As far as other film-making of the time is concerned, I depend here on readings by others of the greatest Hollywood films made in the 'thirties and after that address the subjects of partnership and marriage. I am particularly indebted to the work of Stanley Cavell in his *Pursuits of Happiness: The Hollywood Comedy of Remarriage* (Harvard University Press, 1981) and *Contesting Tears: The Hollywood Melodrama of the Unknown Woman* (University of Chicago Press, 1996). Looking over this study, I notice that the films I have covered were made in the same time-span as those that are the subject of readings in *Pursuits of Happiness*. The earliest film dealt with by Cavell is *It Happened One Night* (1934), and the rest bunch in the late 'thirties and early 'forties, the years of *The Awful Truth*, *Bringing Up Baby*, *The Philadelphia Story*, *His Girl Friday* and *The Lady Eve;* he also engages with a single exception to that period, a film made in 1949 by an established star couple – *Adam's Rib*, the sixth of the nine Hepburn and Tracy films. Of the 28 films discussed at length in this book, 19 fall into the 1933–41 period, and I conclude with another film of 1949, *The Barkleys of Broadway*, the tenth and final Astaire and Rogers film.

The first two chapters deal with the nine films made by the couple at RKO between 1933 and 1939, and set out to challenge the presumption that their plotting is so formulaic or simplistic that tact requires us not to scrutinise it too closely. Given that dance numbers take up a fraction of the running time of the films – about 30 minutes of the 100 or so in most of them – the producers, directors and writers, as well as the stars, must not only have been interested in the quality of the rest of the material, but have believed that it was able to give context and thus meaning to the dances. The audience was intended to take pleasure both in the songs and dances and in what came before, after and between them.

Publicity stills. Rogers on the set of Fifth Avenue Girl. *Astaire in top hat and tails, but not white tie.*

What has affected our viewing of single films has also obscured our sense of the whole cycle: concentration on the dance numbers has caused critics to lose track of the shape of the series, or rather to be uninterested in it, and to be content with terms like 'remake' and 'formula', evidently assuming that while individual films might be variously viewed as successful or not, there was certainly no point in even speculating that they might have a coherent meaning as a cycle. (This has historically had the effect that the one film to be directed by an established *auteur*, George Stevens's *Swing Time*, has been given an attention and respect largely denied to the others.) In successive films, considerations of the couple's situation operate which are not marginal, or accidental, or *post factum* responses to box-office returns, but show a deliberate interest in the changing possibilities for their world as the cycle developed and then drew to its close. This view might be thought of as giving the films back to at least some of the Hollywood professionals who shaped them. A list of the major contributors would include, after Astaire and Rogers, Pandro Berman, who produced seven of the nine, Mark Sandrich who directed five of them, Allan Scott who co-wrote seven of the scripts, and David Abel and Robert de Grasse, the directors of photography responsible between them for seven of the films, as well as the various designers of their sets and costumes. It would be invidious not to mention here also Hermes Pan, who was variously credited but took, with Astaire, a central role in conceiving the dance throughout the cycle.

What I claim for these films – or what, when viewed as whole films in the order of their production, they claim for themselves – is simply that they know what they are doing and do it intelligently. This is said not in a spirit of opposition to those who have written so expertly on the music and the dances, among them Arlene Croce and John Mueller in his invaluable *Astaire Dancing* (Hamish Hamilton, 1986), nor to detract from the sense of the couple's grace and finesse that is so widely shared, but rather to contextualise and so deepen appreciation of it. The song and dance are as wonderful as ever, the films more successful as films than we may have allowed.

The second part of this study looks at the films made separately by Rogers and Astaire in the early 1940s, between their last RKO musical, *The Story of Vernon and Irene Castle*, and the movement into colour filming for both of them in the mid 'forties – relatively obscure periods in their respective careers. (That is, the films are, with a few exceptions, fairly obscure for us today, but it is worth remembering that in the 'forties, Rogers was generally a bigger and more commercial star than Astaire.) These films can be read as revealing a consciousness of the pair's films of the 'thirties, as they continue to address some of their preoccupations while reinflecting them, admitting to change. For Astaire, this involves matters of professional performance weighed against emotional intensity and, arguably, a progressive loss of confidence in his relation to the figure who offers herself as his potential partner. For Rogers, it involves posing her solitariness against a very different world from that of the Astaire-Rogers musicals. The difference might be defined, not so much by the absence of song and dance, as by

Astaire with Grorge Gershwin on the set of Shall We Dance *and enjoying a joke with choreographer Hermes Pan.*

the presence of family. Many of the men who seek to win her are the sons of powerful fathers, and the films involve for the man the subject of being a son, and for the woman what it means to be a mother. There are also questions of how the conditions of the musical continue to echo, or to be invoked, in Rogers's work. Such continuities are also reflected in the ongoing involvement of figures such as Mark Sandrich, Allan Scott and Robert de Grasse in the careers of Astaire and Rogers. The work of the two stars is linked partly through class, of what it means to be an ordinary (democratic, working) American as opposed to an American aristocrat. These subjects receive a particular inflection in the films made by both Rogers and Astaire which directly invoke World War II.

It could be said of the early 'forties work that it explores the subjects of the films that the couple made together, while mainly avoiding direct reference to their partnership. My final chapter looks briefly at the later 'forties work and then at two films that deal with the partnership directly – *Easter Parade* by invoking it, and *The Barkleys of Broadway* by reconstituting it – and considers the significance of having done this a decade after the conclusion of the RKO cycle.

I have not tried to provide a survey of the entire careers of the two stars. Ginger Rogers made 73 feature films, Fred Astaire 40. In my opinion, the couple are best served by detailed discussion of a limited range of work in detail, and I have chosen to concentrate on the films they made together, and to link their RKO partnership to their last film, *The Barkleys of Broadway*, by looking at their separate work in the interim. I have thus excluded Rogers's extensive early filming before *Flying Down to Rio*, and Astaire's one early film, *Dancing Lady* (Robert K. Leonard, 1933), as well as work dating from after their final collaboration in 1949. Within the period of the RKO musicals, the pattern evidently was that while Astaire choreographed and rehearsed the dances for the next film, mostly with Hermes Pan, Rogers was employed by the studio making (usually) more modestly budgeted productions. Between their musicals, Astaire made only one other film, *A Damsel in Distress*, in 1937, while Rogers made twelve. Of these, I have discussed only *Vivacious Lady*, made just as the RKO cycle was drawing to its close but with links to Rogers's immediately following work, and *Stage Door* for its relationship to *Shall We Dance*.

On the set of Shall We Dance: *a focus-puller checks Astaire's position, and Rogers adjusts her make-up.*

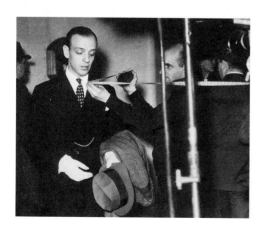

Before looking at *Flying Down to Rio*, I wish to return to my starting point – the naming of Astaire and Rogers as Fred and Ginger. The films themselves encourage us to think of the names of their stars. Astaire's first film, *Dancing Lady*, made at MGM, is a backstage musical in which he appears as himself, credited as Fred Astaire. Fred Ayres, the Astaire character's name in *Flying Down to Rio*, thinly disguises and thus reveals, or offers, the actor's name. Less immediately obvious is the extension of such hinting to Rogers and its occurrence further into the cycle, when characters are given names, or use contractions of names, which seem to mimic the syllabification of Fred and Ginger. Thus we find that Fred and Honey (*Flying Down to Rio*) are followed by Guy and Mimi (*The Gay Divorcée*), Huck and Lizzie (*Roberta*), 'Bake' and Sherry (*Follow the Fleet*). In *Top Hat* the pattern is interrupted by reversing it: Jerry and Dale. Afterwards, as the cycle moves through stages of disintegration towards its close, the names seem to echo this: in John and Penny (*Swing Time*) the convention is observed, but in Pete/Peter/Petrov and Linda (*Shall We Dance*) it is beginning to falter. It has clearly dissolved in Tony and Amanda (*Carefree*) and is unavailable in the biopic that closes the cycle, where the names are determined by the source material. It may be worth adding that such patterns do not appear in the films that Rogers and Astaire made after 1939, other than to resurface for the final bow: Josh and Dinah (in *The Barkleys of Broadway*).

I think that this rhyming is more than just a kind of fun, or play. It acknowledges the connection of the screen roles with one another, giving a hint that the parts played by the pair are variations on a concealed root – Fred and Ginger. Once the special consistency, the very particular potential of a cycle of a number of films built around a star couple is established, it is possible to see its inverse. This is the dissolution of the possibilities of the partnership and of the world that sustained it reflected in the breakdown of the rhyming, until the happy re-establishment of the link for the last performance.

NOTE ON SOURCES

The titles of Chapters One and Two are Shakespearean: the first from *As You Like It*, Act I Sc. III, and the second from the speech by 'Time: the Chorus' which introduces Act IV of *The Winter's Tale*.

In the early 1940s Ernst Lubitsch put forward to 20th Century-Fox 'a project with Ginger Rogers called *A Self-Made Cinderella* [that] didn't get made' (*see* Scott Eyman, *Ernst Lubitsch: Laughter in Paradise*, Simon and Schuster, 1993, p.308). These words provide the title of Chapter Three, although the concept of 'the self-made girl' in American culture can be traced back at least to Henry James's story 'Pandora' (1884).

The title of Chapter Four is lifted from the dialogue of *Broadway Melody of 1940* (the George Murphy to the Astaire character): 'Why do you always have to keep changing the steps on me?'

The title of the final chapter is taken from Byron. The fuller version is this:

On with the dance! let joy be unconfined
No sleep till morn, when Youth and Pleasure meet
To chase the glowing Hours with flying feet

Childe Harold's Pilgrimage, canto iii, v. xxii

CHAPTER ONE

COUPLED AND INSEPARABLE:
THE FIRST RKO MUSICALS

FLYING DOWN TO RIO (Thornton Freeland, 1933)

The status of *Flying Down to Rio* as marking the opening of the Astaire-Rogers cycle is purely retrospective: its audience and its producers could not know of the films to come with which we associate it, and if conditions had arisen to prevent the making of another movie with these two actors, there would be no light thrown on it by the rest of the cycle. The question, then, is what made audiences think that they might like to see this pair on screen again? This is answered not simply by the image of the couple dancing, but also by what the film tells us about this particular dancing couple.

The premise around which *Flying Down to Rio* is constructed – the attraction between a wealthy blond North American man (Gene Raymond) and an aristocratic Brazilian girl (Dolores Del Rio) – does not involve Astaire and Rogers, who are not its leading stars. The plot that develops amounts to no less than the North Americanisation of Brazil, via technology, music and the resolution of the love affair. The Brazilian girl, Belinha De Redenze, finds herself caught between her duty towards her long-anticipated marriage to aristocratic Brazil in the shape of Julio (Raul Roulien), and her passion for American aviator and bandleader Roger. Despite a suggestion to the contrary early in the movie, it is not the girl who does the choosing. The final minute finds the three in a passenger plane, where the 'captain' can perform marriages. Julio gives Belinha and Roger his blessing and then leaves the happy couple to each other by parachuting out.

A sequence about halfway through the film is one of the few in which Astaire and Rogers are allowed – dancing apart – any dramatic business. Its premise is that Fred and Honey, the two members of the band played by Astaire and Rogers, are helping the bandleader to search for Belinha in the streets of Rio. Honey is distracted by the sight of a cookie stand, and this exchange follows:

Honey: Oh Freddie, how do you ask for little tarts in Portuguese?
Fred: Don't heckle me, try the Culbertson system.

(The Culbertson system was a popular technique of bidding in the card game, Contract Bridge.) As Fred speaks, he has spotted Belinha with her duenna, sitting at a table in a smart cafe. He tries to speak to her, is ejected, and lands on the sidewalk in front of the cookie stall, in a sitting position. Honey sits down next to him.

On the street in Flying Down to Rio. *Honey (Rogers) and Fred (Astaire) making entertainment with the locally available talent.*

Honey: Hiya Tarzan. Been having fun?
Fred: Gosh, if you even speak to that girl they throw you out on the sidewalk. Boy, is that class!
Honey: Want a cookie? Take your choice.

The camera's view of the couple is now blocked by the bodies of pedestrians, a reminder of exactly where we are – on the pavement. This scene offers a way of reading a central subject of the movie, one which never quite leaves the films that follow it: the difference between being up in the air and down on the ground.

Butterbass (Eric Blore), Hammerstein (Franklin Pangborn) and Honey await the arrival of Fred in Flying Down to Rio.

There are two invasions of Rio going on here. One is represented by aviation, understood as a form of spectacle and glamour created by money (Roger's personal fortune is mentioned early on), and this forms the background to reading the romance with Belinha. Despite Roger's American image of his own novelty – he describes his wooing of Belinha with the line, 'I'm going to institute some radical changes in your country' – the assurance is that her movement from Julio to Roger represents only a modernisation of the old order, not the crossing of a class line.

The other invading force, represented by Fred and Honey, and tangentially by the other members of the band, has its feet on the ground, recognising 'class' in Belinha and Roger and their world without resentment, even with a certain degree of amusement. Distinctions in the meaning of dress underscore the point. At the posh clubs, Fred and Honey dress apparently like their aristocratic friends, but the tails and the ball gown are professional wear, indicative, as we will see in later movies, of the difference between rehearsal and performance, and so a way of declaring oneself to be at work. (The film begins with a little comedy around uniforms, as the hotel manager's inspection of the pageboys and waitresses is disrupted when one of the latter gives him the eye.) Even the presentation of the characters in the credits sequence touches on this. The five principals are all shown in evening wear, and the shots of the first three billed (Del Rio, Raymond and Roulien) are simple head-and-shoulders portraits. We see the hands of the other two. Fred, in a gesture typical of Astaire's moments of real or feigned embarrassment, is fiddling with his tie, an image clipped from a sequence in which he cannot find anyone to take his top hat and cane at the aviators' club. Honey is preparing herself, polishing her nails. For the aristocrats, their appearance is adequately expressive of their identity. For Fred and Honey, it is costume, which may be acquired, be in need of adjustment, and be discarded.

Consider the final moment of the film in the light of this. As Julio parachutes out of the world of the lovers, we are shown Fred and Honey. They have been saving the day for Belinha's father, a hotel owner, by putting on a show, but it is over and they are sitting down. They are fooling around, trying to look up at the plane, each using one side of a pair of binoculars. They see Julio floating down to earth, and Fred has the final line of the film: 'Gosh, that girl doesn't care who she gets thrown out of what . . .' The reference to his own ejection, or exclusion, reinforces the point that the world of Belinha, Roger and Julio is constructed around a necessity for exclusivity, for confirming the supremacy of the class by throwing people out of places. Compare with this the theme of the one Astaire-Rogers dance number in the film, 'The Carioca', where all the stress is on the inclusivity of desire, on everybody feeling, transmitting and receiving it (a point made overtly in the gags about telepathy with which the sequence starts) so that it can be spontaneously learned and danced by Fred and Honey, and then danced by the couples in the production number. The contrast between 'The Carioca' and the final airborne production number is suggestive. There the marriage of sexual desire and technology is celebrated by an opposite to dance, a spectacle

At the Aviators' Club, Julio (Raoul Roulien) introduces Fred to his Aunt Titia (Blanche Friderici) and his fiancée Belinha (Dolores Del Rio).

of girls strapped and wired to the wings of the planes. The film makes the point that their safety depends on the firmness of these fixings, a reminder that the very condition of being in the air in this way involves the annihilation of a freedom of movement available to those on the ground.

So *Flying Down to Rio* offers us in Astaire and Rogers a couple for whom eating cookies on the pavement represents one kind of good time, a couple for whom the Portuguese language is a problem, a couple with their feet on the ground. I am conscious of the irony, or the surprise, that attaches to speaking of Astaire and Rogers in this way, or through this image. Perhaps it would be proper to say that they are a couple who know that their feet are on the ground at the beginning of the dance and will return there at the end of it. They have, in this movie's imagery, a way of being in the air which is not like flying an aeroplane (it depends neither on technology nor money) and which makes the ordinariness of sitting down together possible, or bearable. They are content to sit because, from their dancing, they – and we – know that they are, or can be, more than this.

THE GAY DIVORCÉE (Mark Sandrich, 1934)

Astaire's career as a musical comedy performer on stage, partnered by his sister Adele, ran from *Over the Top* (first performance November 1917) to *The Band Wagon* (first performance June 1931); Adele Astaire retired with its closing performance in March 1932. In November 1932, Astaire opened in New York in *Gay Divorce*, directed by Howard Lindsay, book by Dwight Taylor, score by Cole Porter. His dancing partners on stage were Claire Luce and later Dorothy Stone. In the summer of 1933, Astaire made *Flying Down to Rio* at RKO, and then starred in the London run of *Gay Divorce*, which opened in November 1933, just before the American premiere of *Flying Down to Rio* (29th December 1933). Astaire tells us in his autobiography that the director Mervyn LeRoy saw *Gay Divorce* in New York but was unable to interest Warner Bros in a film version. Pandro Berman flew to London, saw the show there and confirmed it as the next film in Astaire's RKO contract. (In the course of shooting, the title was changed to *The Gay Divorcée*, but the film was released as *The Gay Divorce* in England.) Thus *The Gay Divorcée* is unique among Astaire-Rogers movies in that it was a filmed version of an established stage hit for Astaire. It is also the first time that Astaire and Rogers appear in principal rather than supporting roles and begins to establish a pattern of Astaire playing a role close to his own life, as a song-and-dance man. In his small first film role, opposite Joan Crawford in *Dancing Lady*, he appears and is credited as playing himself, and one of the changes made from the stage version of *Gay Divorce* was to abandon the identification of his character as a novelist.

In *Flying Down to Rio*, part of the status of Fred and Honey as the supporting couple is expressed in their being presented as old friends and colleagues, so much so that the idea of sexual attachment between them is never explicitly raised, the matter of romance and particularly of a first encounter between lovers being assigned to the principal couple. A defining characteristic of such a couple seems to be that they meet for the first time in the movie, and this will be true of the characters played by Astaire and Rogers in six of their eight following films.

'A third party might spoil this.' Guy (Astaire) with the immobilised Mimi (Rogers) at the beginning of The Gay Divorcée.

The exceptions are *Roberta* and *Follow the Fleet*, where we understand the pair to be meeting again after a period of separation; in both, Astaire and Rogers play alongside another couple who encounter each other for the first time.

In *The Gay Divorcée*, the Astaire character meets the girl played by Rogers for the first time in the second scene of the film. We get there via a prologue which takes place in a restaurant in Paris, in which celebrated song-and-dance man Guy Holden (Astaire) is dining with his friend, English lawyer Egbert Fitzgerald (Edward Everett Horton). Some light foolery takes place, with dolls attached to the fingers of the diners, in tune with the mood of a number, 'Don't Let it Bother You'. A piece of business is now contrived to remind Astaire's character who he is, a matter of lost wallets which requires him to dance, supposedly at first to establish his identity. This turns out to have the not exactly foreseen result that Guy's reluctance melts away. The audience applauds, the management tears up the bill, and the final shot is of Guy sitting down on the dance floor, quite at home.

The first meeting with Mimi Glossop (Rogers) occurs a couple of minutes later (in screen time), after an interlude of comedy involving her aunt, Hortense Ditherwell (Alice Brady), and two exasperated officials. The setting is a customs hall in England, and Hortense has left her niece alone, having unknowingly tucked the flowing end of Mimi's gown into a trunk, which she has then locked. When Guy ambles past, the immobilised Mimi is calling for the porter. The dress has pulled up to slightly above the knee, and the director, Mark Sandrich, uses the image to prompt our awareness of the voyeuristic possibilities of the scene. We understand that Guy wants to help, but he recognises the situation as a delicate one. Of course, he is also responding to the opportunity to help this pretty girl out of trouble, to meet her in circumstances flattering to himself.

But he cannot strike the right note. Meeting coolness from Mimi, he takes refuge in something intended to be witty but which emerges as flippant. Rather than calling Hortense and thus ending the moment, he tells her, 'You know, a third party might spoil this.' Still wishing that she should be grateful to nobody but him, he then tries direct action, his excuse being that what they are doing is like a child's game: 'I pulled a cat out of a well once, when I was a boy.' He tears the dress. Mimi starts to walk away in the coat that he has offered to cover her, and we see him from behind as he moves off in pursuit. In the next shot, he is suddenly in front of her, blocking her way; in its unlikeliness and grace, this resembles a dance move, and will be reprised as exactly that in 'Night and Day'. He now faces her with the only line of the sequence not imbued with flippant self-consciousness, 'Please forgive me', but she avoids answering. She moves away again. He accidentally catches the coat in a swing-gate, so that it falls, and she must pick it up. As she leaves, he looks contemplative – how did it all go so wrong?

The contrast between this and the Paris restaurant sequence should be clear enough. Faced with a mundane problem, Guy is able to prove his identity, and prove to himself by his dance that everybody knows who he is. Faced with this girl, he loses that identity – one could say that he can find no way of dancing with her. He tells her lamely, 'I'm an American too', but does not divulge his name; later on it will be implied that she has never heard of Guy's fame in America.

The matter of their identities is still unresolved at their next meeting. We are in the country – Guy has spotted Mimi in London traffic, and there is a car chase until he corners her. She threatens to drive at his car with hers: 'the air will be full of fenders'. She does not use his name, but he works it into the conversation indirectly – he forgets to ask hers, and when she is driving away, she provides it in a less than romantic shout. He offers her marriage as if it were one of the potions, or props, in his wicker box of cocktails, and she responds by letting the box fall from the running board of her car and smash to pieces.

These scenes of damage have something in common with another, later Hollywood comedy, *Bringing Up Baby* (Howard Hawks, 1938). Both films begin with a sequence in which the central male character is asked to contemplate who and what he is, followed by a meeting with the principal female character which involves tearing her dress and helping to cover up the damage that he has done, and an encounter in which the presence of automobiles leads to the threat or the actuality of bent fenders. Both films acknowledge the sexual attraction between the couple as an explosion of energies that smashes things up – both physical objects and a sense of identity. Both couples now embark on a journey, but their destinations are very different. In Hawks's movie, there is danger and torment to be gone through in the Connecticut woods, before the old order is demolished. For Astaire and Rogers the destination is somewhat different, one that the movie calls Brightburn. (We will see a further set of variations on this theme in *Carefree*.)

The meanings of Brightburn can be summarised as follows:

1) As a seaside resort, it is legitimately a place to have a good time, to meet girls, which is what Egbert tells Guy, and what Sandrich sums up in the first shot of it: a girl emerging from the water.

2) It is also a place for a good time of a less legitimate kind, a weekend with a mistress or a night with a lover – the latter being exactly the scenario that Egbert (as Mimi's lawyer) is organising in a faked version, using a hired co-respondent so that Mimi can obtain a divorce from her husband.

3) It is a place of entertainment, of stages and dance floors for singing and dancing, of performers and audiences, and therefore one where Guy can display his professional talents.

4) As a venue for dance, it also offers something that can replace verbal communication as a way of making sense of the world and of relationships between the sexes.

5) It is at times recognisably a Hollywood sound stage (and our sense of the film need not be disturbed by realising this) the Big White Set in which major production numbers can be staged.

The opening moves of the sequences in Brightburn establish a hierarchy of the different kinds of communication in a place like this. First, Sandrich takes us into a world in which the emphasis is on the possibilities of social dance, with the minor charm of the 'Let's Knock Knees' number in which a girl (played by Betty Grable) vamps Egbert, literally pulling him to his feet and into the dance. This is followed by a sequence that demonstrates Guy's inability to express anything about Mimi in words – 'she's the buzzing of the bees in clover' is an example of it, and even Egbert knows this is not good poetry. And this is followed by a comic set piece, a conversation between Egbert and a waiter played by Eric Blore, which shows that having words at your command does not necessarily help you

Seaside pleasures: Egbert (Edward Everett Horton) and a casual acquaintance (Betty Grable) in The Gay Divorcée.

to know what you want, or how to ask for it. Its key line (Egbert to Blore), 'Your figure of speech has made me forget entirely what I wanted', makes the point for the whole film, as well as perhaps reminding us that these scriptwriters do seem to know what they are doing.

Shortly after this, Guy pursues Mimi to the empty pavilion stage, the setting for the 'Night and Day' dance number. Commentators on this have noticed that it is narrative, that it offers in dance an enactment of Mimi's flight, Guy's pursuit, her acceding to his desire, and their mutual delight. In other words, it grows out of the customs house and car chase sequences, reprising them but with immobility and language replaced by dance and the eloquence of the gaze, by the movement from Mimi's averted face as Guy sings 'Night and Day', to the achieved communication with which the number ends. Mimi is lowered onto a seat as Guy mimes the final notes of the music with his free hand, and the next shot shows her speechless, her gaze resting on Guy, adequately articulating her response to him and to herself.

This defines how far the couple have come, and perhaps touches on their problem, which is also suggested by another quality of the number, its privacy. The stage on which they dance is a public place – we have seen it earlier, full of couples, in the 'Let's Knock Knees' number – but it is now deserted, and within the film there is no audience for the dance. The brief use of shots through Venetian blinds has been taken to suggest something about voyeurism, our privileged access to this scene (*see*, for example, Jim Collins in *Genre: The Musical*, edited by Rick Altman, Routledge, 1981, p.144), but I think it is as much a matter of emphasising the isolation of the couple from the rest of the world. They can dance alone, and now they know it. It is their task to take this knowledge back to the world of language and other people. We see the difficulty of such a transition, as Guy offers Mimi a cigarette, and they talk about their 'aunts'. In a moment of foolishness or embarrassment he offers her the phrase which is one of the movie's gags. It is partly about the emptiness of pretentious language, but the words also function as a kind of spell: 'Chance is the fool's name for Fate'.

The phrase creates the illusion for Mimi that Guy is the co-respondent hired by Egbert. This does not last long, about ten minutes of the running time of the film. Most of this time is spent with the couple in the sitting room of Mimi's suite at the hotel, and the motifs of the opening are repeated – entrapment in a confined space, Guy trying to be the figure who will 'free' Mimi without knowing what exactly he should do, the falling back on childhood behaviour (here reciting capitals of states). By the time Tonetti (Erik Rhodes) enters the suite in his role as the real co-respondent, it is already clear who and what Guy is, and Tonetti's function is to begin the reinsertion of the couple into the world. Guy says, 'I feel crowded, but that's life', and crowded life begins here with the telephone ringing and the family (Tonetti's) on the other end of the line.

The final movement back into the mundane world takes two forms. The first is in the big professional dance, 'The Continental', a production number written for the film: under Tonetti's gaze, Guy and Mimi leave their cardboard shadows

Achieved communication: Guy sings 'Night and Day' to Mimi in The Gay Divorcée.

Public performance: 'The Continental' in The Gay Divorcée.

to dance for the public, in the Big White Set. Guy's and Mimi's skills are thus placed in the context of professional entertainment, expressed in the formality both of the chorus dancers' dress and of the choreography.

The second aspect of this movement appears in the reprise of this number in Mimi's sitting-room set in the last three minutes of the film. All the obvious problems have been resolved, and Guy and Mimi are checking out of the hotel. Guy is finally out of the white tie and tails he has worn for the whole of the central section of the film, and Mimi is in street clothes. The couple dance not just around the room but over the sofas, table and chairs, watched by a group of bellhops. This is a matter of dance transforming the ordinary, of dance being given an idealised relationship to the world in which ordinary life – represented by the furniture the cast has been using – is lived.

There is an obvious connection here with an earlier number in the film, the solo 'I'm Looking for a Needle in a Haystack', in which Guy danced around his London sitting room as he dressed, again dancing over a sofa and on to a chair (the informal audience then being a butler). The movement from this number to the finale suggests the celebration of the replacement of the single man by the couple. But there is a further dimension. This is Astaire's account of the genesis of this number in the stage show:

'It was a spectacular thing on the hazardous side, in which the climax of the number was reached as we waltzed around the room at top speed going over chairs and tables as if they were part of the floor. We took many a fall rehearsing this and occasionally we fell during the show, too, much to the dismay of the audience. When that happened, we would just get up and do it over properly, like the juggler who misses a trick the first time. Then, when it finally worked, the audience would give us twice as much applause.' (Fred Astaire, *Steps in Time*, Da Capo Press, p.176).

My interest here is in Astaire's desire to admit such a number into the show, the implication (of 'twice as much applause') being that not just the possibility but the likelihood of a fall during performance could be thought of as a virtue, as if such a moment rendered the skill of the performers less remote, made them fallible. We might expect this element to disappear in the filmed version of the number, in that we know that we will see the best take. But the nature of the number – danced hazardously over the props of ordinary life – is such that as we watch the achieved grace of the performance we may sense that in rehearsal or in unused takes, the dancers will have stumbled, and that this is part of what is ordinary or mundane about the process of dancing, or of making films that include dancing. I see this as information which Astaire wants to reveal to us. The subjects of rehearsal and miscalculation in the dance, and thus acceptance of the ordinary laws of physics, or even an insistence on the ordinariness of those laws, will be returned to in subsequent films.

The Astaire and Rogers of *Flying Down to Rio* develop recognisably into the couple of *The Gay Divorcée*. The film again begins by placing them in the mundane world, in which we understand courtship to be a difficult or clumsy business. This is not a casual point, but one central to the cycle's interest in romance. It springs from the conception of the characters played by Astaire and Rogers as essentially alone: neither of them has parents or mutual friends, and so no social context exists in which they might meet. In the films in which they meet for the first time, it is always because of a chance encounter in mundane circumstances – borrowing some small change, diving into the water to rescue a dog that might be drowning. They are rarely introduced by a third party, and where this does happen it is either when the couple are in the wrong context, one which might seem to block any hope for romance (doctor and patient in *Carefree*), or there is a joke being made. That the well-meaning mutual friend does not always appear to guarantee happiness becomes part of the point of the mistaken identity gag around which *Top Hat* is plotted.

The Astaire-Rogers films never use the obvious route of bringing the couple together for the first time through one of them being seduced by watching the other perform. (This happens as soon as we move outside this particular couple, for example, when the woman is Rogers and the man is James Stewart in *Vivacious Lady*.) Rather, the opposite is true – where Astaire or Rogers is the audience for the other's solo act, the scenes are often used to express some kind of criticism, or the reservation is implied by the observer not staying on to the end of the performance. Their seduction of each other always depends on their dancing *together*, and involves a degree of abandonment of their sense of themselves as professionals and of their dance as just a professional skill, a withdrawal from a social context in which the world is divided into performers and audiences. It becomes the business of the film to explore how the couple find their way back to the social world, or the solid ground, that is represented by institutions like marriage and divorce.

ROBERTA (William A. Seiter, 1935)

The subject of *Roberta* is implicit in its title, a word which is both a first name and the name of a business. In the film (as opposed to the Broadway musical show of the same name on which it was based, which starred Bob Hope in the Astaire role), it is not made clear how the character called Roberta acquired the name, raising the question of the obscure ways in which names and titles are bestowed and thus what they might mean. The film opens with American band-leader Huckleberry Haines (Astaire) disembarking in Le Havre with his orchestra and his friend John Kent (Randolph Scott), a sports coach. The names already posit a contrast – plain monosyllabic John against a character named Huckleberry, after one of the great assumers of identities in American fiction. On the quay-side they are greeted with choler by restaurateur (and Russian) Alexander Petrovich Moscovich Voyda (Luis Alberni), who thought that he had ordered a band of Indians from the USA, but is confronted by palefaces: 'Huck Haines and His Indianians'. Huck offers Voyda a view, or a joke, about such confusions – 'we don't wear our feathers in warm weather' – but Voyda will not accept less than the genuine article and storms off. The boys head for Paris, where Huck has a childhood sweetheart, an American girl whose name he cannot at this moment

John Kent (Randolph Scott) intervenes in a dispute between Stephanie (Irene Dunne) and Schwarenka (Rogers) in Roberta.

quite recall, and John has a rich aunt, Roberta (Helen Westley), who owns a top fashion house. At Roberta's showrooms, John encounters her young assistant Stephanie (Irene Dunne), the house's principal dress designer, who is hiding the fact that she is a Russian princess – in other words, in one sense of the term, she is 'Roberta'. Huck has the band display their talents in a trick number, and realises that a high-toned customer who is a distant audience to it is none other than his childhood sweetheart, Lizzie Gatz (Rogers). Again, American writing seems flimsily concealed in this script – Gatz was the 'real' name of another self-made American, F. Scott Fitzgerald's Jay Gatsby in *The Great Gatsby* (1925). When Huck is introduced to Lizzie, she is using her assumed identity: of a Polish noblewoman, the Countess Scharwenka. His fun with this pretension is to announce himself as the 'Marquis de Indiana'. Her fun occurs when they are alone:

Scharwenka: Don't call me Lizzie. *[setting up the gag]* You may call me Tanka.
Huck [falling for it]: Tanka.
Scharwenka: You're welcome.

Huck and Lizzie are presented from the outset as a pair who share a past (or a future) which allows them to treat identities as fun, part of the business of entertainment. Lizzie tells Huck that Scharwenka is '. . . just a stage name. You have

Fooling around: Huck Haines (Astaire) presents himself to Scharwenka/Lizzie as 'the Marquis de Indiana'.

Performance: Huck and Lizzie in the sung part of 'I Won't Dance' in Roberta.

to have a title to croon over here'. All this will later be claimed as an extension of the world of their childhood, where Huck once won a beauty contest for Lizzie by showing the voters a picture of Lillian Russell.

The other couple is Stephanie and John. The difference between the two couples is underlined when John is asked if he ever says anything that he does not mean, and he replies 'no' with some surprise. This is not exactly a matter of honesty, but of belief in a world not subject to essential change or revision. (In Stephanie's case, it is one in which a Russian revolution merely displaces a Russian princess geographically, but does not challenge her understanding of her identity.) This is linked in *Roberta* to the confidence of aristocratic culture, a confidence that values breeding but allows that it can also be acquired and learned, implied in the sending of John to an English aristocrat's tailor in the early part of the film.

These two mental worlds are represented by differences in performance styles, for example, the two numbers presented in quick succession in the evening sequence at the Café Russe. The first is Huck's and Lizzie's conversation in song to 'I Won't Dance' which dissolves into Huck's solo tap. It invokes fake, or fun Russianness and costume (the 'guards', who force Huck to dance) and patter and physical comedy, performed as public, commercial entertainment, complete with a specific reference in the lyric to where we might have experienced these entertainers – doing 'The Continental' in *The Gay Divorcée*. This is in sharp contrast to the number that follows it, Stephanie's rendition of 'Smoke Gets in Your Eyes', which proposes an aristocratic world that still believes itself to be the real thing. Stephanie is presented in the robes and tiara of a Russian princess, surrounded by her court in the form of a dinner party. Her singing is not a job of work but the act of an amateur privately entertaining her guests. Her table is set apart from the rest of the Café by the drawing of a veil, a transparent curtain emblazoned with the imperial eagle.

The ground has been carefully prepared for this contrast. 'Smoke Gets in Your Eyes' is Stephanie's third song, the first two being 'Yesterdays' and a Russian folk song, both sung in Roberta's private apartment and accompanied on solo guitar by another Russian aristocrat, Ladislaw (Victor Varconi). On both occasions, the purpose is to lull the ailing Roberta to sleep, and after the second song she dies – the singing is associated both with the passing of a social order and with privacy, or self-reflectiveness. Against this we can place the film's first song from Rogers, 'I'll Be Hard to Handle', performed in the Café Russe in front of an impromptu audience. The song looks to the future both in the tense of the lyric and in the placing of it as a professional activity, practising for something that will be perfect later – it is a rehearsal, a point specifically made in a line from Huck as the song ends.

A different point needs to be made about the dance number which follows shortly after Lizzie's song. As this is the first time in the series that Ginger Rogers wears slacks, the tendency has been to lump the song and subsequent dance number together as a 'rehearsal number' (e.g. in Jane Feuer's *The Hollywood Musical*, Macmillan, 1982, p.11) and consider it under the heading of the 'illusion of spontaneity'. I find it difficult to accept the argument that we are buying these illusions by not acknowledging that we are watching a film. The term 'rehearsal' may need more definition in the context of these musicals than it is often given.

Any Astaire-Rogers number raises the question of whether the narrative has told us that this couple have ever danced this particular dance before, or whether it is stated that they have not. A large number of the dances are apparently invented as they are performed, whether the setting is a private one as in 'Night and Day' or 'Isn't This a Lovely Day' in *Top Hat*, or a public one as in, say, the couple's performance of 'The Carioca'. Equally there are numbers which are set up as public performances by professionals who will of course have rehearsed them to their current state of perfection. There is no need to have seen rehearsals to understand this about, say, the dance-duet version of 'Smoke Gets in Your Eyes' at the fashion show which is the climax of *Roberta*. The matter of the couple's clothes, or the absence of an audience (or at least of a paying audience – waiters, or bellboys), may tell us something about privacy, but it does not answer this question. 'Night and Day' is danced by Rogers in an elaborate evening gown, and 'I'll Be Hard to Handle' in slacks, but neither is strictly a rehearsal. What could such dances be rehearsals for? No dance leads up to, or away from them, no routine is being repeated, or will be repeated later on.

Above: 'A musical fashion show!' Lizzie, Huck and Stephanie plan the extravaganza in Roberta. *Opposite: Huck and Lizzie dance 'I'll Be Hard to Handle'.*

In the case of 'I'll Be Hard to Handle', the articulation of the introduction and conclusion to the dance offer clues as to how to read it. After her song and his comment to the band, Lizzie and Huck sit on the steps next to the orchestra, or rather, he sits, she lies back on the steps. They reminisce about their childhood, the shows they put on in her barn, how they used to fight and how they were in love with each other. He teases her, she makes as if to strike him, he catches her arm with his, and they are dancing – a movement that Astaire refers to in another context as 'we pantomimed our way into a dance' (Astaire, p.75). The dance consists of series of jokes, tricks, perfect harmonies, mimed outrage and injury, and conversations in tap-danced form. In other words, it is reprising the conversation that the couple have just had, appropriating it as a form for their dance together. The relationship between the custom house/torn dress sequence and the 'Night and Day' number in *The Gay Divorcée* is relevant here. The link is the same, the sense that dance can be used to address the world, that something spoken or gestured inexpertly or ineptly can be given form more adequately in dance.

I have already discussed how the ending of 'Night and Day' leaves the couple with the task of finding their way slowly back to the ordinary world. The 'I'll Be Hard to Handle' dance offers the opposite. As it ends, the pair fall into a sitting position on conveniently placed chairs – but in the shot there are not two but three chairs, and the one on to which Lizzie falls has a jacket casually flung over its back. They bow to the applause of their audience, two male waiters and a female

One of Rogers's wonderful back-bends in the danced version of 'Smoke Gets in Your Eyes' in Roberta.

cleaner. In the careful irregularity of these details, we see the means of defining the couple as being in the ordinary world; their dance does not take them out of it further than they want to go.

The dance performance of 'Smoke Gets in Your Eyes' is the first case in the cycle of a public dance duet that can be read as having been rehearsed. This beautiful dance expresses the couple's attainment of a precise rapport (at several points conveyed by their gaze, fixed on each other) in this formal, public setting. As it ends, the camera follows them into the wings:

Lizzie [flopping into a chair that is facing away from the stage]: My, oh my.
Huck [still looking out at the audience]: What?
Lizzie: I said, my oh my, that was lovely.
Huck: It went well, didn't it?

At this point, the couple are not quite talking about the same thing. For Huck, it is what it feels like to be a successful professional, for Lizzie, what it feels like to be in love. Now their conversation continues:

Lizzie: I guess I'll have to give in to you.
Huck: To me? *[she nods]* Why, I didn't say anything.
Lizzie: But I thought you were about to want to marry me.
Huck: Well, I was. *[he takes a last glance at the audience]*
Lizzie: Well, I accept.
Huck: Well, thanks very much.
Lizzie [holding both his hands in hers]: Well, you're quite welcome, my fine–feathered friend.

Lizzie's words are spoken not as if she is raising a question but answering one – 'I guess I'll have to give in to you' – encapsulating the near-redundancy of this conversation after what has happened on the dance floor, as if something allied to a proposal and an acceptance has already been exchanged. The difference is that the woman of the couple knows it completely, and the comedy arises from the man having to be prompted into remembering what has gone on. It is a vital moment, for it is the first time in the cycle that a verbal declaration of love or proposal of marriage operates as an acknowledgement of something that seems already to have happened, to exist somewhere in the couple's past. The problem for the characters played by Astaire and Rogers is not to understand that they are in love, but to realise that this has happened some little time before they find the words to declare it – to make peace between their, or society's, words, and the dance. This configuration will be repeated as the cycle proceeds.

All is not so well, or so easily worked out, elsewhere. The project of *Roberta* is to modernise Roberta's (the business), so that the generation represented by Roberta herself and by Lord Henry Delves (Ferdinand Munier) can give way to the couple of Stephanie and John – in other words the transformation of aristocratic Europe into consumer America, a class order giving way to a new democratic relationship to commodities. (This is hinted at in the climax to the film when Astaire, a representative of consumer America, is given the role of introducing the new season's models at the fashion show through a patter number.) It may also be thought of as a development of *Flying Down to Rio*, in which an American man falls for an aristocratic foreign girl, and the film ends with their implied marriage. But the differences are important. In *Flying Down to Rio*, the third figure in the romantic triangle is male, the aristocrat who releases the girl so that she can marry her American love, and we accept his insight as part of a compliment being paid to the old order in the film. In *Roberta*, the comparable role of Ladislaw, Stephanie's cousin, is reduced almost to nothing, and the important third corner of the triangle is occupied by an American girl, Sophie (Claire Dodd), John's former fiancée. Some of the anxieties which trouble *Roberta* are registered in her treatment.

Sophie seems to be set up as one of the possibilities of the future, the new order that will follow on the death of the older generation. Her first appearance in the film comes immediately after Roberta's death – we see her on an Atlantic crossing reading a newspaper report about John inheriting the fashion house. After this, her role, in summary, consists of three scenes:

1) She meets John in his office and persuades him to think of himself as still being in love with her.
2) She comes to Roberta's to buy a gown, and chooses '*la sirène noire*', a gown that John has rejected from the house collection in an earlier sequence. She is drawn to make this choice by her own taste, assisted by Huck, and with some reluctance, by Stephanie, who are punishing her for snobbish behaviour.
3) She wears the gown to Huck's and the band's opening night at the Café Russe, where John denounces it as vulgar, and they quarrel. She tells him that his views on gowns are worthless: 'you make yourself ridiculous by even discussing them', and storms out of the café, and the film.

It was clearly easy enough for the scriptwriters of *Roberta* to construct Sophie's part so that we understand her to be shallow and self-seeking, but her humiliation through the issue of the dress suggests something more about the film's divided loyalties. Look at the way the dress is introduced in a sequence shortly after Roberta's death, when Stephanie and John (as new owner) are reviewing the house's current collection. Huck and Lizzie (in her role as Countess Scharwenka) are also present. When the gown appears, it is denounced by the two men as too revealing, but not before Lizzie has frankly admired it – 'Doesn't she look wonderful in that' – and we should recall that it has been implied that Stephanie must have designed it. What we see is a backless black evening dress, not unlike gowns that will be worn by Rogers, shown by a model (RKO bit player Jane Hamilton) who does not appear to have been chosen to support a reading of it as vulgar. Its sole fault seems to be that it is a little too plunging at the back, but when Stephanie draws attention to this, John firmly refuses to make any adjustment and orders the dress to be dropped from the range.

The punishment of Sophie in the Café Russe sequence sends similarly mixed signals. Her pleasure in herself and the dress, and the fact that she is the unwitting victim of the frame-up, make John's unhesitating denunciation seem priggish and crude. And can it be chance that as she shows off the dress to him her dropped cape covers the lower part of the back, so that what is on screen is at that moment unexceptionable? Of course, the larger plot of the romance is not to be diverted, and the scripting of Sophie's final speeches ensures that we do not much regret her loss. But the overall experience is of an episode that seems forced, possibly because, as a young and desirable American woman, Sophie represents a type whom elsewhere – that is, in Lizzie – the film asks us to admire. It may not be chance that Lizzie and Sophie never appear in the same sequence, as if we are being discouraged from making any link between them, beyond allowing ourselves to notice that they are the two admirers of the controversial black dress. (Some associated issues, which mostly surface in the film as a series of gags, also relate to the figure of Sophie. They are essentially anxieties about gender roles and commerce, about the powerful role of women as the purchasers of *haute couture*, and about the anomalous place of men in this world, either as designers or as managers of places like Roberta's.)

It may be that the difficulties surrounding Sophie express a wider uncertainty. The likelihood that the world of Huck and Lizzie is radically opposed to that of John and Stephanie is never faced, and the treatment of Sophie may be a way of repressing this conflict, punishing a figure who stands between them, and represents a tension that cannot otherwise be expressed. No choice is in the end made between the two couples. We leave them – but in different places – making their vows to each other, and only by one gesture does the film suggest its preference. After both betrothal sequences, for no pressing reason in terms of the narrative, we cut back to the Big White Set, so that the film ends not with its top-billed star, Irene Dunne, but with Astaire and Rogers performing a brief reprise of the 'I Won't Dance' number. This repeats the movement from Astaire's solo dance to a final duet, the single dancer giving way to the couple, that we have seen in *The Gay Divorcée*.

The central feature of the Astaire-Rogers couple in *Roberta* can be expressed as their sustaining and defining of intimacy. As the plot does not require them to meet for the first time, it allows them to express more fully the familiarity with each other that was sketched out in *Flying Down to Rio*, and 'I'll Be Hard to

Handle', developing out of the final dance over the furniture in *The Gay Divorcée*, is the expression of this in dance. Their intimacy is explained here both by having known each other since childhood, and by the idea that a marriage proposal is not a climax but an acknowledgement of the obvious, or the handing over of an obvious truth to society. The importance of this subject can be measured by its appearance later in the cycle in plots where such closeness is not literally the case, but the project of the couple is to create such a feeling, to learn to behave as if they have always known each other. Which takes us on to *Top Hat*.

TOP HAT (Mark Sandrich, 1935)

There seems to be a measure of consent that *Top Hat* is the climax of the Astaire-Rogers musicals – the couple's most perfect, or enduring, or typical performance. The brilliance of the Irving Berlin score is clearly important. Merely listing 'No Strings', 'Isn't It a Lovely Day (To Be Caught in the Rain)', 'Top Hat, White Tie and Tails', 'Cheek to Cheek' and 'The Piccolino' makes the point, although arguably the score is rivalled by the Kern-Fields numbers for *Swing Time* and Gershwin's for *Shall We Dance*. *Top Hat* is also sometimes referred to as a remake of *The Gay Divorcée*. The connection between the films is emphasised by the connection between the casts, the reappearance of Eric Blore, Erik Rhodes and Edward Everett Horton, and the use of Helen Broderick in a part that seems to echo the role taken by Alice Brady in the earlier film. The mingling of romance and farce works similarly in the two films to create an apparent antagonism between the man and the woman as soon as they meet, to let them seduce each other with the dance, to let there be a misunderstanding over who or what he is and to let that misunderstanding be resolved. Looking at the widely divergent ways in which the films approach these premises helps reveal what is particular to *Top Hat* and why it is so often identified as the climax of the series.

First, I want to consider the differences between the worlds created by the two films. *The Gay Divorcée* opens by presenting a series of locations that relate to the activities around which ordinary life is organised – the restaurant, the customs shed, Egbert's apartment, London streets. Another world is represented by the various Brightburn sets – the pavilion, Mimi's hotel suite, the dance floor – all of which make much less pretence (or claim) to be realistic or mundane in any way. *The Gay Divorcée* is shaped by the journey to and the thought of the imminent return from Brightburn, the return to the everyday world that marks the end of the comedy. (This shape is familiar from examples in classical comedy – Brightburn might be thought of as an equivalent of, say, the Forest of Arden in *As You Like It*.)

Although there is a superficial change of location in *Top Hat*, the differentiation between types of setting is not so strong, and the effect is to set the whole of the film in one kind of world. We can see this in the ways in which the spaces occupied by the Edward Everett Horton character in the two films are treated. In *The Gay Divorcée*, Egbert's rooms are a domestic space, where it appears that residence is relatively permanent. (Roberta's rooms in *Roberta* are a similar case). In *Top Hat*, the equivalent space is the kind of interior that recurs throughout the film: the hotel suite. In all, we see six of them in Venice and London, and the point is their distance from domesticity. In their impersonal imitation of it, they evoke the theatrical or film set. There is no suggestion of any of them being permanent, personal residences; all the action takes place in locations which are essentially stages for display. (This sense of display means that when we arrive at an actual performance within the narrative, a further distinction becomes necessary. Astaire's solo number 'Top Hat, White Tie, and Tails' is performed on a traditional, proscenium arch stage.)

The move to the Venice Lido in the middle of the film thus becomes not a change of world, but rather a further insistence that these events are taking place in a world with no connections to the outside. (We could call it a world created wholly by money and lacking other forms of social dimension, arguably a reasonable definition of one kind of Hollywood set.) Even gestures to the existence of another world, as in the back-projected images of the seaside in some sequences of *The Gay Divorcée*, have virtually disappeared. The same distinction can be seen in the change in the approach to *haute couture* from *Roberta* to *Top Hat*. In *Roberta*, it is a business, and the film continually returns to the fact that the dresses are manufactured for sale. In *Top Hat* such issues are an irrelevance: there is no interest shown in either selling or buying the gowns, which exist solely in the realm of the sensuous pleasures of designing or wearing them, or, for the spectator, in looking at women wearing them. I shall argue that money, or what it can symbolise or create – call this confidence – is indeed important.

This means that *Top Hat* poses for its couple a different problem from that of *The Gay Divorcée* or *Roberta*. As no part of *Top Hat*'s world is one where ordinary lives are led, the lovers have to put some work into finding out, or defining what this place is, where (apart from Hollywood) they are. We see them trying out such terms as paradise, or heaven.

Some of the differences between the two films are also expressed in the roles played by Erik Rhodes. His very distinct mannerisms offer a temptation to conflate the dress designer Beddini in *Top Hat* with Tonetti in *The Gay Divorcée*, as the comical foreigner/immigrant figure, defined by his malapropisms and identified as a figure of comedic sexuality, surrounded by energies greater than his own. The joke about his being a cuckold in *The Gay Divorcée* is replaced in *Top Hat* with the joke about his parentage: 'My father killed a man just before I was born'. But in *The Gay Divorcée*, Tonetti is a harmless, amiable worker in the co-respondent business – when he thinks he is being supplanted by Astaire, his gag line is, 'Are you a union man?' A devoted family man, he is scared by the thought of the aggression of angry husbands. In *Top Hat*, Beddini is aristocratic, given to postures of violence, and, most crucially, rich – which is the first reason that he offers to Dale Tremont (Rogers) for marrying him.

This is part of a consistent interest in *Top Hat* in the importance of the differences between the principal players in terms less of social class than of wealth. Up to this point in the cycle there has been no difference between Astaire's characters and Rogers's in terms of their affluence – in *Flying Down to Rio* and *Roberta* both were, as entertainers, equally liable to be rich one moment and poor the next, and in *The Gay Divorcée*, playing opposite Astaire's successful song-and-dance man, Rogers seems to exist in a world of easy access to cash, even if its terms are not specified. The different emphases of *Top Hat* could be said to be encapsulated in Dale's line to Beddini in her first scene with him: 'Up to now our relationship has been purely a business one, but if you start interfering with my private life, I'll go back to America and live on the dole.' (*Top Hat* is the only film in the cycle where there is a wide difference in the financial positions of the Rogers and the Astaire characters.)

Dale's line expresses an exact awareness of their relationship, her dependence and her independence. There is no suggestion here that censorship is concealing the idea that she is Beddini's mistress, their behaviour with each other being founded precisely on the fact that there is no sexual attachment. As the beautiful model for Beddini's exotic dresses, she is necessary to him (one gag has him protesting 'never again will I allow women to wear my dresses'), but her position is that of a Cinderella. While she has the appearance of a wealthy society woman, this illusion, as her practical friend Madge Hardwick (Helen Broderick) knows, needs to be converted into permanency by Dale finding herself a 'reliable husband'. In the context of this search, what connects Jerry Travers (Astaire) and Beddini is the power of money. What distinguishes them is their rhetoric (Beddini is continually codified as full of emptily rhetorical gestures, his family motto and his posturing with the sword, as opposed to Jerry's directness), which is in turn a way of raising doubts about Beddini's sexual desire, of characterising it as narcissism. Alongside this is Beddini's occupation – some of the prejudices about dress designing and masculinity that are evident in *Roberta* are being played to here. Compare this to the way in which Jerry's occupation is established as a display of power, in the solo performance of 'Top Hat, White Tie and Tails'. The number is a celebration partly of the power of money expressed as social class, partly (as has often been noticed) of his phallic potency, and partly of his standing as a massively successful professional. The last is stressed by Sandrich's presentation of the number, with shots of Jerry taking a curtain call and continuing his

Dale (Rogers) confronting Jerry (Astaire) in Top Hat, *after he has woken her by dancing 'No Strings' in the room above hers.*

teasing of the members of the Thackeray Club. These are the clutch of patriarchs with which the movie began, in a sequence in which Jerry broke the silence of the Club, establishing that the power of the talented performer is expressed in his belief in his right to tease other figures of authority.

The torn dress sequence in *The Gay Divorcée*, which is the couple's first encounter, is about wanting to seduce the girl but being unable to the display your great skill (you cannot dance with a girl who is in effect tied to a trunk). The parallel sequence in *Top Hat* begins in the hotel room of Horace Hardwick (Edward Everett Horton). Jerry is talking to Horace, his friend and producer, about his unmarried state. From the very beginning of the sequence, the music is already introducing us to Berlin's melody. Jerry starts to sing and then goes into the tap routine of 'No Strings'. The camera moves downwards, and we discover that Horace's room is above Dale's and see her waking from sleep at the racket on her ceiling. We may notice that this time Jerry is already dancing when he meets Dale, or, rather, his dancing finds her and holds her attention before he does. In the era of the implementation of the production code, the idea of these male tap-dancing rhythms penetrating a woman's bedroom, is mildly risqué. The literal annoyance produces aggression and yet creates an intimacy, bringing the couple face-to-face with each other in a context in which they are made aware that at least the physical barriers dividing them are thin ones. When the device was used with the gender roles reversed, in Lloyd Bacon's *Cain and Mabel* (1936), this intimacy was again disguised as sarcasm: the dancer (Marion Davis), asks the indignant figure at her bedroom door (Clark Gable), 'what am I supposed to do, make you hot milk?' – later in that film, the proffered image of intimacy is her frying pork chops for him.

Finally, consider how the nature of the film's spaces is established. A possible camera movement might take us out of Horace's window, down the side of the building, and then into Dale's room through her window, but this is not the case here. Rather, the camera movement passes, with a minimal dissolve, through the floor and ceiling, reminding us that one of the places we are in is Hollywood, that this is a sound stage as well as a hotel.

Dale comes to Jerry's room and catches him fooling about, dancing with a statuette in his arms. Their conversation is also fooling around – he claims that his dancing is an affliction, underlining the fun by calling it 'St Vitus Dance'. When he tries to claim that his dance can be stopped only by having someone's arms around him, she shows that she is entering into the spirit of these matters by topping the gag: 'I'll call the house detective and have him put his arms around you.' Here we have a scene in which Astaire's character is suddenly disconcerted when he realises that Rogers is watching him, followed by a scene of verbal sparring which suggests such rapport that we might think that these characters had known each other before – not a version of the encounter in *The Gay Divorcée* but something close to a repetition of the couple's meeting in *Roberta*. The similar spirit of this encounter is registered in the pleasure on Rogers's face as she walks back to her bedroom and then her smile as she sits on her bed – quite unlike her retreat in *The Gay Divorcée*.

This is followed by the sandman sequence, the pianissimo reprise of 'No Strings'. Dance becomes enchantment as, in order to send Dale back to sleep, Jerry turns down the lights in *his* room, scatters sand on the floor and dances his way into her dreams again. There is a shot of a drowsy Dale, establishing that she is receiving this communication through her ceiling, and Horace, Dale, and finally Jerry fall asleep.

The note is both of a spell or charm and of the world of childhood, of the nursery in which a child is sung to sleep. The connection is introduced as the sandman sequence begins and ends in the musical phrases from 'Rock-a-bye baby' that frame Astaire's dance, and arguably in the set dressing, in the unusual design of Dale's bed, which sits with its side rather than its head against the upholstered wall. Can it be chance that it tentatively suggests a cradle on legs? All of this connects with Astaire's song, not just as being the credo of the unattached man, but as expressive of the freedom, or the polymorphousness, of childhood.

The subject of childhood, that is, of a couple constructing, or experiencing, what it might be like to have had one together, is at the centre of the gazebo sequence, the dancing of 'Isn't it a Lovely Day (to Be Caught In the Rain)'. It invokes the little girl who is frightened by thunder, prompting a nursery story from the man, 'When a fluffy little cloud . . . ' – an allusion to how you explain to children the world of sexuality (the old nursery standby of the stork will come into the film a little later on). The dance which follows Jerry's nursery lesson is not a seduction in the sense that 'Night and Day' is, but what Arlene Croce describes as a 'challenge dance' and Rogers in her autobiography calls 'shadowing', essentially dramatising the couple's ability to operate in exact harmony, to follow each other's every move. Since such a dance is not about flight, it cannot end in capture, in something that might resemble the triumphant gesture with which Astaire settles Rogers on the sofa at the end of 'Night and Day'. Rogers recounts the story of Astaire and his choreographer Hermes Pan being unable to find an appropriate ending, and claims the last moves (the couple dancing to the edge of the gazebo, feeling the rain, sitting down, shaking hands) as her contribution (*see* Ginger Rogers, *Ginger: My Story*, Headline, 1991, p.124). Perhaps Rogers realised most clearly the articulation of the note of the ordinary here, that the point of the dance would not be made in a final embrace.

There turn out to be two ways of reading this dance. The one that I have given is that it is inventing a past, playing like children, or at being children. The other dismisses a need for a past: the idea that in Dale's mind the dance has created a new world, and defined the couple, too, as new in it, is made clear in the next sequence. In her conversation with Beddini, she stumbles across the fact that she does not know her dancing partner's name, and christens him Adam. When Beddini asks her what she will wear if she marries Adam, she naturally replies: fig leaves. All this is important to reading the confusion that follows it. Dale's mistaken belief that Jerry is in fact Horace Hardwick (that is, a married man, her best friend's husband) is not simply a trick of the lines of sight in the hotel lobby, the switching of accessories and the identical clothes of the two men that are necessary for the mechanics of the plot. These are what enact it, but not the condition that makes it possible. This is Dale's insistence that she does not need, or perhaps does not want, to know her partner's social face, that she can give him an identity which assumes that they are the only couple in the world. So her trauma at the loss of this Eden is correspondingly severe – when he tries to remind her of their invented past, she slaps Jerry's face, convincingly hard.

Two of Rogers's costumes for the Venice sequences of Top Hat, *including the problematic ostrich-feather dress for 'Cheek to Cheek'.*

The reactions of the couple to this crisis are shown in juxtaposed scenes in the two hotel rooms. Dale is standing, miserably attempting both to dismiss the humiliation of the presence of the concerned management and to deny the whole business '. . . nothing matters, nothing's happened'. Upstairs Jerry lolls comfortably in a chair, one leg over its arm. In response to Horace's worries about his actions, he offers a series of mild gags. His confidence is absolute: 'If anyone's going to buy her anything, I'm going to do it.' The distinction between their respective states can be expressed as the difference between denying that something ever existed (something like awaking from a dream), and denying that any impediment to desire could possibly exist, a confidence in power, which at times in this plot can be called money.

The couple have one more scene together before 'Cheek to Cheek'. In it, Dale, her composure apparently regained, intends to punish the man she thinks is

Horace for his apparent infidelity to Madge by claiming to be what Horace calls a 'designing woman'. She will remind him of a supposed past, a love affair in Paris, and so frighten him 'that he'll never so much as look at another woman'. Jerry is meanwhile being warned by Horace that there are such creatures as designing women, and that he believes Dale to be one of them, with designs on Jerry. So when Jerry and Dale meet, she does exactly what he has expected, or been warned about. She now takes her turn in telling him a story, one that claims they were lovers, that she has known him intimately in the past, but again it is a story such as children might invent, involving supping on tea and muffins. Far from being frightened by such a performance, he goes along with it enthusiastically (while offering a hint for her consideration about what they are doing):

Jerry: You weren't calling yourself Dale Tremont then.
Dale [by now very uncertain as to where she is being led]: Wasn't I?
Jerry: You called yourself , er . . . *[pausing, adopting a pose of thinking]* . . . Madeline! That was it . . . I called you Mad for short. You've put on a little weight, haven't you?

In other words, he tries to tell Dale that he knows that she is playing a game, and consents to play it with her while not understanding, or caring, what it is about.

But Dale cannot take the hint, or see the point – the movie proceeds as if she is under a spell, in which the characters are doomed to feed her illusion with lines and gestures which support her belief not only that Jerry is an adulterer (after the teasing quoted above she nonetheless goes back to her room with the impression that there was a Madeline that Jerry/Horace met in Paris), but also that Madge is actively encouraging her into an affair with him. The business at the table as the 'Cheek to Cheek' number begins – Jerry's line, 'Madge instinctively knows the kind of girl that interests me', and the two wonderful comic shots of the gestures with which Madge encourages Dale to surrender to Jerry's charms – are vital in setting up the number as a dramatised, helpless surrender to the dance, against the logic of the world as Dale believes she understands it.

Another difference between this film and *The Gay Divorcée* can be identified here. In the earlier film, Rogers danced with Astaire before there was any confusion over his identity and afterwards, but not during, the illusion. The effect of positioning the central duet of the film here is not to compromise the perfect harmony of the couple, but to offer it as the transcendent effect of the dance, the creation for Dale of a place where her puzzles over Jerry's identity do not exist.

Where are we? This place is not a private ground of sexual seduction, as the pavilion of 'Night and Day' is, or an Eden, or a playground, from which you might be expelled. In Jerry's lyric it is called heaven, and it is established visually by Sandrich's direction, in which the other couples in the frame gradually disappear, and Jerry and Dale cross the bridge dividing the two halves of the set and move into their duet. The gorgeousness and strangeness of this place is emphasised by the wardrobe department, in Rogers's ostrich-feather dress, as suggestive of the exotic as Dietrich's costume of black cock-feathers in *Shanghai Express* (Josef von Sternberg, 1932), but calling on an opposite set of associations with respect to sexuality: of innocence, pliancy. But possibly the dominant note is one of its hopeless impracticality for anywhere else. Dietrich's costume is a statement of who she is, like a badge of office or a uniform – something Sternberg's

'Cheek to Cheek': Dale and Jerry dance across the bridge between the two halves of the set in Top Hat.

Misunderstandings and explanations in Top Hat.

Left: Horace (Edward Everett Horton), Jerry and Madge (Helen Broderick).

Opposite: Horace, Madge, Bates (Eric Blore), Dale, Jerry and Alberto (Erik Rhodes).

film has quite a lot of. Rogers's feathers express where she is: in a place which makes no claim to connection with the mundane world.

The impractical dress may conceivably have been a factor in the brilliance of the sequence in another way. Given the dramatic importance of Dale's negative feelings that the dance engages with and overcomes, the well-known anecdote from the making of *Top Hat* told by both the principals seems to fall into place. It is a story of a performance surrounded by tension – the untried dress shedding feathers in rehearsal, the filming undertaken in a spirit of anxiety and in the face of Astaire's and Sandrich's objections and impatience, and then reconciliation, the viewing of the rushes and the triumph of the finished product as seen on the screen. (The film may even be able to afford an insider's intimacy about this. Consider the look of knowledge that passes between the couple in the hotel room sequence before the dance, when Jerry has taken over the narrative of their supposed affair and is reminding Dale of 'that little blue dress I bought for you'. I realise that this occurs before we have seen the dress, but there is no reason to suppose that the scenes were shot in sequence, and Rogers tells us that the problematic dress was blue.)

After 'Cheek to Cheek' the action moves towards reconciling the lovers before Dale can give herself sexually to Beddini, whom she has married, or rather believes herself to have married, in a fit of loneliness. The truth about the confusion of identities is revealed, not to Dale but to Jerry. He heads for the bridal suite and, after an encounter with Beddini which produces comedic exchanges rather than explanations, leaves again – after glancing up at the ceiling. Now, at the exact moment when Beddini and Dale are, with evident awkwardness, about to embrace, Jerry executes the tap routine on the floor, a signal sufficient to constitute an assurance that there will be some kind of explanation that will make all this end happily. She consents to leave the bridal suite and the next glimpse we have of her is with Jerry in a gondola. Perhaps what is most striking about all of this is the couple's air of confidence that the right outcome will follow – the moment of explanation can be postponed because it is required only as a gesture, not something truly necessary. There is no interest in the issue of unfaithfulness,

41

and a song that would have expressed such doubts, 'Get Thee Behind Me, Satan', which was at one point planned to fit in here, was cut and used in *Follow the Fleet*.

How will such lovers find their way back from RKO's Venice Lido to an ordinary world? By now the principals have all taken to the water, and ordinariness seems to be resurfacing as Beddini catches a cold and Horace falls asleep among the catch on a fisherman's boat. But throughout there has been one irreducible link to the mundane in the figure played by Eric Blore. In both *Top Hat* and *The Gay Divorcée*, he addresses the difficulties of the lovers. In *The Gay Divorcée*, he is the waiter whose interest in rocks results in the recognition of Mimi's geology-professor husband and the revelation that he has a mistress, so solving the impasse of Mimi's botched divorce arrangements and providing the necessary release. In *Top Hat*, he is Bates, Horace's manservant: in formal terms, he is an *eiron* figure, a clear descendant of the tricky slave of Roman comedy. Bates is mysteriously acquired from The Salvation Army (Horace: 'I sent them a pair of very old shoes.' Jerry: 'Oh I see, the shoes came back and Bates was in them'). He is instructed by Horace to follow Dale (Horace: 'Whither she goes . . .' Bates: 'Thither I, Sir'). The language here sends a sufficiently clear hint that we are to read him as some kind of guardian, an earth-bound Puck. He appears throughout the Lido sequences in various 'disguises', the common quality of which is that among the *soigné* extras on the set he sticks out extravagantly, floundering in the ordinary (on two occasions, the medium is water itself, once when he swims desperately past Dale and Madge, the other when, masquerading as a gondolier, he falls from Jerry's and Dale's gondola).

We might think that Bates is not necessary to the ending of this comedy, at least in the way that he is necessary to the happy ending of *The Gay Divorcée*. After all, the unconsummated marriage of Beddini and Dale is no real obstacle to happiness. The problem was Dale's believing that Jerry was Horace, and that has been cleared up, and the explanation is about to be given to Beddini. Bates's final performance reveals him as the spirit of comedic reprieve, telling us that something that might have to be undone literally can be dissolved magically, by repeating the gesture of the turning round of a collar and tie. This act, in raising the fact that there was no marriage, that a collar turned around does not make one, invites us to consider what constitutes marriage, what kind of tie it is. The pun on 'tie' haunts *Top Hat*: Bates is introduced on the note of the breach with Horace brought about by his passionate views on different kinds of tie, Jerry sings first 'No Strings' and then about tying up his white tie, Bates puts himself in the position to solemnise a marriage by concealing a tie. Finally he performs this strange ritual: by reversing his tie again he unmarries the couple of Beddini and Dale, reversing their tie – we see Dale discreetly taking off her ring. But he also, visually, becomes a priest again, perhaps reminding us that this is the most like a priest that any actor in the movies becomes. Looking at the final moments of this sequence, we may be struck by how it looks a little like a wedding group, as Dale and Jerry face the clergyman of the moment, Beddini rises to his feet to give the bride away, and Madge and Horace look on.

But even if we do not (quite) see a marriage in *Top Hat*, the film reaches out from the subject to be the most searching exploration so far of different kinds of bond or tie: the marriage bond is one, and that between a star couple and other supporting actors who perform together on successive occasions is another. There seems to be a direct allusion to this in that there is another way to read the final shot of this sequence, another link between these figures. Visually, it resembles a curtain call. The principal players, five of whom appeared in *The Gay Divorcée*, could be thought of as taking their bow, and this is followed by the principal couple performing their encore, a brief coda of Astaire-Rogers dance.

What we see in *Top Hat* is the way in which the earlier films of the cycle deepen the meaning and extend the possibilities of the plot. We accept both that the couple are meeting for the first time and that they wish to create an intimacy that consists in their pretending that they have always known each other. (If we remember that the first part of Astaire's career was built around performing with a figure he had known since earliest childhood – his sister Adele – it becomes less of a surprise that he is good at creating this feeling, and how important it might have seemed to him.) The ability to combine the charge of a new romance with the sense of intimacy is at its peak here, and subsequent films in the cycle move away from it.

FOLLOW THE FLEET (Mark Sandrich, 1936)

Of the nine musicals that Astaire and Rogers made at RKO, *Follow the Fleet* is the fifth, and numerically speaking the central point. It was conceived and made after the substantial success of the earlier films, and the rehearsals for it commenced on the day before the release of *Top Hat*, so it was made in the light of the great success of that film. Astaire writes of it in this way:

'*Follow the Fleet* looked like a good show. Ginger and I were enthusiastic about it but we also wondered how long it would be safe to carry on this cycle of team pictures. We didn't want to run it into the ground and we discussed the situation with each other frequently. Irving Berlin had agreed to write the music for *Fleet*, so we decided it was best to do this one and talk of other plans later' (Astaire, p.212).

So the film can be thought of both as a highpoint, the crest of a successful commercial and artistic wave, and as a vantage point, from which it was possible to contemplate the danger – to use the pervading nautical metaphor of this film – of running aground.

It is immediately clear in the film that there is a sort of self-consciousness new to the cycle: the subject of a dance team and their future has been worked into its plotting. It is announced at the beginning by a new kind of prop, the publicity still of Astaire and Rogers that is accidentally dislodged from the locker as ordinary seaman Bake Baker (Astaire) prepares to go on shore leave. The printing on the reverse of the photo establishes its status as a professional calling card, 'Baker and Martin: High-Class Patter and Genteel Dancing'. What we now learn is that Bake had asked Sherry Martin (Rogers) to marry him, and that she turned him down. Bake's response was to break up the team, and later to join the Navy. The narrative of the film begins at the point at which they meet again and it is clear that Sherry has not achieved the big break of a prestige solo act. Bake offers to help her do so. All his apparently well-intentioned actions in this direction turn out to be impediments: he causes her to lose her job, then unwittingly ruins her audition just as she is about to be offered a contract. For reasons that are grounded elsewhere in the plot, Bake and Sherry now put on a scratch show in a boat; Bake has made sure that a powerful producer is in the audience. He offers the couple a contract, but Bake insists on one condition, something that he has predicted, or anticipated, earlier – Sherry must now ask him to marry her. She does so, with an evident sense of its being a tax on her patience: 'Well, will you?'

One aspect of marriage is that it is a contract, and *Follow the Fleet* invites us to compare the qualities of the marriage bond with those of some other contractual relationships: an agreement to dance as a couple, or what is involved in the business of restoring a grounded ship or captaining a seaworthy one. Equally, the choice of a solo career is related to the refusal of a marriage proposal. In contrast we are offered matters which exist outside, or refuse the world of the contractual: a sailor's sexual fun with a divorcée, the behaviour of a pet animal, the injunction, in the words of Berlin's number, to 'let yourself go'.

The film works out these issues around two couples, one played by Astaire and Rogers, and the other by the second leads, the couple who meet for the first time: Bilge Smith (Randolph Scott), a sailor on Bake's boat, and Connie Martin (Harriet Hillyard), Sherry's schoolteacher sister. As in *Roberta*, Scott combines a beautiful physique with attitudes that are felt to be homespun, but whereas in the earlier film he is presented as almost comically upright and committed to

Below: Bake (Astaire) and the crew arrive at the Paradise Ballroom in Follow the Fleet. *Right: the dominant male – Bilge Smith (Randolph Scott) towers over Connie Martin (Harriet Hillyard).*

marriage, here the simplicity takes the form of not being able to see past his physical appetites, a sailor's right to love and leave women – the refusal, not of a particular girl, but of the entire prospect of marriage. This is established in his first scene: learning that Bake once proposed to Sherry, he replies wonderingly, 'Imagine asking any girl to marry you'.

The point of Bilge's scenes with Connie is his blindness to the nature of her intention, her desire not for a sexual partner but for a husband. Just as he cannot recognise her as the same girl in her two forms of dress – two sequences are designed to show his indifference to the dowdy girl he sees at the entrance to the Paradise Ballroom (a dance hall patronised by sailors), and his fascination with the same girl when dressed up and made over – he cannot read the meaning of the setting when she takes him back to her apartment. She makes him food, they talk about his mother and, as they look at the model of Connie's grounded ship, the *Connie Martin*, about her dead father. Now he is abruptly awakened by her use of the word 'husband', and understanding that marriage is being imagined, or even proposed, beats a hasty retreat into the arms of divorcée Iris Manning (Astrid Allwyn), who stands – naturally, only as far as censorship conventions will allow it to be implied – for sexual pleasure without complications.

Much of the remaining plot shows Bilge preferring Iris's charms to Connie's. Connie, aided by Sherry, decides to refloat the *Connie Martin*. A father figure, Captain Ezra Hickey (Harry Beresford), organises this work for them, but risks his own job in the process. In order to save him by paying off the money owing on the boat, the scratch show is mounted, and just as it is about to begin Bilge appears on board. This is another sequence involving his blindness. He has to be told where he is by Bake, that the ship he has boarded is the *Connie Martin*, and that it was refloated for him. This is the basis of the brief final scene where the couple are united and talk of the seas they will sail together as man and wife.

The conclusion that presses on us is that Bilge has been persuaded to surrender his freedom not for Connie Martin but for the *Connie Martin*, that, as a current of *double entendre* in the film implies, theirs is a version of the marriage contract in which she becomes the 'vessel' and he is the Captain. The connection is more than just the hint given through the naming of the ship. It is contained in the parallel between the remaking of the girl's appearance at the beginning of the film and the refitting of the ship towards its close – both become objects of desire to this man only when suitably made over, in clothes and make-up, or canvas and paint.

The re–encounter between Bake and Sherry, which takes place in the Paradise Ballroom setting and is intercut with the scenes in which Bilge fails to recognise Connie after her makeover, has as its keynote the idea of likeness, or equality. This is first expressed in a series of verbal exchanges which risk banality in order to make the point that this pair are content to find themselves repeating one another's lines. (As in, *Bake:* 'What a surprise seeing you here' *Sherry:* 'Kind of surprised to see you here too' *Bake:* 'I've missed you' *Sherry:* 'I've missed you too'. This is taken to the point of becoming a conscious gag, carried in the line 'I'm glad to see you' which is delivered five times until Bake caps it by saying, 'Gosh, you're glad to see me'). The first dance number also takes on these qualities as the couple exchange quips about keeping up with each other, and Sherry executes a single movement which elegantly brings her into unison with her partner as the dance begins.

Costume is important here, too. The 'naval' slacks and blouse worn by Rogers for her number are plausible – this is a sailors' dance-hall – but they also distinguish her from almost every other woman in the place, from the other dance-hall girls wearing gowns, from Connie in 'schoolteacher' and 'dance-hall girl' costumes, and from the other dancers on the floor. (A variation on the outfit is worn by the three girls who form her chorus in the number, but they are shot in

Bake and Sherry (Rogers) dance to 'Let Yourself Go' in Follow the Fleet.

such a way as not quite to show their slacks. A single glimpse of one of these chorines, actually Betty Grable, in the dressing room is the only shot that confirms the similarity of their costumes to Sherry's.) The effect, enhanced by Sherry's cap and cravat, is to present her visually as wearing a likeness of Bake's uniform.

Sandrich also annotates this with matched physical gestures – for example, when Bake and Sherry first greet each other, their arms are identically out-stretched. The shots of Bake and Sherry's reunion, sitting side by side at a table in the dance–hall and treated equally by Sandrich's camera, present a sharp visual contrast to the sequence that immediately follows. This is Bilge's first meeting with Connie after her transformation into dance-hall girl, and the geometry of the camerawork, particularly the high angle from behind Bilge's head that Sandrich uses to photograph Connie, emphasise Bilge's dominance. The camerawork reminds us that Bake and Sherry are of similar size and height and suggests the meaning of the opposite situation for Bilge and Connie. Finally, there are the messages of the songs – Sherry's call to pleasure in 'Let Yourself Go' contrasting with the idea of physical arousal as threat in Connie's ballad, 'Get Thee Behind Me, Satan'.

At this point, a way in which Bake and Sherry are possibly unequal is raised. Bake's way of claiming a form of authority is to assert that he can further Sherry's career by organising an audition for her with Nolan (Russell Hicks), a powerful producer. Part of what follows expresses the emptiness of this: as Sherry's 'manager', the title he gives himself, Bake is ineffectual. The arrogant act of talking to the owner of the Paradise Ballroom in such a way as to lose Sherry her job is followed immediately by a reminder that Bake is subject to naval authority (the fleet unexpectedly leaves port), and his belated arrival at Nolan's office shows him as an impotent figure. He cannot gain access to Nolan – we never see them together – and his situation is expressed through the attitude of Sullivan (Brooks Benedict), Nolan's subordinate, friendly but finally unhelpful. So Bake resorts to crippling the opposition by spiking the drink of the unseen auditioning singer with bicarbonate of soda (note the pun on his name, bi-carbonate of soda being otherwise known as baking soda). Of course, the singer

Bake boasts to Sherry about the bicarbonate of soda gag in Follow the Fleet.

was Sherry, and in the next sequence we see her getting even: she disguises an out-of-uniform naval officer as a civilian (by borrowing and concealing his Naval Academy ring) and goads Bake into a fight with him so that she can reveal his rank at a crucial moment. What the two actions have in common is the acknowl-edgement that the way in which this pair can effectively wield power – by manipulating the power structures that surround them indirectly, by trickery – indicates their larger powerlessness. It is this that makes them evenly matched.

The sung duet 'I'm Putting All My Eggs in One Basket' continues to stress the note of resemblance or similarity in the couple, both in the costume (Bake in navy fatigues, Sherry in sweater and slacks that also appear grey on screen) and the delivery of the song. Each gets a full verse to sing to the other, versions of the same sentiments couched in similar words. Once they move a few bars into the dance, the opposite might seem to be the case, for the number is built around a series of gags based on mistakes resulting from the couple not being in synch with each other. This is set up in an exchange of dialogue about not having rehearsed the dance fully, but as the number proceeds it becomes a more and more anarchic miming of aggression, indifference, pleasure, resignation. A point of reference here is the dance section of 'I'll Be Hard to Handle' in *Roberta*, which also invokes something like fighting. The difference is that in the earlier number, the devices are contained within the dance and do not seem about to disrupt it to a point of disintegration. Here the gags, described by Hermes Pan as 'every old vaudeville trick in the world stuck into one number', take over the dance, pushing it much further towards a kind of improvisation in which mistakes can act as opportunities, allowing the couple to explore how it feels to be out of synch and then to find pleasure in being back in synch again. This is like the plot of *Follow the Fleet* as it concerns Bake and Sherry so far – the number is another example of a dance being a kind of ideal reprise of the action of the film.

The placing of the number is also interesting. As it ends, with some difficulty, after a long gag about knowing which is the orchestra's final chord, and what pose to assume, there is no inserted shot of the appreciative audience of sailors or chorus-girls. (The parallel number from *Roberta* is obviously different in this respect.) Since there is no question, narratively speaking, of privacy here, the effect of omitting the shot is to underline the directness with which the number addresses the cinema audience. Bake has introduced the whole sequence with a challenge : 'I can see you fellas don't appreciate high art'. Is he challenging us, reminding us that the intricacy and delicacy (and the search for exactly the right note) that we have been exposed to here can be so thought of?

'Let's Face the Music and Dance', the number which is all we see of the stage show mounted on the *Connie Martin*, suggests that a number of points are

'Every old vaudeville trick in the world': Bake and Sherry about to dance 'I'm Putting All My Eggs in One Basket'.

now being consciously made about what Astaire and Rogers are expected to do, and what they do superlatively well. An expectation (that is also part of the claim of Bake and Sherry's act to be 'high-class') is being satisfied: that the film will find a way finally to get the couple into evening dress. The number replaces the big production numbers of the previous four films in the cycle; it is as if Astaire and Rogers are saying that a performance like this, which simply reeks of class, is what audiences want of them. Further, the dance's miniature drama (with both Astaire's and Rogers's characters on the point of suicide) creates a situation where we see a couple who know nothing of each other meeting in unprecedented circumstances, and we have to trust in the qualities of Astaire's character as he seduces Rogers into the dance: this recalls 'Night and Day', and 'Cheek to Cheek'. The positioning of the number here, at the climax of the film, makes a claim for the importance of this mode of dramatically charged dance for the couple themselves, especially as it is deliberately and self-consciously detached from the main narrative of the film.

It could be argued that 'Let's Face the Music and Dance' is about power (or money), about letting go and finding out in the process that you now have power of a different kind. The final aspect of the film that I want to consider is how it invokes the power structures of the navy and the entertainment business, and points to the connections between them. The link is suggested in the scene of Bake and Sherry sitting together at the table in the Paradise Ballroom, both wearing 'sailor' costumes expressive of the institutions to which they are contracted – she is as much in uniform as he.

This is the first film in the cycle to give Astaire a role in an organisation and a fixed rank in it alongside his professional role as a song-and-dance man, and it begins with the fleet itself and the contract involved in joining the navy. The opening number shows seafaring life in its traditional role as a bargain in which escape from women, or rather from commitment to specific women, is bought at the price of submitting to command. But, of course, the presentation of the 'navy' here continually insists on it being a fabrication: just a set and a range of costumes and roles for the male chorus. The lyrics of 'We Joined the Navy (To See the World)' protest the hollowness of a dream of freedom and a fantasy of heroism while the dance is celebrating the brio and energy of the male group, as they scoop Baker up and set him down, and throughout the film the navy is always both a place of power and command and a site for 'entertainment'.

(*Follow the Fleet* continually works by joking with, and so probing, the distinctions between its different worlds, acknowledging that we are being asked at once to make distinctions between them for the sake of the narrative, and acknowledge their common status as props for the musical comedy. When Bake needs costumes and scenery in order to mount his scratch show, he approaches Sullivan, who agrees to lend the material from an unsuccessful Nolan show. Bake's reply is 'Thanks – and if you ever need a battleship – you can have mine'.)

This film knows that the places where the business of entertainment is conducted are also sites of power. Consider how the subject is presented in the first sequence set in Nolan's offices. When Bake arrives, Sullivan looks at his uniform and greets him with 'What's with the costume, Baker, new act?' Bake's reply makes a distinction and a connection: 'Yes, an Act of Congress'. Immediately after this, we see Nolan auditioning Sherry for her solo act in an inner office set which is decorated prominently with stylised maps of the world, as if to claim that the domination of space by this enterprise can be indicated in the same way as it might be in a naval commander's headquarters. (Perhaps behind the narrative's surface, the presentation of the world of stage production, lies the thought of another power structure, the Hollywood studio. Is it relevant to notice that Nolan is played by Russell Hicks, an actor who had been a director of silent Hollywood film?)

In its concern with power, *Follow the Fleet* is the first of the Astaire-Rogers musicals to pay consistent attention to father figures. There are the benign characters who are either dead (Sherry's father) or nearly powerless (Captain Hickey). Alongside Nolan we can place the other figures of authority in the film, the owner of the Paradise Ballroom and the captain of Bake's ship. And there is the figure of Bilge, deliberately working his way up the ranks to become a 'master'. We can read Bake's role as challenging or defying them, but the film is aware that he is ultimately unable to evade their power to bestow advancement or punishment. In the closing scene, Sherry points out that they cannot take up Nolan's offer of a contract until 'Mr Baker gets out of the brig, which is one thing he can't fix'. This line is followed by the business of the marriage proposal: when Sherry takes the traditionally male role of making the proposal, Bake takes the woman's part. His reply, the last significant line of dialogue in the film, is 'You'll have to ask father'. Who is he talking about? Is his facetiousness admitting the power of these patriarchs or seeking, comedically, to evade it?

With *Follow the Fleet*, a movement in the Astaire-Rogers cycle ends. It is the most self-conscious of the films to date. Part of this is in its awareness that their lengthening history together makes it easy to acknowledge Astaire and Rogers as a dance team and to draw on their familiarity with each other. The film draws a parallel with the history of Astaire and Rogers, in that it both gives them a substantial professional past and locates that past in America. But it is also conscious that another element of their success is their ability to produce charged, dramatic dance, and it is aware of the necessity of finding a structure that will include this. It achieves both intimacy and drama, represented by 'I'm Putting All My Eggs in One Basket' and 'Let's Face the Music and Dance' respectively, by detaching the dramatic dance from the main narrative, so that the couple can still meet for the first time, as it were, in a dance within a show within the film. This is the only time that the couple find their drama in this way. From now on their own situation will provide it.

A distinct shift could now be said to take place in the cycle. Of the five films we have looked at thus far, two turn on a comedic convention in which the mistakes of a weekend and their resolution show Astaire and Rogers, as the film ends, in the act of becoming a couple, and a dance team for the first time – *The Gay Divorcée* and *Top Hat*. Of the other three, two turn on a couple already familiar with each other, and the brio of the acknowledgement that the partner they find themselves dancing with is the right partner, which the films claim is like finding themselves to be married to the right partner. (These are *Roberta* and *Follow the Fleet*, and there is a primitive gesture towards this structure in *Flying Down to Rio*.) In the films after *Follow the Fleet*, the couple's lengthening history as dance partners will be explicitly acknowledged, and the tension will emanate from the sense of an ending, the anticipation or the enactment of the breakdown of the couple's dancing lives together.

CHAPTER TWO
THE ARGUMENT OF TIME:
THE LATER RKO MUSICALS

SWING TIME (George Stevens, 1936)

Each of the Astaire-Rogers musicals strikes a balance between innovation and the retaining, or retrieval, of production elements from the earlier films. *Swing Time* redeploys actors from *Top Hat* – Helen Broderick and Eric Blore – and the score is by Jerome Kern, who had written *Roberta*. A screenplay credit is given to Allan Scott, whose involvement in the cycle runs from his uncredited contribution to *The Gay Divorcée* through to *Carefree*. On the side of innovation is the appearance of two actors in significant roles: Georges Metaxa as the bandleader Ricardo Romero and Victor Moore as 'Pop' Cardetti. Metaxa is a variation of a previous figure, the foreigner who hopes to wed the Rogers character, and Moore, as a kind of father to the Astaire character, is a new departure, although anticipated by the

Left: jumping a train. Lucky Garnett (Astaire) with 'Pop' Cardetti (Victor Moore) in Swing Time.

Opposite: getting acquainted. Lucky borrows from Penny Carrol (Rogers).

interest in father figures in *Follow The Fleet*. A partial innovation (she had written two numbers for *Roberta*) is Dorothy Fields as lyricist. But perhaps the most important shift is from Mark Sandrich, who had directed *The Gay Divorcée*, *Top Hat* and *Follow the Fleet*, to George Stevens.

The cycle has so far developed around two easily distinguishable types of plot. In one, the couple have known each other – which is to say, have danced together – in the past; the plot contrasts them with a second couple, and as the series progresses we can see the status of this couple shift from that of the main focus of attention (*Flying Down to Rio*), to a parallel romance (*Roberta*), to a couple whose relationship is offered as inferior to that of Astaire and Rogers (*Follow the Fleet*). There does not seem to be an agreed shorthand for this group – I will call them 'dance team' films.

In the other plot structure, Astaire encounters Rogers for the first time and pursues her. Their mutual seduction through dance is complicated by misunderstandings which are resolved in time for the couple to emerge and dance publicly together in the number which ends the movie ('The Continental' in *The Gay Divorcée*, 'The Piccolino' in *Top Hat*). These films do not involve a second pair of lovers. In their concern to find the right partner for a young woman they might, for my purposes, be termed romances. Up to this point, the cycle has alternated between the two structures.

Given that Howard Lindsay, the writer with Allan Scott of the screenplay of *Swing Time*, had directed *Gay Divorce* on Broadway, it is not surprising that *Swing Time* begins by returning to the plotting of *The Gay Divorcée*. Again we see a chance meeting between the Astaire and Rogers characters, John 'Lucky' Garnett and Penny Carrol, in a mundane public place. He annoys her – she calls for an

'Pick Yourself Up' in Swing Time, *a number about doing something over and over again.*

official, this time a policeman rather than a porter. The scene ends with her re-treating in disarray, and he pursues her to a place from which she cannot flee. This time it is not a country road but a dancing academy run by Mr Gordon (Eric Blore). Lucky reminds her of where they had started by quoting her own earlier call for help back to her. His 'Officer?' on the dance floor here is a recollection of Guy's rhetorical 'Porter? Porter?' as Mimi is threatening to ram his car with hers in *The Gay Divorcée*, as if to ask her to consider what such cries for assistance are for – what do you want to be saved from? She begins to relent.

Now the structure departs from the earlier model. The couple sing 'Pick Yourself Up' together, a song about doing something over and over again. We can read it as being about what we know Astaire and Rogers do – endlessly rehearsing dance to a point of perfection – while reminding us that this involves something as ordinary as falling over. They perform in front of an audience of one, the astonished Mr Gordon, who immediately organises a tryout for them at the Silver Slipper night-spot. The difference from the previous two romances can be seen by comparing the contexts of the couples' first dances. A keynote of 'Night and Day' or 'Isn't this a Lovely Day (to Be Caught in the Rain)' is the couple's privacy, and our access to that privacy. Here the dance is a professional occasion, designed to impress an audience and retrieve a lost job (Gordon wants to sack Penny) and resulting in a desired professional break. The ending encapsulates the difference, a striding 'offstage' at the end of a performance, not a tableau of repose or an intimate handshake. Suddenly – though familiarity with the history of Astaire and Rogers means that it does not feel sudden – they are a dance team. Pandro Berman's comment on the pair at this point was: 'The minute the names of Astaire and Rogers go up on the marquee, the audience knows they belong together' (quoted in Croce, p.109).

Thus, the business that occupies most of the plot of the romances, from the first meeting to the fusing of the couple into a dance team, is condensed into a few minutes. It is as if the audience's knowledge – that of course the couple can dance wonderfully together – means that the charge of discovering this will no longer sustain the whole movie, so the result is that the romance plot dissolves into the dance-team plot, becoming a brief prologue to it. One of the ways in which this is expressed is that the film now implies the passing of a significant amount of time, during which the couple quarrel, make up and live a life of professional dance together. (Compare this with the action of *Top Hat*, which takes place over a single weekend, or the few hours that constitute the last half of *The Gay Divorcée*.) An element of the central part of the film is to display this life by showing professional routines performed by Lucky and Penny on the public stage: the context for 'Waltz in Swing Time'. It is the third number in the film, and the difference in structure can be measured by seeing that as a polished public show it resembles the numbers at the end of several of the earlier films. 'Bojangles of Harlem', Astaire's blackface solo number with a chorus, is also presented solely as a professional turn performed by Lucky at the Silver Slipper; it has almost no other function in the plot of the film.

There is another shift away from previous patterns. The second pair of lovers in the dance-team films were always distinguished from the Astaire-Rogers couple in that their romance generated occasions not for dance but for song, or ballad – Irene Dunne's three songs in *Roberta*, and Harriet Hillyard's two in *Follow the*

Lucky and Penny dancing 'Waltz in Swing Time'.

Fleet. (This is not simply a matter of pointing out the distinction between songs that lead into dance and songs that do not, but of noticing the subjects and occasions of Dunne's and Hillyard's singing as having reference to the past or to loss, or death.) If we read *Swing Time* against the structure of the previous dance-team movies, we find that the second couple has disappeared, but that songs which are not introductions to dances remain, now given to Astaire and Rogers; these are 'The Way You Look Tonight', and 'A Fine Romance'.

The context of 'The Way You Look Tonight' relates to the film's implication that these events are taking place over weeks, not hours. It is one of intimacy, or domestic ordinariness, an implied life together. The plot here is that Lucky has missed the initial tryout at the Silver Slipper because he was not able to assemble the right costume (a running gag in the film). He and Penny have quarrelled, and a reconciliation is finally brokered by Mabel (Helen Broderick). Now Lucky enters Penny's hotel suite and they talk through a closed door, while Penny, wearing a bathrobe, massages shampoo into her hair. When she believes him to have left, she begins washing her hair in earnest. He sits at the piano in the living room and starts to sing. (This is evidently as much domestic intimacy as the censors were likely to allow. Croce quotes Howard Lindsay as saying that the scene as originally written had Penny dishevelled after cooking dinner for Lucky, but 'the producers lacked the courage to do this'.)

The Kern-Fields song, which won the Academy Award for Best Song in 1936, needs to be heard in full for the quality it brings to this sequence to be properly understood. Here I can only stress its subject, which is the belief that there can be such a thing as a benign, retrievable past. It imagines an unspecified point – 'some day' – as a place of firm vantage, from which a specific joy – 'the way you look tonight' – can be recalled, not as loss but as energy: 'a glow/Just thinking of you'. Its relation to time, looking forward to looking back, is a sentiment entirely new to the cycle.

If we think of the singer as Lucky rather than Astaire, then this is a small progression in the romance and a gentle gag, a love song about how a girl looks, addressed to a girl he cannot see. (It is perhaps a little odd for Lucky to be thinking in these terms about a romance which still seems close to its beginnings, but this will be explained later in the film.) If we think of the singer as Astaire – and we are encouraged in this reading by the intimacy of the setting and the sense that the pair are much more at ease with each other than the literal progression of the plot can account for – then it becomes a pivotal moment in the cycle, the first explicit recognition, or imagining, of an ending. It celebrates the couple's achievement while recognising it as both transient (because of their mortality) and enduring. Such a reading may also have a force for us that it cannot have offered in 1936 – Astaire's 'some day' is now, and the predicted glow, ours.

Any account of the sequence must consider how it is directed by George Stevens. Stevens shows us the working dancer that is Penny, with a couple of shots of her massaging her scalp and telling Lucky off. But as Astaire's song transforms the occasion, he transforms her. The cap of white suds becomes a perfect wig made of some unlikely material, combining an idea of ordinariness with the sense of carefully wrought perfection: these suds sculpt the head as real suds never do. (Rogers in her autobiography tells of the considerable difficulty of achieving exactly the right effect.) Stevens photographs the song by cutting between shots of Lucky at the piano and four memorable close-ups of Penny's face as she moves through the space, which are unlike anything to be found in the earlier Sandrich films. When she finally touches Lucky and he turns to her, neither of them quite smiles or laughs. The sequence is remarkable; it might stand for something that Astaire and Rogers do consistently well, the capturing of an impression that is simultaneously part of the mundane world recorded by the cinema – a girl with shampoo on her head – and part of another world that it also records, a briefly perfect image of beauty.

Now Stevens makes a significant cut, to the Silver Slipper Ballroom. The last lines of the number are reprised, in a very different style, by bandleader Ricardo Romero, partly into a microphone and partly to Penny. A figure leans across and speaks into the mike, concluding the radio broadcast of which the song was a part. This explains what Lucky was doing – not improvising, but singing a popular hit of the day – and in this respect excuses the sentiment of the lyric by placing it slightly outside the narrative in a way that could be related back to the placing of the emotions of 'Let's Face the Music and Dance' in *Follow the Fleet*. But while this explanation makes literal sense of the narrative, it leaves the song the more easily read as Astaire's song to Rogers than Lucky's to Penny.

In the romances, we see the lovers finding themselves transported to another place in order to work out their fates – a place designated as 'Brightburn' or 'Venice'. The 'New Amsterdam' sequence of *Swing Time* can be viewed as a parallel to this movement and an interrogation of it. Here the journey to a holiday resort becomes a brief interlude in a place both hostile (a derelict hotel and band-stand, freezing cold and falling snow) and enchanted (the musical score, and falling snow on a Hollywood sound stage, at which the principals arrive in an anomalously open car). 'A Fine Romance' expresses this sense of enchantment. Singing about their difficulties becomes a celebration of the fun of the couple's intimacy, that this truly is, as the ambiguity (the play on the meaning of 'fine') in Fields's title allows, a fine romance, and again the song floats between reference to Lucky and Penny and reference to Astaire and Rogers. (The nearest thing to it earlier in the cycle is the sung part of 'I Won't Dance' in *Roberta*, which Fields was also involved in writing. The note of jokey reference to other films is one link: 'especially when you do the Continental', referring to *The Gay Divorcée*, in the

'Does she dance very beautifully?' The introductory dialogue between Lucky and Penny for 'Never Gonna Dance' in Swing Time.

earlier song, and here 'we don't have half the thrills that the March of Time has'.)

The sequence also expresses the hostility of the world and the vulnerability of the Rogers character. Pop functions as a senex figure (the parental figure common in traditional comedies whose role is to block the flowering of the romance), first by interrupting Lucky and Penny and then by telling Penny of Lucky's engagement to another girl. This is the first occasion when the roles in this plot are reversed, and there is a striking change in tone from those occasions when Astaire's character had learned that Rogers's character was engaged or about to be married. For Penny, the engagement is a disaster – Astaire's optimistic sense that of course such difficulties can be worked out is replaced with Rogers's sense of her own powerlessness and vulnerability, her belief in her inability to move the Astaire figure except within the spell of the dance, a mood that will reach its climax in her tears in *Carefree*. And something is beginning to be confirmed here about the loss of the gaze that bound the couple together in the earlier films. Following 'The Way You Look Tonight', in which the couple literally could not see each other, most of the lines here are sung as one of the pair, back turned, walks away from the other.

The final move in the plot redeploys and develops a configuration from *Top Hat* – the Rogers character, deceived as to the real status of the Astaire character, agrees to marry another. The degree to which this threatened marriage is a much more serious matter than before may be seen by comparing Romero to Beddini in *Top Hat*. Stevens treats Romero with some generosity; his foreignness is not presented comically, his sexual performance is never in question, he is played as tactless but never a fool, and he will be generous in defeat. So the threatened loss of Penny to Romero has a substance that the loss of Dale Tremont to Beddini never had, and the crisis produces the following dialogue as the final number begins. Stevens has Lucky and Penny standing a little apart, looking into each other's eyes:

> *Penny:* Does she dance very beautifully?
> *Lucky:* Who?
> *Penny:* The girl you're in love with.
> *Lucky:* Yes, [*pauses, with great earnestness*] very.
> *Penny* [*her gaze falters for a second as she realises where this has taken them*]: The girl you're engaged to, the girl you're going to marry.
> *Lucky:* Oh, I don't know. I've danced with you. I'm never going to dance again.

The first four lines demonstrate, and insist on, the connection between dancing very beautifully and being in love, as if they can be understood as the same thing. This is related to what I have said about the couple's acceptance of the inevitability of their marriage in previous films, as if something that they think of as marriage had already happened to them. The next exchange sums up ordinary engagement and marriage as something that exists somewhere else, in a world that is not known (or cared?) about. Lucky's last two sentences can be read not as a threat, or a *cri de coeur* but as a definition of dancing – it was what I did with you, whatever else I do will be something else, but it won't be dancing.

What follows is Lucky's song ('Never Gonna Dance') and the couple's dance. The following can be observed:

1) It does not end with an embrace, but with Penny dancing off into the wings leaving Lucky alone in a pose of yearning and loss. It is thus neither a dance of reconciliation nor a rejection of Penny's choice of Romero.

2) There is no audience whatever to the dance – it celebrates the couple's privacy in a public space, and the perfection of the present moment (the melody of 'The Way You Look Tonight' is worked into the orchestration at the point of the beautiful stroll that becomes the dance number.) This is a reversal of the pattern of the romances – the larger movement is now from public to private dance.

3) The song, and then the dance, involve a pantomime of retreat and pursuit, Penny walking away in the initial parts of the song, and moving as if to retreat again as one movement of the dance number ends.

4) In all three of these respects, the number to which 'Never Gonna Dance' can be most related is the one which initiated the major part of the cycle, the couple's first duet, 'Night and Day'.

5) Stevens includes two shots of Rogers, alone on the stairs, framed by stars, as if to insist on her status as central to what is being lost, and celebrated, here.

The account that I have given so far has emphasised the film's move into a bleaker, if no less rich, world. But there are strategies to overcome this melancholy, for example, the use of magic, or trickery. It begins with a card trick, performed by 'Pop' Cardetti, to which nobody is paying attention, and the opening dialogue is about innovation, about changing the act, an impulse that we learn comes from the Astaire character: 'He says, straight magic is too old-fashioned'. The next sequence defines a kind of magic and continues the subject of what is and is not in fashion. Lucky is about to marry Margaret (Betty Furness), the wrong girl for him. His fellow dancers cast a spell – a couple of lines are quickly drawn on to a photo in *Esquire*, and he is persuaded, or allows himself to be persuaded, that he cannot possibly get married in 'last year's trousers'. Obviously this trick, taken at face value, would only fool a child. We may consider that perhaps Lucky's desire to get married isn't so great, that last year's fashions are a laugh, and that laughter is infectious. And what of the desire here, almost the anxiety, not to be thought old-fashioned? The film begins and ends with a gag which has to do with the repudiation of the past, or one's own connections with the past, as if it is hiding the determined, frantic desire to be thought to be facing only towards the future.

The film is aware that such an insistence makes for hysterical behaviour, as the reprise of the trousers gag shows. Lucky and Margaret discover that they are both in love with someone else and burst into simultaneous laughter. Pop and Mabel arrive, and the laughter spreads to them. Now Lucky and Pop visit Romero, in order somehow to prevent his marriage to Penny. Romero suggests 'maybe you should call me Lucky', wiping the smile from Lucky's face. But what the film calls luck, or magic, is on Lucky's side; on the table is the identical copy of *Esquire*. Laughing helplessly, Lucky and Pop pull the 'last year's trousers' gag on him. The wedding sequence is structured by the reduction of the characters one by one to hysterical laughter, first Mabel (who is still in hysterics from the previous sequence), then Pop (producing the confiscated trousers like a rabbit out of a hat), then Lucky, and finally Penny. Stevens organises the editing of the sequence so

Dissolving into laughter: Penny, Lucky and Ricardo (Georges Metaxa), the victim of the 'wrong trousers' gag, in Swing Time.

that we are waiting for her reaction, yet another instance of his direction underlining the importance of Rogers. Penny announces, through her laughter, that 'there isn't going to be any wedding', agrees with the obvious fact that she's going to marry Lucky, and the final reprise song begins, each character taking a line, led off by Romero. So that we can see the snow dry up and the sun come out, the couple move to the window, and the fade-out takes place on a duet of the two previous songs without dances: 'A Fine Romance' sung by Lucky against 'Just the Way You Look Tonight' sung by Penny.

This tide of laughter might be thought of as a species of intoxication (something you cannot control) and an infection (something you 'catch' from those around you), but is it a response to the stress of a difficult situation? Moments earlier, we have seen Margaret in tears, and Mabel starts to laugh, commenting, 'I know just how you feel: I've been divorced a couple of times myself.' *Swing Time* is plotted with care, and the idea of laughter being a response to an unbearable situation has already emerged twice, once in the New Amsterdam sequence, when Penny (sadly) corrects the description of Lucky as 'aloof' to 'a laugh', and once in an earlier moment of crisis, when Penny's tearful exit line was 'Why don't you laugh – it's all so very funny'. Laughter does indeed solve the problem of the plot, but does this leave a suggestion that the only response to these problems is to overwhelm them? In 1930, Freud wrote in *Civilisation and Its Discontents* of 'powerful deflections, which cause us to make light of our misery', and offered physical intoxication as an option in an otherwise insoluble world. The intoxication here is not chemical (the issue will be raised again, in those terms, in *Carefree*), but an uncontrollable bodily response needed to banish the melancholy of the film.

The changes in both mood and structure make *Swing Time*'s use of the couple quite different from that of the first part of the cycle. If there is more of a sense of the value and uniqueness of their achievement here, there is also more awareness that whatever strategies are adopted to postpone it, sooner or later the cycle will conclude. Paradoxically, although the film contains four immaculately successful dance numbers by Astaire and Rogers, dance seems no longer absolutely, or solely, at its centre. By introducing for the Astaire-Rogers couple songs which are not also dances, it finds drama in the question of how, or why, the couple may *not* dance (or not quite dance: a look at the choreography of the sequence that includes 'A Fine Romance' reveals the thinness of the line dividing these movements from a dance number). The raising of such issues is the first sign of something that will develop in the ensuing films, a gradual withdrawal of conviction in the capacity of dance to redeem the negative elements of the world of the film, associated with an increasing sense of the hostility of that world.

Another question raised by *Swing Time* is the change in the kind of attention given to Rogers. Is it mainly a matter of George Stevens being a director more sensitive to her responses than Mark Sandrich had been? It is true that she seems more sympathetically photographed in some of the later films – Rogers attributed this to the cinematographer Robert de Grasse, who worked on nine films with her, including *Carefree* and *The Story of Vernon and Irene Castle*, between 1937 and 1940, although *Shall We Dance* was to be a return to the combination responsible for several of the other films in the series, Mark Sandrich as director and David Abel as cinematographer. Perhaps the different treatment also has to do with the changing mood. The awareness of the possibility of the end of the partnership focuses attention on Rogers, in that (until the issue is resolved in quite a different way in the final film) it implies the loss or withdrawal of the Rogers figure, and the sense that she is irreplaceable.

SHALL WE DANCE (Mark Sandrich, 1937)

The last major number of *Swing Time*, 'Never Gonna Dance', made a drama of the subject of an ending. Could the interrogative title of *Shall We Dance* – a late choice, replacing working titles like *Stepping Toes* – be a deliberate allusion to that number, a sign of an intention to answer its negativity, but with a degree of tentativeness? Certainly, *Shall We Dance* represents a further substantial departure from the pattern of the earlier films. This is not in the plotting of the encounters between the principals, which follows the established pattern of the romances: the first meeting, the initial antagonism, the misunderstandings, the emergence as a dance team. It is in the matter of characterisation and situation. These events are happening to different figures, or rather figures who understand their worlds differently. I can explain most easily by summarising the innovations of the film:

1) The film deals with the difficulty of casting the couple as ingénues of the dance, by constructing a plot in which they are experienced dancers, but not a team. Both the Astaire and the Rogers characters have been at the top of their respective branches of the profession for some considerable time, enough to feel firmly established – we are asked to read them as stars. The plot is that Petrov (Astaire) is a star of the classical ballet and Linda Keene (Rogers) is a Broadway dancer and

Classical dance meets Broadway dance: 'Petrov' (Astaire) greets Linda Keene (Rogers) as her manager, Arthur (Jerome Cowan), looks on in Shall We Dance.

singer. That the Astaire character is a star is implied in *The Gay Divorcée* and stated in *Top Hat*, but the same has never been true of the Rogers character. It is as if we are meeting Lizzie/Scharwenka from *Roberta* some years later in her career.

2) For both of them, success is measured in some part by public recognition, and the penalty of this is a life lived in public. The press, which has no substantial presence in the earlier films (a brief headline for a plot point in *Roberta* is about all) has a central role here.

3) The plot involves a transatlantic crossing which both the principals, who are Americans (Petrov, real name Peter P. Peters, is a stage Russian, like Scharwenka earlier), understand as an act of returning home. The earlier films either took place in America or made journeys away from it to exotic locations (Rio, Paris).

4) The previous films in the cycle make no mention of children (other than the childhoods of the players), and virtually no children appear in them. Apart from a newsboy, no child has a speaking role in *Shall We Dance*, but the film continually returns to the subjects of pregnancy and birth, in both plotting and gags. No-one is actually pregnant, but it is as if the subject of pregnancy cannot be evaded.

5) The meaning of the threat of the marriage of the Rogers character to some-one other than the Astaire character has changed. The two previous instances, in *Top Hat* and *Swing Time*, show Rogers agreeing to marry another because she has lost the Astaire character, believing that he is already married or engaged to be married. One of the opening moves of *Shall We Dance* is Linda's announcement that she is returning home to get married, and this is conceived as a retirement from Broadway, the end of a career. At this stage she has not yet met Petrov.

6) The changed significance and scale of the use of images of Rogers. In *Follow the Fleet*, we see her with Astaire in their professional 'dance team' photograph. In *Swing Time*, she appears in a studio portrait in the dance academy, and twice as a reflection in a mirror. *Shall We Dance* insists on the repeated reproduction of the image of Linda. She appears as the figure in the flip book that Petrov is playing with in the opening minutes of the film, as a dummy with a detachable head, as a series of newspaper photographs (shots of both Linda and of the Linda dummy) and as the image on the masks of Linda worn by the chorus in the final number.

7) Previously the extent of relationships between the star and his or her entourage, followers or managers or friends, was represented by the link between the Astaire and the Edward Everett Horton characters in *The Gay Divorcée* and *Top Hat* and, minimally, the Victor Moore character in *Swing Time*. Here the Edward Everett Horton role remains unchanged, but otherwise the relationships are of a different kind. The men involved with Linda are her manager Arthur Miller (Jerome Cowan) and her putative fiancé Jim (William Brisbane). There is a parallel in the women who attach themselves to Petrov: Denise (Ketti Gallian), a former prima ballerina making a comeback, and Harriet Hoctor, the ballerina who plays herself, dancing with Petrov in the closing ballet. Arthur Miller and Harriet Hoctor are also similar in that their connection to the respective stars is mainly professional, while Jim and Denise are their opposites and wish to enhance their own status by marrying a star. It is made clear that for Linda and Petrov figures like these are simply a function of fame. There will always be ballerinas wanting to marry Petrov, and playboys wanting Linda. There is no emotional connection to them: the feelings circulating around Margaret and Romero in *Swing Time* are dense by comparison. Petrov dismisses Denise with a reference to 'all the trouble she caused', and no attempt is made to substantiate any idea of feeling between Linda and Jim, who represents a joke, or an escape route, or a sense that marriage can be a catastrophe.

8) There are betrothals but no wedding ceremonies in the cycle before *Swing Time*. That film approaches the moment twice, taking us to a place where a ceremony is

due to be performed but the weddings (of Lucky to Margaret, of Penny to Romero) fail at the last moment to find both parties ready to consent. In *Shall We Dance*, the aspect of Petrov and Linda with which many of its characters are concerned is not their love but their marriage, that is, not their private feeling but a public acknowledgement of their commitment to each other. The film includes Petrov and Linda's marriage. What we actually see and hear is not their vows, but a shot of the Justice of the Peace filling in the certificate, the public document that defines their social relation to the world.

9) The music and lyrics are by George and Ira Gershwin. Astaire's connection with the Gershwins dated back to the stage musicals *Lady Be Good* (1924) and *Funny Face* (1927) and Rogers's, also on the stage, to *Girl Crazy* (1930). But the immediate past is as important. George Gershwin's latest work was *Porgy and Bess*, which opened in New York on 10th October 1935 and played into 1936, with a total of 124 performances. The Gershwins arrived in Hollywood in the late summer of 1936, and in her autobiography Rogers tells us that she started work on *Shall We Dance* on Christmas Eve of that year. The significance of the Gershwins' music at this point in their career cannot be separated from the response to *Porgy and Bess* (a critical but not a commercial success on Broadway) and the ensuing argument about the common ground between the opera and Broadway, leading George Gershwin to point out (in a letter to the *New York Times*, 20th October 1935) that 'Carmen is almost a collection of song hits'. It seems probable that this debate cannot have been far from Allan Scott's mind in inventing the 'marriage' of popular and high culture in New York as a main plotline of the film.

The plots that operate to separate the Rogers and Astaire characters in the previous romances, the misunderstandings that turn on who they are, or whom they wish to marry, are no help as models for *Shall We Dance*. This can be demonstrated by asking if there is any point in the film where Linda's projected engagement to Jim is felt as even the slightest impediment to any other relationship. The answer is clearly no – the impediment is of a different sort, and relates to the kind of life allowed to figures who are felt to be public property.

After their first meeting, Petrov has discovered that Linda is sailing home and pursues her, booking a passage on the same boat. They clash as soon as they board – Petrov's 'Russian' act is dismissed by Linda as 'one of the games little American boys play'. This is followed by a sequence in which Linda repeats to Arthur her plans for marriage to Jim and retirement from the dance: 'I'm tired of being pawed.' (It is one of two scenes in the film in which dialogue about marriage is misunderstood by a casual listener – here a ship's steward who reads Linda as the virtuous woman, refusing the role of mistress to Arthur. This indicates how like that of a kept woman Linda's role is, and could also be a way of saying how easy it is for her position to be misunderstood.)

In the events leading up to Linda's first flight from Petrov, the sequence of the boat's departure, showing Linda's and then Petrov's relations to the press, establishes the crossing as a form of flight or rest from their public roles. Astaire's solo number, 'Slap That Bass' emphasises this, being not a professional performance but an improvised number in the ship's engine room. The note of the ordinary is continued in the next stage of his wooing of Linda. The context is one of the ways in which life on board ship imitates, or asserts its connection with, the

Consummate skill: Petrov and Linda stroll their way into the dance of 'They All Laughed' in Shall We Dance.

routines of daily life: passengers with dogs can take them for a walk on deck. The action is split into three sections, a first unsuccessful encounter with the couple in evening clothes followed by a second, successful one in casual dress. Here Sandrich photographs Rogers in a medium close-up that emphasises her private enjoyment of this everyday moment. In the third section, the couple are together and back in evening dress, and Petrov sings the light, slightly narcissistic number 'I've Got Beginner's Luck', while Linda listens politely. It is a good example of how Rogers is able to perform the act of listening to a song so as to indicate the exact state of her emotions.

Here Linda is interested in Petrov, but the couple have not yet danced together. The absence of a number at this point to sweep the romance forward is one of the ways in which *Shall We Dance* extends something raised in *Swing Time*, the drama of the couple's *not* dancing. The choreography of the pair strolling up and down seems to be teasing the audience's expectations of Astaire and Rogers, playing on our impatience, our feeling that they might dance if only these dogs were got out of the way. And the presence of fine incidental music, written by George Gershwin, intensifies the effect. We are in a world where dance, and what it implies for this couple, is difficult to achieve.

What happens next is that the private lives of Petrov and Linda are subjected to the public gaze. A rumour of a secret marriage circulates around the boat, and they stand, uneasy and uncomprehending, as the other passengers sing 'for he's a jolly good fellow'. Worse is to come – they have been seen sitting together, with Linda knitting what is in fact a coat for her dog but looks suspiciously like a baby

garment. The ship's bulletin archly announces 'it is rumoured that a blessed event is imminent'.

Linda reacts with fury, smashing one of the cabin windows when Arthur attempts a joke, angrily rejecting the crew's congratulations, and fleeing the scene. We have not seen evidence of her feeling for Petrov being other than genial interest, and there has still been no dance. To say that Linda is in love and that her rage is some combination of her repressed desire and her humiliation at finding out that she has (as she thinks) been 'used' by Petrov to get rid of another woman seems insufficient to account for such anger. There is also the question, which is often implicit in the plotting of romances that turn on such misunderstandings, of why the wronged party does not simply speak out in plain denial, and what exactly such a denial would involve.

Her outrage is provoked when she opens the ship's newspaper at the breakfast table in her cabin, a set of circumstances that will be more or less repeated, with the same meaning, later in the film. It is her privacy that is being violated – less a matter of a fine romance with Petrov, or anyone else, than a sense of being denied a private world in which such a romance might possibly take place. We can distinguish between her responses to the newspaper's claims. The marriage can be spoken of, and Linda will deny it at intervals in the rest of the film, until she is finally in a position to confirm it. But the matter of pregnancy is one of which she never speaks. Even her rage at Cecil Flintridge (Eric Blore), the manager of her hotel apartment, who has taken the liberty of filling her bedroom with toys, is wordless. The film suggests that marriage exists in the public

Jim (William Brisbane) finds Linda and Petrov together in Shall We Dance.

realm and may be subject to assertion and denial there, but that pregnancy is emblematic of the woman's privacy, and it is her right to choose when and how to make known something that stands at the core of the intimate. Such a distinction could suggest that the knowledge of pregnancy, and the sharing of that knowledge, might be thought of as a private act which precedes the public knowledge of the institution of marriage. Pregnancy, rather than functioning as a literal state, comes here to represent privacy.

The conflict between private and public continues when Linda arrives in New York to a montage of newspaper headlines proclaiming her marriage to Petrov. The scene in Arthur's nightclub uses the business of stars having, with real or faked reluctance, to acknowledge their status as public property by doing a turn for the audience. Linda's song, 'They All Laughed', is offered as something the singer expects, or is at least not surprised, to find herself doing, and she knows that she can give a good performance. The 'surprise' dance with Petrov (a surprise to Linda, but obviously a set-up between Petrov and Arthur) is very different. Sandrich photographs Linda so as to give the narrative of her reactions, from her confusion and her consciousness of the risk in this situation to consent and relief. The dance represents the ideal resolution of the tension between intimacy (making the dance up as you go along) and the acknowledgement of the public role (achieving harmony in the public eye). The tension is at its sharpest and most touching in the moment of the transition from song to dance, as the couple learn their first moves from each other. This crux in the structure of the number, the

Ordinary Americans: Linda and Petrov sit on the grass in Central Park.

drama and brio of which can be traced back through analogous moments to the couple's first duet, appears here for the last time in the cycle.

This sequence has a link with the event that follows it, Arthur's faking of proof of the marriage by sneaking into Petrov's bedroom with a dummy of Linda and passing the posed 'intimate' photographs to the press, and Linda's and Petrov's reaction. The connection is that in both cases the couple are faced with evidence of their intimacy without quite understanding the route through which this state has been achieved, as if part of the process of knowing each other has been misplaced or lost. They also discover that they do not exactly object to where they find themselves, which is a further confusion, and a source of comedy. Jim's arrival in the apartment to remonstrate with Linda is an example of it. In her bedroom, he finds Linda in her negligée and Petrov in his dressing gown, quite as if this is a continuation of the life represented in the photos in the morning paper, and the comedy springs from the failure of the couple to remember that they are doing anything other than behaving naturally. It is as if all three submit to the spell cast by the image in the newspaper, as if Petrov and Linda are indeed married.

It is now that we see the couple escape to work out their relationship. This follows similar moves in some of the earlier films, but instead of an escape to an exotic or an enchanted place, here the world of nightclubs and swanky apartments is abandoned, via the back stairs, for the urban ordinariness of Central Park. The couple visit the zoo, row on the lake, and finally roller-skate together – a sequence introduced by the sight of a few skating children, an allusion to the games the couple might have played as children. (In Rogers's account, the genesis of the roller-skating idea occurred as her interruption of Hermes Pan's reminiscences of his childhood [Rogers, p.160].) They sing 'Let's Call the Whole Thing Off', a love song which proposes that the only difference between lovers could be how they choose to pronounce words, and celebrate the relocation of their skills in the quotidian world by performing an Astaire-Rogers duet on roller skates. The ending of the number neatly underlines the tension around which it is built, between the ordinary and the quality of honed performance. Intoxicated by the dance, the pair skate at speed towards an imaginary stage exit, and come crashing down on the turf, their hardest landing in the whole cycle. (Perhaps this is indicative of the distance to be covered here between being up in the air and having your feet on the ground. It has been anticipated in the choreography of 'They All Laughed', which ends with a series of movements in which Petrov sits Linda down and then raises her to her feet again, and by their bumpy landing as they first sit down in their skates here.)

It is while they are seated on the turf that Linda realises that the way to solve their problem is to make a private arrangement that will correspond to the public reality. They will marry secretly, so that she can then start divorce proceedings. Now for the second time, a conversation about marriage is overheard, this time by a passing policeman:

> *Petrov:* . . . well, I don't know.
> *Linda:* You got me into all this, the very least you could do is marry me.
> *Petrov:* Wasn't my fault any more than it was yours.
> *Linda:* All right, it's my fault. But *[emphatically]* you've just got to marry me.
> *Petrov:* Well now, I'd like to think it over.
> *Linda:* But why, there's nothing to think over.
> *Petrov:* All right . . .

The presence of the policeman allows Sandrich to include reaction shots that underline the perceived meaning of this conversation. It is a return to the subject of pregnancy, the cop assuming that the girl must persuade her reluctant boyfriend into marriage. The effect is to give the couple a place in ordinary life where such events happen (and are governed by mundane laws embodied in an ordinary cop). The other point, clearly established by now – in *Roberta, Follow the Fleet, Swing Time* – is that making a proposal of marriage for this couple is the business of the woman.

In the wedding to which the sequence cuts, the stars are without their stage identities: Linda Thompson marries Peter P. Peters. The admission of these names also points to the problem – that neither Linda nor Petrov can hold on to these ordinary identities for more than a short period of time, in this unlikely place. What follows, as they return to New York, is close to a dream sequence. It takes place in a mist, in a floating space (literally the ferry to Manhattan), with the couple apparently alone and Petrov singing 'They Can't Take That Away From Me' to Linda.

An important song delivered by Astaire to Rogers and not leading into dance suggests a link to *Swing Time*, when Lucky sings 'The Way You Look Tonight' to Penny. Both songs speak of the Astaire figure's awareness of the possibility of the loss of the Rogers figure, and both celebrate their belief in enduring memory. They operate on two levels, addressing the situation of the couple in the film and in the cycle of Astaire's and Rogers's career together. The difference is in the point the narratives have reached. Here the situation is closer to the 'Never Gonna Dance' sequence of *Swing Time*, when the loss of the Rogers figure seems imminent. The Gershwins' song does not dispel the sense of waste, which continues to the end of the sequence. In his direction of the number Sandrich, perhaps following Stevens's lead, gives Linda one emphatic (if too brief and thus somehow clumsy) close-up on the climactic phrase 'the way you've changed my life'. More successful is the direction of the gaze. As the scene begins, Linda is speaking while looking away from Petrov, and after the introductory verse she does not look directly at him again. Given the force of the couple's gaze in major numbers earlier in the cycle, this immensely increases the melancholy of the moment.

Petrov's song is a way of trying to create, or claim, a life with Linda, a life which combines mundane detail – 'the way you wear your hat', 'sip your tea', 'hold your knife' – with singing and dancing – 'the way you sing off key', 'danced till three', a lyric that brings Peter P. Peters and Linda Thompson into contact with Petrov and Linda Keene. It is also a way of wooing her, of suggesting that something positive could come of the marriage they have just contracted. The couple arrive back at their adjoining hotel suites, and Petrov refuses Linda's invitation to come in for a drink, perhaps trying to tell her that such an obvious ritual of courtship is unnecessary, that if she thinks about it she may realise that they have already related to each other in a way that could be understood as marriage, and that the ceremony that they have just been through is only a matter of being able to behave openly as if this is the case. At any rate, the couple retreat to their rooms, and Linda is visited by Cecil Flintridge, the representative of censorship in the film. Cecil represents both the public and the private aspects – he is both the guardian of the public morality of the hotel, and 'troubled in my mind'. Linda is able for the first time to confirm the marriage – unhappily, Sandrich lets her deliver her line with her face turned away from the camera, so that we are denied the sight of her pleasure in it. Cecil, perhaps recalling Blore's role at the end of *Top Hat*, gives her what he terms the 'new key to your happiness': it will unlock the communicating door between the two suites. At this point, Sandrich takes his camera outside the building, to present the door as a line dividing the screen in two, a shot that would have presumably been clear to his audience in 1937 as a reference to the comparable barrier in a film that was famous at the time, the blanket in *It Happened One Night* (Frank Capra, 1934). Such a barrier was part of the currency of mid-'thirties film-making, as in *Forsaking All Others* (W.S. Van Dyke, 1934), in which a folding screen separates Robert Montgomery from Joan Crawford. Perhaps there is also an allusion here to the hotel ceiling in *Top Hat*.

Once again, the Rogers character finally takes the initiative in the matter of a marriage proposal; it has to be Linda who chooses to open the door. When she finally does so, she starts a further twist in the plotting with the discovery that Petrov is not alone, but (innocently) with Denise. Now she falls into playing a strange role, as if she is compelled to act out the drama of an ordinary marriage:

71

'I'll never divorce him.' Denise (Ketti Gallian) and the newly wed Petrov and Linda in Shall We Dance.

she plays the wronged wife, coolly accepting the evidence of her husband's latest philandering – 'Why have you been so secretive about this one, Peter?' – and indicating that she is not the kind of wife who will lose him to this new woman – 'I'll never divorce him'. (That something of this was intentional is supported by the costuming of Rogers and Ketti Gallian which emphasises their roles as deceived wife and glamorous new erotic temptation.)

There is no trace of comedy in this moment, and the broad outlines of what follows are easier to understand if we can accept that a movie like this can work within traditional cultural myths of death and revival in romance, if we can think of *Shall We Dance* in the same breath, and operating with some of the same terms, as Nathaniel Hawthorne's *The Marble Faun* or Shakespeare's *A Winter's Tale*. (Those who find this unlikely may be persuaded by the knowledge that Allan Scott, the film's screenwriter, was a Rhodes scholar who had worked for the Theatre Guild as a lecturer on Eugene O'Neill.)

Of course, there are many divergences, but *A Winter's Tale* in particular seems to have been in the minds of the creators of *Shall We Dance*. The consistent interest in the subject of pregnancy, and in the telling of tales – now called stories and reported in newspapers – are some apparent common ground. The thread I am interested in picking up here concerns the resolution of Hermione's situation, and the ending of Sandrich's movie. We may recall that in Shakespeare's play Hermione is falsely accused of sexual impropriety by her king, Leontes. She is imprisoned and then, after swooning in his presence, is believed by him to have died and disappears for many years. After this interval, Leontes, now in 'greediness of affection', is taken to see a likeness of her – a curtain is drawn back and he

The recognition scene in Shall We Dance. *Petrov with Linda and two of the masked girls.*

sees 'Hermione standing like a statue'. Music prompts her revival (the play's words are 'Music, awake her') and she steps down and embraces Leontes. He ends the play with a reference to one of its recurrent subjects, time: 'this wide gap of time, since first/We were dissevered'.

The final scenes of *Shall We Dance* can be considered in this light. After her encounter with Petrov and Denise, Linda shuts and locks the door between the suites, and immediately flees from the hotel. Her image is replaced on screen in the next sequence not by a statue, but by something that might recall one, the Linda dummy, the wax figure which falls over – Jeffrey calls this act fainting – when the accusation of the public notoriety of the marriage is put to it. It is implied that some time now elapses, enough to prepare and then stage a musical show, but we never learn where Linda has gone and never see a shot of her in another place. In an idea inspired by the sight of the dummy, Petrov has announced that he will dance with Linda by having the chorus girls wear masks of Linda's face.

On the first night of the show, Linda reappears, sees the chorus of girls in masks, and demands to be taken backstage. She emerges on to the stage, hiding at first behind a mask of her own face. The drama that follows is of Petrov being unable to locate the true Linda among the false ones. He moves along the chorus line, pulling the 'Linda' masks away from the faces of the girls, one by one. When he reaches Linda, her hand is touching her chin as if she were still holding the mask, which she has now discarded. Thus, as Petrov touches her, her empty hand moves away from her face and is held out to her partner to offer not a mask, but an unmasked self. It is as if she has cast away a graven image of herself, revealing a living image beneath it. Astaire choreographs a brief hesitation here, as if, like a statue coming to life, this moment is not easy to grasp or accept. Then the couple move into their final triumphant dance.

But is it Linda Keene who has returned? Or is it Linda Thompson, or Linda Thompson Peters, which is the name on the divorce summons she is holding? Petrov's claim, 'I'm going to dance with Linda Keene', is made as if dozens of Linda Keenes can be produced to order, as if their existence is simply a matter of surfaces. This is related to one of the film's opening moves, when dozens of images of Linda, the pages of the flip-book which Petrov is manipulating, dissolve into the figure of Linda herself on screen for the first time in the film, drawing attention to the link between the multiplication of nearly identical images and a filmed image. (The connection is a reminder that such difficult negotiations between images of the self are a familiar problem for a movie star, a point taken up in another film from 1937, William Wellman's *A Star Is Born*). Here we have learned that some part of the public image of Linda Keene was a mask, or what Jeffrey called a 'practical dummy'. The couple are reunited through Linda's act of assuming a mask in order to be able to discard it, and the power of desire in bringing about this revival is celebrated in dance.

The final number reminds us that the problem of what is gained or lost here can be thought of in terms of time. The song is 'Shall We Dance?', and the fifth line of the first verse of Ira Gershwin's lyric is 'Stop wasting time!'. The fifth line of the refrain is 'life is short; we're growing older'. The two phrases, taken together with the song's injunction '. . . dance little lady/dance, little man/dance whenever you can!' drive home a point that is present in the whole of *Shall We Dance*, a consciousness of lives, in Henry David Thoreau's phrase, 'minced into hours'. (The film is more than usually conscious of clocks, the image being conspicuously initiated by the large timepiece in the set of Linda's Paris apartment.) The film's final position is to accept the vulnerability of the public face, and the difficulty of sustaining access to the private one, but to demand that dance take place nonetheless, as a matter of urgency . The song claims that to dance is to triumph over time, that the harshness of the world can be – the Gershwins' voice insists, must be – laid aside, in what time remains to the dancers.

Following up the subject introduced in *Swing Time*, this film presses further the awareness, if not of the cycle's end, then at least the pressure of time upon it. It considers the stress and complexity of being a star with a directness that is new to the cycle, perhaps also with an awareness that Astaire and Rogers have to bear the weight of our expectations of them. Its exploration of the problem of identity in marriage has a density unique in the cycle.

TWO ASIDES

A Star Is Born and *Stage Door*

A contrasting film which supplies a way of contextualising some of the elements in my reading of *Shall We Dance* is William Wellman's *A Star Is Born*, also released in the late spring of 1937. The common ground is the subject of stars, of private and public worlds, and of the baleful presence of the press and publicity machines. As in the Astaire-Rogers film, this is focused around the subject of marriage, and how a marriage considered to be public property by pressmen is reclaimed for the

Leading lady Anita Regis (Elizabeth Jenns) remonstrates with an inebriated Norman Maine (Frederic March) in A Star Is Born.

private realm. Like Petrov and Linda, Wellman's Norman Maine (Frederic March) and Vicki Lester (Janet Gaynor) journey a short way from the city to marry under their own names, Alfred Henkel and Esther Blodgett. Both couples try to find a place for their marriage in an older America, one which is ignorant of Broadway or Hollywood, but this privacy cannot be sustained for longer than one sequence: the ferry to Manhattan and Astaire's song in *Shall We Dance*, the honeymoon in the trailer in *A Star Is Born*.

One of these marriages will be unendurable both in public and in private. Marriage in *A Star Is Born* is signalled as a negative state tightly bound to a view of society which stresses its violence and repressiveness. Wellman shows Norman proposing to Vicky at a boxing match, the dialogue intercut with the vicious fight, and the wedding takes place in the area behind a courtroom, the background to which is the bars, and the inmates, of a jail. At the end of it, Norman makes a verbal slip, saying to the judge 'see you again'. The couple laugh this off, but it is preparing us for the climax of the film, the scene in which they find themselves in another courtroom, the night court at which Norman is released into Vicky's 'custody' after a drinking binge. In this scene, the judge asks Vicky if she understands the responsibility that she is undertaking 'to this court and to the commonwealth', and, standing next to her husband, she replies 'I do'. The point of the Dorothy Parker/Alan Campbell script in forcing this response from the woman is to suggest a question. Is she marrying him anew, and in what terms?

An answer here is to be found in the woman's relationship to parental figures. From the opening sequence of *A Star Is Born*, Vicky's life is controlled and directed by her grandmother, by the manager of her Hollywood hotel, and very pointedly by the benign producer, Oliver Niles (Adolphe Menjou). The marriage presents Norman as a failed patriarch – one act of violence apart, he is consistently presented as infantilised by alcoholism. Thus the final 'remarriage' in the night court represents the acceptance of the husband as if he were a child, and the sequence immediately before his suicide clearly repeats the point, with Norman overhearing from his bedroom the arrangements being made by his 'parents', Niles and Vicky. After Norman's death, Vicky's resurgence is entirely achieved by the reappearance of the grandmother (who in effect repeats her role in the opening of the film), and the film's final scene at the premiere positions Vicky securely between parent figures, her grandmother and Niles. We are presented with a world in which all relationships, including those of marriage, turn into ties between parents and children.

In *Shall We Dance*, Linda has no parental figures. The casting of Jerome Cowan as her manager suggests a brotherly rather than an authoritative role, and when an obviously patriarchal figure does finally appear, at the very end of the film, it is as a redundant functionary, or employee – Linda's lawyer. The result of this difference, that Linda has nobody to speak for her, to act on her behalf, is that the films present themselves in ways apparently at odds with our expectations of them.

Wellman's world may be dystopian, but it contains no apparent threat at any point to Vicky Lester. Surrounded by those who support her, she is never truly at risk from the effects of the marriage, or criticised by the film. (A memo from David O. Selznick, the film's producer, makes it clear that, even in the early stages of the project, the idea was to stress that Norman's fall preceded the marriage, and nothing would be presented as Vicki's fault: *see* Thomson, *Showman: The Life of David O. Selznick*, Andre Deutsch, 1993, p. 218). The world of *Shall We Dance* appears as more benign, but we notice how alone the Rogers figure is, how completely her acts are her own and not dependent on the presence of a grandmother, or a mother or father figure. I pointed out much earlier that an important part of Rogers's persona is that she is almost always without parents to defend (or oppress) her. Where figures who might occupy this role are to be found in her films – an example would be Pop in *Swing Time* – they seem to be kept at a distance and not invited to offer fatherly advice. In the central part of the cycle – *Top Hat, Follow the Fleet* and *Swing Time* – there is some support offered by an actual sister or a sister-like figure, but in *Shall We Dance* this figure has dwindled into the virtually non-speaking part of Tai (Emma Young), Linda's maid.

A final point of connection between these films is provided by *Stage Door* (Gregory La Cava, 1937). Here we see Menjou in a part closely related to his role in *A Star Is Born*, as theatrical producer and patriarch, attempting to seduce the young actress played by Rogers. Her response – getting hopelessly drunk – expresses her inability to know how to deal with a man who presents himself simultaneously as a father and a potential lover. The point is underlined by the juxtaposed scene of the wonderfully deft outmanoeuvring of Menjou by Terry Randall (Katherine Hepburn), who is established as thoroughly familiar with the operations and ambitions of father figures.

It is possible that Vicki Lester is more oppressed than Linda, being trapped inside a system of nurture which unwittingly denies the possibility of relationships of any equality. Linda's final gesture, unmasking herself in order to reveal herself, captures both the vulnerability of her isolated condition and her willingness to take the risk involved in making this avowal in public, her understanding that this is where she has to make it, that the stage is the only world where it means anything for her. (It is not a coincidence that the other proposals in the cycle take place in the glow of a successful number.) We should notice here the relevance of 'They All Laughed'. Ira Gershwin's lyric begins with a catalogue of those who risked public humiliation, attempting in different ways to overcome unbridgeable distances (Columbus, Edison, the Wright brothers, Marconi). It describes Linda's risk, and her triumph. Its chorus, sung by the couple, forms the final seconds of the film.

The high plateau of achievement in the Astaire-Rogers cycle can perhaps be marked by the fact that Rogers was not assigned to other films in the interval between *Follow the Fleet* and *Swing Time* or between *Swing Time* and *Shall We Dance*. The four films made between *Shall We Dance* and *Carefree* are marked by two changes of emphasis. One is obvious, the move away from a mode in which dance is central to one in which musical numbers and dance have a part, but not a crucial one in defining the couple. We see Rogers briefly sing and dance in her three films but not necessarily with a lover, while Joan Fontaine was evidently cast as the object of Astaire's love in *Damsel in Distress* (George Stevens, 1937) despite her limited abilities as a dancer. Astaire's dance partners there are a couple (George Burns and Gracie Allen), anticipating the moment when he will form part of another trio in *Broadway Melody of 1940*.

The second change of emphasis is perhaps less obvious. It is the renewed insistence on differences of social class. I have suggested that in the Astaire-Rogers cycle this difference, particularly between the pairs of lovers, is subdued or absent

Aristocratic America: Kay (Andrea Leeds), Miss Luther (Constance Collier) and Terry (Katharine Hepburn) in Stage Door.

The resolution of class difference: Jean (Rogers) and Terry in Stage Door.

– in the films made in this interval it is at the centre. In *Damsel in Distress*, the Marshmorton family are landed English aristocrats. In *Stage Door*, Terry is the American equivalent of this, a moneyed daughter from an old pioneer family, whose father turns out to be 'the wheat king'. Instead of a plot centred on lovers, *Stage Door* offers the energy of the repartee between the Hepburn and Rogers characters, which proceeds from their perception of the other's class status, and much of the film is built around this opposition.

Democratic America in *Stage Door* is represented by the majority of the girls in the Footlights Club, from Jean (Rogers) and Judy (Lucille Ball) to the maid Hattie (Phyllis Kennedy). They are associated with the communal loyalties of the chorus line, and their closest approach to individual achievement is in couples: two Tyrolean dancing girls, a Rogers/Ann Miller dance number. They are also wryly but firmly associated with the desire for marriage, through such characters as Judy's lumberman suitor, Jean's boyfriend, who appears for one sequence, and even Hattie's suitor from the butcher's shop. An alternative ambition for a poor girl in the city is to become a rich man's mistress, the role played by Linda (Gail Patrick), another figure who is continually sparring verbally with Jean. But in these exchanges there is always the background of understanding that their condition is a shared one. Both recognise that acquiring a 'grandfather' is a possible form of escape from the economic punishment of the depression, and in the centre of the film Jean will briefly experiment with it. In contrast, Jean recognises Terry, with her money, expensive clothes and actual grandfather, as on the other side of an apparently absolute class divide.

The values of aristocratic America in *Stage Door* are associated with 'serious' theatre – Shakespeare, the memory of Sarah Bernhardt, a play like *Enchanted April* – with devotion to 'art' rather than domestic ambitions, with the ambition to be a theatrical star as opposed to a song-and-dance star and thus with individual rather than group achievement. The position is embodied by Terry, but elements are present in Kay (Andrea Leeds) and Miss Luther (Constance Collier). In many respects these three are felt as negative, offering boorishness and egotism (Terry in the theatrical rehearsal sequence), neurosis and collapse (Kay as she moves towards suicide) and self-deception (Miss Luther).

The plotting of *Stage Door* achieves an uneasy resolution of this opposition. In her lead role in *Enchanted April*, Terry is seen to triumph in her theatrical ambitions, but her performance is dependent on a wave of emotion that arises out of Kay's suicide and unites Terry with Jean and the weeping girls from the Footlights Club who are in the audience to the play. We are invited to accept that Terry has, through her triumphant performance, 'become' Kay, and thus the distinction between them – which is that Kay was destroyed because she was a penniless victim of the system run by tycoons like Anthony Powell (Adolphe Menjou) which cannot touch an American heiress like Terry – can be abolished, or ignored. Most remarkably, Miss Luther is given a speech stressing the collective nature of the theatre, telling Terry that she must succeed in her role in order to keep the rest of the company, 'the ushers, the property-men, the old women who clean up the theatre', in their jobs. Thus individual success is awkwardly reconciled with collective survival.

The final note is a generous one. The closing sequence in the Footlights Club is notable for its suspension of judgement. We are offered a number of 'roles': the wife (Judy, leaving for her marriage in Seattle and carried to the threshold of the Club by Terry and Jean), the unattached actress (Terry, who suggests that actors are 'a different race of people', and Miss Luther, silent in the background of these events), the attached actress (Jean, in the process of phoning her boyfriend), and the kept woman (Linda, going out to meet Powell). In their trading of various sentiments and wisecracks, we see La Cava's refusal to imply that any of the different lives embodied here are superior or inferior to another.

Class difference is also central in Rogers's two other films made between *Shall We Dance* and *Carefree*. In *Vivacious Lady*, which I will be considering in some detail in the context of Rogers's work in the 'forties (pp.103-106), she plays a New York club singer who marries a young university teacher (James Stewart). In *Having Wonderful Time*, Rogers plays an office girl, and her lover is Douglas Fairbanks Jr, a lawyer. The latter film is very slight, possibly the weakest in Rogers's major period. It seems plausible that she was assigned to it only because Stewart's illness had caused the suspension of shooting on *Vivacious Lady*. Its interest is that it is an early instance (a later one is *Kitty Foyle*) of a screenplay for Rogers which erased all Jewish elements from its source, here an Arthur Kober play entirely set in the Jewish part of the Bronx.

CAREFREE (Mark Sandrich, 1938)

Accounts of Astaire's and Rogers's partnership tend to locate the period following the release of *Shall We Dance* at the end of April 1937 as the beginning of the public loosening of their association. This is usually linked to the appearance of films in which Rogers or Astaire appears without the other: Rogers in *Stage Door* and Astaire in *A Damsel in Distress*, released in October and November 1937 respectively, a season in which, as Arlene Croce points out, 'for the first time in three years there was no Astaire-Rogers fall release' (Croce, p.130).

The nature of these developments becomes clearer if we take a closer view of Astaire's and Rogers's patterns of work. One of the differences between the couple's film careers in the 'thirties is that Astaire worked almost exclusively on the Astaire-Rogers musicals, while Rogers was continually used in films with other stars. During the period of the Astaire-Rogers partnership at RKO, Astaire made only one other film, *A Damsel in Distress*. Rogers made ten films: four minor features between *Flying Down to Rio* and *The Gay Divorcée*, and then *Romance in Manhattan* (Stephen Roberts, 1934). *Roberta* was followed by *Star of Midnight* (Stephen Roberts, 1935). After *Top Hat* she made *In Person* (William A. Seiter, 1935) and, after a run of three films with Astaire ending with *Shall We Dance*, she made *Stage Door*, *Having Wonderful Time* (Alfred Santell, 1938) and *Vivacious Lady* (George Stevens, 1938), before starting on *Carefree*. So, for Astaire, *A Damsel in Distress* was a decisive break, ending his run of seven features with Rogers. For her, the change can be measured in part in terms of quantity – three features rather than one between films with Astaire – and working with two substantial stars, Katharine Hepburn in *Stage Door* and James Stewart in *Vivacious Lady*.

Financial considerations are also illuminating here. The RKO archives give figures for production costs, world gross film income, and a profit and loss figure which evidently takes into account post-production costs, as it is not arrived at by subtracting production costs from income. The figures generally support the claims that the films were very profitable for the studio, especially as the cycle reached its peak in 1935-36. This period covers the four most substantial hits, with profits of $770,000 (*Roberta*), $1,295,000 (*Top Hat*), $930,000 (*Follow the Fleet*) and $830,000 (*Swing Time*). The decline in commercial success is equally clear. At $413,000, the profit from *Shall We Dance* was less than half that of its immediate predecessor, and *Carefree* and *The Story of Vernon and Irene Castle* showed losses of $68,000 and $58,000 respectively.

The figures for production costs show that the musicals were relatively expensive to make; they constituted some of RKO's largest investments, as well as delivering their largest profits. While the cost figures do not contradict the wider picture of profitability, looking at them alongside the profit/loss figures demonstrates the common problem that, as costs escalated in the late 'thirties, some of the films began to look less successful when returns were considered in terms of the studio's very large investment. The series opened with films that made profits of around their production costs – *Flying Down to Rio*, made for $462,000, showed a profit of $465,000, and *The Gay Divorcée*, made for $520,000, a profit of $583,000. After two films where the production costs were relatively stable – *Roberta* at $610,000 and *Top Hat* at $609,000 – there was a series of steep rises, with the result that the $930,000 profit of *Follow the Fleet* has to be seen in the context of a production cost of $747,000 and *Swing Time* showed a smaller profit ($830,000) than its production cost of $885,000.

This pattern became more pronounced towards the end of the cycle. The modest profit – for an Astaire-Rogers film – of *Shall We Dance* ($413,000, a figure smaller than any of the other profit figures up to that point) relates punishingly to a production cost of $991,000. The last two films both cost over a million dollars: $1,253,000 for *Carefree*, and $1,196,000 for *The Story of Vernon and Irene Castle*. It was these figures, rather than falling box-office receipts, that resulted in the losses. The totals of the foreign and domestic box office for the two films were $1.7 m and $1.8 m respectively, which, while not nearly as high as the peak figures (*Top Hat* took $3,160,000 at the box office and *Follow the Fleet* $2,685,000), compared fairly well to the earlier films. The box office for *The Gay Divorcée* was just under $1.8 m, so the difference between its $583,000 profit and the small losses of the final two films can be attributed mainly to production costs. (Considerations of cost were doubtless involved in the last-minute production decision to abandon the plan to make *Carefree* in colour.)

The situation in the winter of 1937 is also illuminated by the commercial fates of the films in which Astaire and Rogers appeared without the other. The studio's unremitting use of Rogers is doubtless connected with the fact that her mid 'thirties films were consistently profitable: *Star of Midnight* made the studio $265,000 (production cost, $280,000) and *In Person* $147,000 (production cost, $493,000). Her two major productions of the 1937-38 season reflect the pattern of escalating costs, and both returned tiny profits on their large investments: *Stage Door* (despite its reputation as a substantial hit) made only $81,000 on a cost of $952,000 and *Vivacious Lady* $75,000 on a cost of $703,000. Astaire was less successful with *A Damsel in Distress*, where the figures are rather similar to those for *Carefree*. The film cost $1,035,000 to produce, made just less than $1.5m at the box office and returned the same small loss as *Carefree*, $68,000.

The background of decreasing profitability may help to explain why *Carefree* appears to return to the models provided by the early part of the cycle, particularly *The Gay Divorcée*, for the structure of its numbers. This is the pattern in which Astaire dances a solo number, then he and Rogers dance together but otherwise alone and without a formal audience. Then their dance takes them into the public world, the company dancing with them, and finally the focus of the dance returns to the couple again (sometimes, as in *Roberta* or *Top Hat*, in a brief coda). This fits

Tony (Astaire), Amanda (Rogers), Stephen (Ralph Bellamy) and Cora (Luella Gear) take some outdoor exercise in Carefree.

Release from inhibitions: Tony and Amanda dance 'The Yam' in Carefree.

Carefree: to take the numbers in order, Astaire's golfing routine 'Since They Turned "Loch Lomond" into Swing' is the solo, the dream sequence 'I Used to Be Color Blind' is the private duet, 'The Yam' at the country club the public dance, and 'Change Partners' a final duet.

If the numbers reflect the progress of the lovers, the shape of the film can be read roughly as follows. The golfing dance would be a celebration of Astaire's character first desiring Rogers's, 'I Used to Be Color Blind' their private commitment to each other, 'The Yam' their public announcement of this commitment, and 'Change Partners' a final celebration of their love in dance. But such expectations are consistently defeated: *Carefree* has a familiar structure in terms of the numbers but a plot which gives those numbers an entirely unfamiliar context and radically changes their meaning.

Astaire is cast as Dr Tony Flagg, a psychoanalyst who recalls that in college he wished to 'escape reality' – 'I wanted to be a dancer'. Rogers is Amanda Cooper, a radio singer and dancer who continually resists the marriage proposals of Tony's friend Stephen Arden (Ralph Bellamy). Stephen sends Amanda to Tony for analysis, and her first act of aggression, insisting on sitting in the doctor's chair and making Tony position himself as the patient, provides a hint of the governing idea of the film. The woman here has some kind of access to and understanding of what she desires, whereas the man has no access whatever to his own psychic life – clearly a neat gag about psychoanalysts. This premise, and the idea of a film in which the woman educates the man into wanting her, is not a surprising one, given that the original story for *Carefree* was written by Dudley Nichols and

Hagar Wilde, the scriptwriters of *Bringing Up Baby*, which had been released a few months earlier in 1938.

Professor David Huxley (Cary Grant) in *Bringing Up Baby* is another man who believes himself to be educated. His movement is from an apparently coherent professional role (reconstructor of skeletons, raiser of donations) into a world in which he is involved in tearing clothing and wearing forms of fancy – or fanciful – dress, throwing stones at windows, pursuing dogs and leopards through the Connecticut woods and being arrested. Defining this world very simply as the one he inhabits with Susan Vance (Katharine Hepburn), we can apply the formulation used by Stanley Cavell about another couple (Clark Gable and Claudette Colbert in *It Happened One Night*) in his analysis of the Hollywood comedy of remarriage, 'What this pair do together is less important than the fact that they do whatever it is together . . .' (Cavell, 1981, p.88).

The difference between the worlds of *Bringing Up Baby* and of *Carefree* can be measured by considering the uses made by the two films of changes of setting. In *Bringing Up Baby*, the movement is from the social spaces of the couple's world (museum, golf course, restaurant) to the more private (their apartments) and then crucially to what, following Northrop Frye, Cavell calls ' "the green world", a place in which perspective and renewal are to be achieved' (Cavell, 1981, p.49). The larger part of the working out of David's and Susan's situation takes place there, with a coda which expresses their changed relationship to the world of the museum. *Carefree* begins with a strikingly similar movement, when after the initial antagonistic exchanges in Tony's consulting rooms, the couple meet again at the country club. Here we see Tony's golf practice disturbed by his consciousness of Amanda's gaze and his inability quite to master the situation through his solo dance – Amanda leaves before it is over. After a brief interlude on bicycles, the film follows the couple through a social space (the smart restaurant, here a part of the country club) to a more private space (Amanda's apartment). But at this point the move to a place which would be a 'green world' equivalent to the Connecticut woods of *Bringing Up Baby* fails to materialise. The next sequence is set again in Tony's consulting rooms, and later the characters return to the country club's dining rooms. Much of the rest of the action switches between these two locations, with some uncomfortable interludes in the chambers of Judge Travers (Clarence Kolb). The fact that *Carefree* is the first film in the entire cycle not to invoke some substantial form of travel may also be expressive of this entrapment: the characters cannot flee this repressive world in any sense.

(A blocked promise of renewal does appear briefly in the early bicycle-ride sequence. The couple are talking about fear and marriage. Amanda has to put one foot out to steady herself on her bicycle, but Tony's cycle turns out to have no brakes, and he crashes spectacularly but harmlessly into some bushes. The couple are now on the ground and laughing together, accompanied by a pair of ducks, which seem to be a sign of what is going on – nature taking its course. But the film immediately cuts to the country club, and nothing comes of this excursion.)

Elsewhere in *Carefree* some attempts to evade the grip of polite society are made, but these forms of behaviour turn out to have been relocated inside the practices of its world, and no longer operate as effective escapes. A comparison of the smart restaurant sequence and its subsequent development in *Bringing Up Baby* with that in *Carefree* will express this. In *Bringing Up Baby*, Susan's impulses create mayhem through a series of accidents – dropping the olive on which David slips, mistakenly taking the wrong handbag, tearing David's jacket – until his exasperation spills over into his accidental contribution, tearing the back off the skirt of her evening dress. They are forced into a position of apparent intimacy. As they abandon the orderly social world and have to do so physically locked together (*Susan*: 'Get closer' *David*: 'I can't get any closer'), it is tempting to see their actions as parallel to what is represented by dancing, particularly by the inclusion of slapstick in the dance, earlier in the Astaire-Rogers cycle. The subsequent apartment scene, with Susan photographed in profile sewing the torn jacket while David explains his troubles, is a knowing snapshot of an almost domestic intimacy.

In *Carefree*, Amanda, Tony and Stephen dine at the country club with Stephen's Aunt Cora (Luella Gear). There is eccentric behaviour here, but it is understood by them as medical practice. When Tony prescribes for Amanda a diet designed to make her dream, only the waiter is scandalised. Back at Amanda's apartment, she can achieve an intimacy with Tony in a place which is free of the social order, but it is of a different kind from David's and Susan's, being accessible only when she sleeps. This dream sequence is the Astaire-Rogers duet 'I Used to Be Color Blind'. The dance of seduction appears here as a return to the earlier part of the cycle, but with a new kind of privacy, confirming Amanda's desire but also indicating her isolation. When she is back in the context of Tony's consulting rooms, she finds that it cannot be shared with him even as a narrative.

Amanda's diet is one example of a recurrent interest in *Carefree*, the subjection of the body to forms of medical or other treatment, or to a narcotic drink or a food, followed by the results of this subjection. The other instances of it are:

1) Where the film starts, with Stephen drunk outside Tony's offices and trying to steady the sign on the building.

2) Aunt Cora is given a sedative by Tony's assistant Connors (Jack Carson) and, following up his visit, which she believes to have been a dream, starts the day with another helping of the dream diet prescribed by Tony.

3) Amanda is given an anaesthetic by Tony and another doctor to effect a temporary release from any inhibitions – apparently some kind of gas, though the film is a little coy about this.

4) The rumble-seat of a car closes on Connors and he is trapped inside. When released by Cora, he can hardly stand.

5) Tony uses a stroboscopic light to hypnotise Amanda, so that he can plant the idea that she loves Stephen and that Tony should be 'shot down like a dog'. She then finds a gun and tries to shoot him.

One of the marked connections between these occasions is the degree to which they result in isolation for their subjects. I have given Amanda's dream sequence as an example of this, and it is also true of her behaviour under the influence of the anaesthetic which begins with her running away from Stephen. She is seen smashing a sheet of plate glass on a passing lorry, insulting the sponsors of her radio show and kicking a policeman. The moments are performed as mild fun, but we should notice that they are only for Amanda's amusement (and ours,

Subjecting the body to treatment: Tony and Dr Powers (Walter Kingsford)
prepare to anaesthetise Amanda in Carefree.

enjoying Rogers's performance of freedom). No character in the film shares the
jokes with her, and the later, related instance of medical invasion of Amanda –
the hypnotism with the strobe light – seems to want to stress that such practices
can result in behaviour that frightens almost everybody in the film, including
Amanda. Nichols and Wilde, in the absence of Howard Hawks, dramatise a kind
of playfulness here which is the opposite of that which dominated *Bringing Up
Baby*, one which creates no shared world.

This quality is most marked in connection with Amanda, most particularly
where it is related to treatments emanating from the consulting room. The film
seems more relaxed about getting drunk, which delivers Stephen into the hands

of his friends, or eating lobster, which conjures up the dream vision of Tony for Amanda and in comedic imitation, the 'vision' of Connors for Aunt Cora. The closest that the film comes to showing such experiences being enjoyed together – and thus to the world of David and Susan in *Bringing Up Baby* – is in some of the business associated with Connors and Aunt Cora. For example, the sequence in which, after Connors is released from the rumble-seat of the car, the two of them are getting happily drunk, oblivious to the events around them which show the rest of the cast at their most divided, as Amanda attempts to shoot Tony with Stephen's gun.

The two characters who never allow themselves to be drunk, drugged or hypnotised are Tony and Judge Travers, who have in common a blindness, or a willed refusal to acknowledge their own desires, for example in the judge's reactions to Cora. As the Rogers character's female friend, Cora is in the position occupied by another aunt, Hortense, in *The Gay Divorcée*, and the two figures played by Helen Broderick, Madge in *Top Hat* and Mabel in *Swing Time*, but what distinguishes her from them is her manipulation of her male partner. Hortense's manoeuvring of Egbert into marriage is presented as a comical celebration of her power and Helen Broderick is cheerfully linked to complaisant men in both her films, Horace in *Top Hat* and Pop in *Swing Time*. In *Carefree*, Aunt Cora is unmarried and the running *double entendre* of her scenes with Connors underlines her interest in men. Her putative male partner is clearly the judge, who is a bachelor. A recurrent subject in the film is Cora's impatience with him, expressed as so often with the couples in these films by an image of physical aptitude or ineptness. Here it takes the form of her continually telling him to sit down (or to sit up, the line with which the film ends). Like the earlier female friends, Cora is aware that for the Rogers figure to marry the wrong man would be a catastrophe and she actively assists Tony in the denouement, but her own situation is not retrieved. Compare the tone of the material dealing with Cora to that given to Helen Broderick or Alice Brady. Here the woman's affection for the man remains, but it is touched by disappointment, by a sense of his inaccessibility, the impossibility of ever bringing him to a knowledge of his own desires, and her impatience with him comes out of his obliviousness of her except as a social convenience. (This shift might have been particularly evident for the actress playing Cora: Luella Gear had created the role of Hortense in the Broadway production of *Gay Divorce*.)

It is as if the film wants to set out for us the limits of Rogers's power, whatever she may do, to move the Astaire character. This can be seen most clearly in the public dance. 'The Yam' recalls 'They All Laughed' from *Shall We Dance* in that it begins with one partner reluctant to perform and ends on a note of triumphant harmony, but the difference in what follows is exemplary. In the earlier film, the dance confirmed the couple's intimacy, in a way which they were unsure how to grasp. Here, it confirms Amanda's knowledge that she is in love with Tony, but it appears to have no effect on him whatever. A moment later, he blandly congratulates Stephen and Amanda on their engagement, and Aunt Cora's horrified reaction drives the contrast home. In the sequence in his consulting rooms that follows, his impenetrability moves Amanda to tears, and his next action is to demonstrate to himself that her feelings can be treated as a mechanism, just a set of mental responses to be manipulated under hypnosis. When Tony does become

'Won't you change partners and dance with me?' Tony (dancing with Cora)
sings the Irving Berlin number to Amanda (dancing with Stephen) in Carefree.

aware of his desire for Amanda, it is a crucial limitation that he does so in a conversation with himself – with his reflection in a consulting-room mirror – rather than in any exchange with her. (Does he partly reverse this in the very last moment of the film, by saying the 'wrong' thing to the hypnotised subject? In the terms of his own practice so far, he should be implanting a feeling by asking her to repeat that Amanda loves Tony, but instead he makes a declaration on his own behalf: 'Tony loves Amanda'.)

The other Astaire-Rogers film to end with an imminent marriage ceremony at which Rogers is about to accept the wrong man is *Swing Time*. Compare the sense of growing release in that film, as the trousers gag communicates Lucky's intentions to Penny and the infection of laughter takes over the cast, with the more sombre mood here. It is caught in Sandrich's shooting one of Berlin's most touching sung numbers, 'Change Partners', to emphasise the social milieu's claustrophobia, the impossibility of doing anything unless the jostling crowd of people can be somehow dismissed. The second, dance duet half of the number, thrilling as it is viewed simply as movement, echoes the opening dream duet in that we understand that Amanda cannot see, this time because she is moving under hypnosis. At the very end, a small detail carefully underlines the melancholy that this comedy cannot quite dispel. The uncredited Hattie McDaniel, playing a maid in the act of arranging Amanda's wedding dress, reminds us that engagements are often to be preferred to marriages.

In most of the cycle, the sense of a hostile social order is set against delight in the couple's privacy and the belief that the intractability of this opposition can

Stephen separates Amanda and Tony at the end of the 'Change Partners' dance in Carefree. *Cora and Judge Travers (Clarence Kolb) look on.*

be made bearable by finding a place in which it is possible to be at home and yet to have a role in the world. This place is some kind of stage or dance floor on which the couple offer their skills – their singing and dancing being simultaneously for themselves and their audience. 'They All Laughed' might be the best example of what I mean, but the mode dominates the closing dances of the films from *Roberta* to *Shall We Dance*. *Carefree*'s world, which offers no closing dance, is one in which the Astaire and Rogers role as, in effect, professional entertainers is reduced to a single number ('The Yam'). It is one in which the social world, represented by country-club culture and forms of professional practice, law and medicine, is more repressive than in any of the previous films in the cycle. The idea of a private space for the couple is differently felt, existing either quite outside the physical world (in Amanda's dream) or within it but in a strikingly embattled context. We can see this in the 'Change Partners' duet, the first occasion in the cycle when the passing of time represents a threat, in the form of the imminent return of other members of the cast.

Perhaps when Rogers considered the script of *Carefree* to be 'better than anything I had seen before in the RKO musical scripts' (Rogers, p.179), she was understanding that the subject of Astaire-Rogers dance was not quite at its centre. Rather than being a continuation of the movement in the cycle in which the value of the couple's partnership is emphasised through a melancholic realisation of what would one day be lost, *Carefree* suggests a faltering belief in its central importance. An objection commonly made to *Shall We Dance*, that it contains possibly only one great Astaire-Rogers duet, could be answered by saying that the film still understands the importance of that dance. It teases us, but finally delivers its promise in 'They All Laughed', and its rhetoric in 'Shall We Dance'. In *Carefree*, the dancing – not the quantity or quality of numbers, but the meaning that the film is able or willing to ascribe to them – seems to be receding into the distance.

The attenuation of effects compared to the previous films is also true of song. I have already discussed how the delivery of 'Change Partners' – yet another song directed at a figure who cannot return the singer's gaze – serves to stress only the negative qualities of the country-club society, and the number contains no affecting transition from song to dance, replacing it with some comic business. The rest of the Berlin score is relatively unmemorable. This falling away of interest in song will become almost complete in *The Story of Vernon and Irene Castle*.

THE STORY OF VERNON AND IRENE CASTLE
(H.C. Potter, 1939)

The trends that I have signalled in my reading of *Carefree* become decisive features of *The Story of Vernon and Irene Castle*. The presence of song is reduced to background music and one sung number, and the couple's dance largely ceases to be presented as highly specialised or idealised, something an audience inside or outside the film would receive as the performance of stars, but is shown rather as a teachable social skill – a democratic force. This change of focus divides the film sharply from its predecessors: it is a biopic with dance, followed by a war-time melodrama. Of course, this is not to argue that either genre is beyond the reach of Astaire's and Rogers's skills, or those of the director, H.C. Potter.

The source of the narrative, the career of Vernon and Irene Castle, was a case of fame achieved very rapidly over a short period – about four years – followed by a much longer period in which popular memory of the couple as a dance team and as dance teachers remained potent. It can be summarised as follows. In 1911, they performed to much acclaim at the Café de Paris. They left France and re-turned to New York in the autumn of 1912, becoming successful and widely celebrated in America and opening their own cabaret, the Sans Souci, in New York in late 1913. In 1913, they also starred in a Broadway show, *The Sunshine Girl*, and then in the first revue to be entirely written by Irving Berlin, *Watch Your Step*, which played for 175 performances in the winter and spring of 1914-15. The production went on tour, but the couple's career was cut short in the December of 1915 when Vernon Castle left the cast to study aviation. An Englishman, he became a Royal Flying Corps pilot, a combatant in France and then an RFC instructor in Canada. In February 1918, while working as an instructor, he was killed in a flying accident.

In 1919, Irene Castle published a memoir, *My Husband* (Scribners), a short account of their marriage supplemented by extracts from Vernon's letters. It was this book to which RKO bought the film rights in 1936, and, according to Astaire, the story was announced as 'the farewell film for Astaire and Rogers' in September 1938. Looking at this material and other accounts of the Castles it is possible to speculate on the ways in which their career might have been felt to be partic-ularly appropriate material for Astaire and Rogers.

1) Irene Castle wrote that 'in the evolution of the modern dance Vernon played a great part'. This was not only a matter of exhibition dancing: in the world of social dance the couple were known as technical innovators and popularisers of new styles. In representing them, Astaire and Rogers could be thought to be implicitly acknowledging their own contribution to dance, to its technicalities and to the popularising of it in another medium, while connecting themselves to the couple who most clearly represented the democratisation of modern dance, its availability to the ordinary man and woman.

2) In the account of the Castles in his *Steppin' Out: New York Nightlife and the Transformation of American Culture 1890-1930* (University of Chicago Press, 1984), Lewis Erenberg tells us that the press portrayed the Castles 'as aristocrats, claiming that Irene came from a privileged background and that Vernon had noble forebears' (pp.161-162). It is not difficult to see how one part of this image suited Astaire. Vernon's Englishness could be represented as an aristocratic quality, but of an unspecified kind that did not deny its possessor the common, popularising touch, thus remaining acceptable to an American audience.

3) The perception of the Castles as refined depended on their being perceived as a newly married couple doing something that might be taken as an extension of ordinary bourgeois life, the act of dining out. Writing in *My Husband* about their treatment at the Café de Paris, Irene points to the innovation of their always starting the act from the table at which they had dined, as opposed to emerging from 'somewhere behind the piano'. She sums up the impression that they created in a single sentence: 'We were young, clean, married, and well-mannered' (p.41). The specific matter of a married dance team is important in the film.

4) A dominant subject of *My Husband* is Vernon's death and the heroic circumstances surrounding it. (These are to do with Vernon choosing to fly in the front, and thus more dangerous, seat of the plane while training pilots: the detail was used in the film.) Clearly, the story offered the possibility of a film that would mark an end to the series with the death of the Astaire figure. It could present this in benign terms, both allowing the audience to anticipate the event from their own knowledge and insulating it from any charge of melodramatic excess as the story was true.

5) The remoteness of the period (1911-18) must have seemed considerable by the mid-'thirties, separated from it by both the Depression and the Jazz Age. Was it thought appropriate to end the cycle by associating Astaire and Rogers with an America which evoked a vision of a lost past?

The threat, or the possibility, of Vernon's death can be seen as a key issue which divides the film into two parts. It is absent from the first part – the narrative of Vernon's and Irene's meeting, courtship and marriage, Vernon's move from vaudeville comedy to dance, their Paris success and the conquering of America, ending with a sequence in which Astaire and Rogers dance across a map of the USA, metaphorically leaving all America dancing in their wake. The second part of the film starts with two announcements: the Castles tell their manager Maggie Sutton (Edna May Oliver) that they wish to stop touring, and simultaneously we hear of the outbreak of World War I, as if the impulse to settle down is to be posed

Courting couple: Vernon Castle (Astaire) and Irene Foote (Rogers) in
The Story of Vernon and Irene Castle.

immediately against a massive disruptive force. The second part of the film now
details Vernon's joining the RFC, his combat experiences in France and his death.

The first part variously conforms to and departs from elements of the previous
films. Take the occasion of Rogers's solo dance. The context for this is the young
Irene, on first meeting Vernon, trying to impress him with an act, an imitation
of Bessie McCoy's 'The Yama Yama Man'. The joke is about male entrapment,

Irene dances 'The Yama Yama Man' for Vernon.

Vernon's chance encounter with Irene turning into a scene of the family anxiously subjecting him to more than one performance of vigorous amateurishness. The desire to insist on the experience as an embarrassment for Vernon has something to do with the requirement to establish Irene's youth, but we may also recall here the sabotaged audition sequence in *Follow the Fleet*. The link is the establishing (of course by quite different means in the two cases) that Rogers's solo performance has no future, or rather that if her future is to be found in her dance with Astaire, the cost of this will have to be the abandonment of her ambitions for herself. The message of Astaire's solo dance is significantly different. Here (as previously), its point is promise, the suggestion that dancing like this needs only the addition of the right partner. The sequence of Astaire dancing to 'By the Light of the Silvery Moon' and 'Who's Your Lady Friend' is a culmination of a movement in the cycle. The couple were separated by a balcony for the solo in *Roberta*, by a hotel ceiling in *Top Hat*'s 'No Strings', and by a balcony again in *Carefree*. This is the first time that the Rogers character is physically on the same level, a clearly present audience for an Astaire solo, staying to the end of it.

The film is aware of the complex relationship in the cycle between dance, seduction and the idea of what a marriage is and means. After she has watched his solo dance, Irene goes to New York to see Vernon's show and is horrified to find that his stage role is a burlesque act with Lew Fields (who plays himself in the film). When she confronts him, her 'I won't have you doing it' is interpreted for us by Vernon's reply as sexual interest: 'What makes you so excited about me?' The film now moves through a familiar configuration in which we see Rogers's ability to look after herself, as she coaches her suitor, prompting him with a picture of Niagara Falls when they are looking at images in a stereoscope. The final movement of the seduction is marked by the film's one original song, 'Only When You're in My Arms', sung by Astaire. During its final lines, the couple find each other in the darkened set and stroll across the room. It is predictable that at this point in the cycle, their stroll does not dissolve into a dance number. It is as if the film can no longer allow Astaire and Rogers the intense, erotic privacy of dancing together and alone, and the point becomes the insistence that its audience should feel the possibility of this, experiencing the absence of the dance here. Apart from the film's closing seconds, the only example of the couple dancing when they are technically alone is a very brief sequence in Irene's parental home, and this is specifically presented as a rehearsal, a performance to a potential audience.

This is symptomatic of the final confirmation of an important change of emphasis. The idea of professional, public dance was previously balanced against the idea that dance was a way in which the couple communicated with each other, a form of private conversation which might, but need not, take place in private. In *Shall We Dance* and *Carefree*, it is becoming increasingly remote. Here the mode has almost disappeared, its intimacy reduced to the two moments when Astaire says 'Dance with me' to Rogers as they move into a number.

This is related to the appearance of the fact of marriage. For the first time in the cycle the couple are actually married early in the film. This is marked neither by the ceremony, which we do not see, nor by Irene's loss of her parents: it is true that they now disappear from the film, but characteristically for Rogers's roles, they were never important – in no scene has Irene appeared alone with either one or both of them. Furthermore, the marriage causes no disruption to another domestic tie, that between Irene and Walter (Walter Brennan), who accompanies the couple on their honeymoon and lives with them in Paris. He is nominally a

Proposal sequence: Irene prompts Vernon with a stereoscopic picture of Niagara Falls.

At the Café de Paris, Maggie (Edna May Oliver) with Irene and Vernon.

family servant but played comedically as a male 'manager' figure with no sexual relationship with Irene, and thus slightly reminiscent of Arthur (Jerome Cowan) in *Shall We Dance*.

The apparently easy transference of Walter from his place in Irene's parental household to his role with the Castles points us towards the reading of this marriage as symbolic of the ordinary, of the couple being part of the everyday world. In the sequence immediately after the unseen wedding, Vernon and Irene attempt to start their dancing career by showing a number to Lew Fields, who justifies his refusal to take it on by saying, 'Who is going to pay money to see a man dance with his wife?' as if the marriage robbed the dance of any erotic, and thus commercial, quality. The sequences of the Castles' triumph in Paris prove Fields wrong and extend the point by continually stressing that the successful dance emerges precisely out of the mundane world in which this marriage is lived. Maggie Sutton's discovery of the Castles takes place in the domestic context of their Paris apartment, where they disturb her (once again, through a ceiling) while creating the 'Castle Walk' as a way of finding mutual courage in adversity. In the Café de Paris, the acceptability of the Castles' dance comes from their combining respectability (the marriage bond) with modernity (inaccurately in one sense, Maggie Sutton calls them 'two Americans') and accessibility. Even the name given to the dance implies an enhanced form of ordinary movement, and the other diners are immediately able to imitate the Castle Walk in their own dance when they return to the floor.

The Café de Paris sequence uses details to mark some of these points. Irene's wearing of her bridal gown expresses her newly married status. The presence of a Russian nobleman seems an ideal contrast with the couple's American/English marriage and their representation of democratic societies. And the business of his tip – he wishes to give them 300 francs, which Vernon refuses but Irene then accepts – seems to express the balance between Astaire's dominance as creator of the dance and Rogers's grasp of their position in the world in which dance takes place, the world of money, patronage and managers. These details feel correct for Astaire and Rogers, but are not created in the scriptwriting: they are laid out in Irene Castle's memoir. Perhaps this only confirms the appropriateness of the source material, how well some aspects of the Castles' story fitted the couple.

The aspect of the Castles most obviously omitted is any mention of the Broadway musical, which in the 1910s was growing out of vaudeville and revue. The film presents the vaudeville farcing – Vernon and Lew Fields in a barber-shop sketch in *The Hen Pecks* – and the Castles' exhibition dancing with its marketing spin-offs, not only as if they were completely separate worlds, but also as if they were the only entertainment contexts in which the couple worked. However, Irene Castle tells us that Vernon had delivered a sung number ('It's Not the Trick Itself, but the Tricky Way It's Done') in *The Hen Pecks*, that in their Paris revue work they had sung Irving Berlin's 'Alexander's Ragtime Band', and I have already mentioned their big contribution to Broadway history, when they starred in *Watch Your Step*, the first complete musical to be scored by Irving Berlin, which opened on 8th December 1914 and was commissioned specifically for them by the producer, Charles Dillingham. At about the time of Vernon's enlistment, Irene also appeared as a solo dancer in *Miss* (5th November 1917), a show with lyrics by P.G. Wodehouse, and music by Jerome Kern and Victor Herbert, and with George Gershwin as its rehearsal pianist (David A. Jasen, *Tin Pan Alley*, Omnibus Press, 1990, p.164).

I should also mention that the film gives no account of the importance of black music and musicians to the Castles' work. In her autobiography, *Castles in the Air* (as told to Bob and Wanda Duncan, Doubleday, 1958), Irene claims that the decision to have Walter, who was black, played by a white actor was a studio strategy 'to satisfy Southern exhibitors' (p.247).

This data is assembled not to condemn the film for failing to include it – although I admit to a twinge of regret for the loss of another film which Astaire and Rogers might have made, using some of these words and music – but to consider the effect and purpose of the omission. Included, it would have formed the link between the musical culture of the period before World War I and that of the 'twenties and 'thirties, and thus between the world of the Castles and the musical stage occupied by Fred and Adele Astaire and that of the screen occupied by Astaire and Rogers. The effect of omitting it is to insulate the two couples from each other, to assert more clearly that Astaire and Rogers are playing roles. Perhaps the omission can also be connected with the film's interest in the ordinary – for this account of the Castles is of people who create dances or hair-styles, or market products like shoes and hats for a world of consumers, but who do not create, or enter into, fictional worlds. In other words, Astaire and Rogers are no longer inhabiting a fantastic, or a fantasy, world – as we might say they have in all the eight preceding films – but are shown trying to find, or make, a place for themselves in an ordinary America.

It is possible to read the second part of the film as addressing itself almost entirely to this subject, through the image of leaving the entertainment circuit and settling down, and the film now replaces the world of the stage with a new threat in the form of the war and the risks involved in early aviation. Melodrama dealing specifically with a couple in which a woman remains on the ground while the man she loves risks his life in the air was a subject very familiar to contemporary audiences. A rich seam of 'thirties film-making deals with this subject in various contexts: warfare (*Today We Live*, Howard Hawks, 1933), flying mail planes (Howard Hawks's *Only Angels Have Wings*, released in the same year as this film) and experimental flying (*Test Pilot*, Victor Fleming, 1938) are a few examples. *The Story of Vernon and Irene Castle* uses a series of sets – the interior of a railway carriage, the Castles' country home, their Paris apartment, and a hotel near Fort Worth – in a way which denotes an embattled domestic world. Looking at the detail here suggests the consistency and density of these concerns. The homely railway carriage set, with armchairs, elaborate curtain hangings, table lamps and pictures, and Walter exercising a newly acquired pet dog, forms a setting for Vernon and Irene to announce to Maggie their desire to settle down, and is contrasted visually with the bustle of the station exterior reflecting the outbreak of war. It is immediately followed by a brief sequence in the Castles' country home, a retreat which is threatened by war and its images: the newspapers, and the prop uniform that Irene finds Vernon trying on. The next domestic setting, in wartime, is a single night at the Paris apartment. Irene's line here is 'You even thought of coming here instead of the Ritz, or some place that might not feel quite like home', but the bareness of the space is evident, and most of the sequence takes place outside, on the apartment's balcony. When the couple are apart, all domesticity disappears. The sequences of Vernon's service in the RFC significantly include no shots at all of interiors.

The final scenes are set in the hotel near the aerodrome where Vernon will die, and Potter makes delicate use of comedy around the film's interest in marriage as a symbol of the ordinary, the idea of it as opposite to the erotic. Vernon is the first to arrive, and his desire to create a romantic setting for his meeting with Irene is set against the cynicism of the hotel manager, entertainingly performed by Donald MacBride. Adapting a turn-of-the-century catchphrase ('A hot bird and a cold bottle' was shorthand for a late-night supper with a chorus girl), he assumes an assignation. The manager is baffled to discover that this man is proposing to entertain his wife, but adjusts his act appropriately, proclaiming to Maggie that the hotel 'caters only to the family trade'. The romantic reunion never takes place, and Potter ends the film with Irene alone in this unstable imitation of an intimate space.

Against the embattled or failed domesticity of these interiors, Potter poses scenes which express the destruction of family life. The sequences in the train interior and the Castles' home are followed by a benefit show for the RFC at which Vernon dances alone and then with a man in drag, as if he is already at the front line. Even as Irene watches the show from the wings, this world is asserting its ability to deal with the absence of women. Perhaps Potter's most adept use of *mise-en-scène* is at the end of this sequence. Vernon has finally succumbed to patriotic feeling and enlisted, and Irene has pursued him through the theatre. She confronts him in its basement prop room, where the doom facing their ambitions is effectively expressed through the image of a jumble of domestic objects in the shot. The sense of the threat to Vernon's life is made with great visual

Vernon reads a newspaper announcing the outbreak of World War I.

economy – just before they embrace, we see that he is standing in front of the theatre's collection of mantelpiece clocks.

The image that ties all this together is a key trope of melodrama, a figure looking out of a window. Potter's shot of Vernon and Irene, framed by the curtains of the railway carriage as they learn that the world is at war, is echoed in a shot of Irene alone near the end of the film, looking out of the hotel window at the planes in the sky, and by the final image of her looking out into the garden at an imaginary, transparent version of Vernon and herself dancing. The sequence was possibly suggested by the use of the couple at the end of *Maytime* (Robert Z. Leonard, 1937), but in that film the image reverts from transparency to solidity as the couple offer a triumphant reprise of the film's central song. Here the couple remain the transparent figures of Irene's memory until they fade from view at the end of the shot.

The effect of the whole of the second half of the film is to argue that the couple cannot find the domestic world that they desire, but only insecure, temporary versions of it, and of course the blame for this is attributed not to either of them but to the war. Their perfected togetherness exists only in the dance and therefore lasts only for as long it does. The final sequence in the cycle goes further in stressing the importance of the imagination by locating the last, ideal dance in the imagination of a specific character (in that respect it is doing something clearer than *Maytime*) and also, in locating the transparency as a 'special effect', reminding us that film is a place where this ideal world of movement can exist.

Vernon and Irene on Vernon's one night of leave from active service.

I have suggested that the progression discernible in the Astaire-Rogers cycle is not unintentional. Far from being a series of random plot variations and decisions to 'remake' earlier films, it is a set of precise responses to the situation of the couple and to the slowly growing weight of their previous films as well as an acceptance that the meaning of a given configuration – say, when the couple first meet – can change. It is capable of celebration of their achievement and of expressing melancholy at the prospect of an end to the cycle, which is one way of establishing its importance.

Let us return to one of the images with which my discussion started, that of Rogers and Astaire sitting together on a Rio pavement in *Flying Down to Rio*.

The final sequence: the couple dance in Irene's memory.

One of the questions that the films pose for this couple is what place there is for their intimacy. Is there a context where it can exist for more than a moment? (You can sit together on a pavement, but not for long, as the crowding bodies in the frame here remind us.) This question is one that the opening films in the cycle are happy to answer positively with their variations on the use of the Big White Set, the place which writers on musicals have talked about as the site of 'entertainment', the hotel dance floor in *The Gay Divorcée*, the fashion show set in *Roberta*, the Venice Lido of *Top Hat*. The question of what it means to leave this world for somewhere else, evident in *The Gay Divorcée* and *Roberta*, falls away in *Top Hat*, which consequently feels like the breathless peak of the cycle. Here the couple briefly exist in a place – Irving Berlin's lyric calls it heaven – which involves no thought of returning to the ordinary.

From here the cycle begins to ask a series of questions about a different world that the couple are to inhabit. The word that generally describes this place is America – the first four films were substantially set elsewhere, and the last five are predominantly set in the United States. In *Follow the Fleet*, the couples exist inside various kinds of power structure: power is held in this film by men, and one form of it is marriage, the power of husbands. *Swing Time* reminds us that all marriages constitute a loss of something and can easily go wrong, but that they can be retrieved by luck and laughter.

Up to this point, the films' worlds could not be described as predominantly hostile. *Shall We Dance* suggests that society renders the creation and the sustaining of intimacy well nigh impossible, but the insistence on its importance is sustained, and the final position is one of imagining the triumph of desire. In *Carefree*, the balance seems to tilt the other way, towards the conclusion that in a society as repressed as this, we are left with the oblique or the interrupted or the marginal, or engagements that are better than marriages. *The Story of Vernon and Irene Castle* goes to a past, lost America (and back to Paris) in order to find a benign society for the now-married couple. But it is clear that they can no longer find a place that is equivalent even to the Rio pavement. The progressive disintegration of the contexts of dance and song leaves them positioned in a world that is either an unspecific exterior (the whole of America, in the montage of their dancing across the map of the USA) or a set of variations, shown to be unsustainable, on the private domestic world. There is nowhere that dance can proceed from or return to. Vernon's death is a narratively neat way of drawing a line under this.

Another way of viewing the cycle involves its use of time. In the early films, the past may be represented as the period when the couple were children together; if they did not share a childhood, they may choose to behave like children with each other, as if to invent a past for the purposes of the present. This remains a possible mode up to the most delirious exposition of it, the 'I'm Putting All My Eggs in One Basket' number from *Follow the Fleet*. About here the mode changes, and it is marked by the mood of 'Let's Face the Music and Dance', the concluding number of the same film, which offers dance as a way of overcoming paralysis in the face of a history of adult life, while also understanding it as a means of rejecting the terms in which that life is usually experienced. The motif of simultaneously turning both away from and towards something that is carried in the lyric of the number is central. The subject of dance as a way of making time bearable lasts through *Swing Time* until the end of *Shall We Dance*, after which it is no longer present.

The unique achievement of the Astaire-Rogers RKO films nowadays tends to be obscured by a combination of the difficulty of viewing the whole cycle in the way that was available to its original audiences and an understandable admiration of the brilliance and verve of the dance numbers. But stand back far enough to see it, and the shape, the intelligence and seriousness are clear. The cycle is an opportunity to question what is understood by marriage, what constitutes the beginning or middle, or ending of one, and what conditions inform such encounters or farewells.

CHAPTER THREE

A SELF-MADE CINDERELLA

GINGER ROGERS FROM 1938 TO 1943

The films covered in this chapter begin with *Vivacious Lady* (George Stevens, 1938) – at the point when an end of the Astaire-Rogers cycle was starting to seem likely – and end with *Tender Comrade* (Edward Dmytryk, 1943). During this time, Rogers made thirteen full-length features including the two final films with Astaire. They can be divided into three groups.

The earliest is a cycle of romances: *Vivacious Lady*, followed by *Bachelor Mother* (Garson Kanin, 1939), *Kitty Foyle* (Sam Wood, 1940), and *Tom, Dick and Harry* (Garson Kanin, 1941); *Roxie Hart* (William Wellman, 1942) is related to this cycle.

Substantially overlapping chronologically with these, but crucially not beginning until after the last of the 'thirties Astaire-Rogers features, are three films involving the principal writer of the Astaire-Rogers musicals, Allan Scott: *Fifth Avenue Girl* (Gregory La Cava, 1939), *Primrose Path* (Gregory La Cava, 1940) and *Lucky Partners* (Lewis Milestone, 1940).

Finally, there are three films which pursue the impulses of the earlier films while acknowledging that America is now actively involved in a world war: *The Major and The Minor* (Billy Wilder, 1942), *Once upon a Honeymoon* (Leo McCarey, 1943) and *Tender Comrade*.

1. FATHERS AND SONS

The treatment of the central couple in *Vivacious Lady*, *Bachelor Mother* and *Kitty Foyle* departs from that in the Astaire-Rogers films in two important respects: the interest in the man's family and the difference between the lovers being viewed as a matter of class or money. In these three films the Rogers character is a woman without a family, or with a disabled or vestigial one, who finds herself in a romance with a man whose world, by contrast, seems to be determined by his family. The Rogers character's pointed solitariness – both *Vivacious Lady* and *Bachelor Mother* draw attention to it with an early line of dialogue – associates her with the atomised working world of the city, while her lovers are heirs to substantial family interests, in two cases a family business, and in one an educational institution (presented almost as a family university).

Central to these films is the apparent ordinariness of the leading men compared with their powerful, confident fathers. This raises the obvious question – obvious,

Peter (James Stewart) and Francey (Rogers) in Vivacious Lady *arrive in Peter's home town, supported by Peter's cousin Keith (James Ellison).*

that is, to the sons themselves – of their ability to take over the empires (retail, financial or educational) that they will inherit, of whether they have the ability to follow their fathers. What qualities are required to sustain such enterprises other than simply echoing the father's strengths? How does such a son establish his independence in his father's eyes?

What these fathers did in creating their empires is the one thing that the sons cannot do. They must show themselves to be worthy by a different act of grappling with the world. This is what lies behind their choosing and being chosen by the Rogers character, as opposed to the high-toned girl the family has in mind for them. This choice can express the son's likeness to the father (*Vivacious Lady*), the hope that America can protect these sons from the deadly effects of inherited wealth (*Bachelor Mother*) or the fear that it will fail to (*Kitty Foyle*).

In each case, the idea that access to money brings with it a kind of positive magic that will successfully transform the world is undermined. In both *Bachelor Mother* and *Kitty Foyle*, sons use their wealth to achieve a physical transformation of the Rogers character, disguising her class background with a stunning ball gown. But Rogers cannot be won, or purchased, by such means, and the success or failure of the romance can turn on the man's ability to give up the power, or extraordinariness, that money confers. In *Vivacious Lady*, this is symbolised by the act of throwing money away (the father and son deliberately wreck their car by placing it on the tracks in the path of an oncoming railway train).

An important context for reading these films is the figure of Cinderella. I am not thinking of any particular version of the story, but taking it as a venerable collection of materials presented in many forms that use some, but invariably not all, of the elements available in it. (For a discussion of this, *see* Marina Warner's chapter 'Absent Mothers: Cinderella' in her *From the Beast to the Blonde: Fairy Tales and their Tellers*, Chatto & Windus, 1994, pp.201-217.) Here the relevant details are the familiar narrative about social class – the poor girl sought by the rich suitor – and one about loss, the frequent identification of the Rogers character as motherless. In her self-reliance, the Rogers character is a typically American Cinderella. Her solitariness should not be taken as suggesting that she is somehow a waif, a helpless victim of the city, and the films acknowledge that the possibilities open to her characters are not limited to relationships with these men. Towards the end of *Vivacious Lady* we see her, convinced that her marriage has no future, board a train to return to New York, where, it can be inferred, she is will resume her job as a nightclub singer and dancer. She is upset at the collapse of her love affair, but not distraught – she can at least think about eating a sandwich. As the final act of *Bachelor Mother* begins, Rogers is preparing to take her adopted child and begin a new life in another place. At the end of *Kitty Foyle*, she has survived a disastrous affair and become a successful businesswoman. Her characters are prepared to find romance but equipped to survive its loss and find a workable form of domesticity or ordinary life outside marriage.

This self-reliance means that the Rogers character does not need much in the way of help from a (god)mother figure, another common element in the Cinderella story; in early versions of the tale, Warner points out, the lost mother returns, embodied in, say, the fairy godmother or the animal helper, but in more recent versions 'on the whole, the absent mother no longer returns' (Warner, p.206). Here the situation is somewhere in between. While there are no fairy godmothers, in each case there is a muted suggestion of an alliance between the Rogers character and an older woman, a minimal suggestion of the replacement of the lost mother.

VIVACIOUS LADY (George Stevens, 1938)

Vivacious Lady is the earliest film of this group, made between *Shall We Dance* and *Carefree*, before the Astaire-Rogers cycle was complete. (There is some evidence that it was conceived earlier, but delayed by James Stewart's being ill.) Rogers plays Francey Brent, a nightclub singer and dancer who encounters an assistant professor of botany, Peter Morgan (James Stewart) when he is sent by his family to rescue his cousin Keith (James Ellison) from the enticements of the city. In the early sequence of Francey's and Peter's mutual seduction, Stevens stresses the role of New York, its energy and promise of renewal, specifically through exteriors – the top of an open bus, the newly washed streets at dawn. The couple marry and board a train that will take them to Peter's home town. Francey asks

Peter, in Vivacious Lady, *tells his father, Dr Morgan (Charles Coburn), that he is married.*

Peter to carry her over the threshold into their compartment. He demurs ('People did that a thousand years ago, that's old stuff') until she stops him talking with a kiss. He carries her into the confined space, only to find that it is already occupied by a different vision of marriage, an older couple who are casually familiar with each other and lurch in and out of violent conflict.

In emphasising the crossing of a threshold, Stevens is prompting us to consider the meaning of this image of marriage. This relates to the distance to be travelled between the world in which these lovers have found each other – essentially the streets of New York – and the world in which their marriage will be consummated and lived. The train compartment represents a possible setting for erotic fulfilment, legitimate or otherwise, which is alluded to in the older wife's gibe about her husband: 'when I'm not along, something always happens . . .' It is also an image of domestic claustrophobia, of living out a marriage within a cramped space, resulting in a kind of cramping of the self.

The central sequences of the film follow up these moments by showing, in Peter's failure to face his parents with the news of his marriage, his inability to find a way to take his new bride across the threshold of the family home. Peter's parents resemble the couple on the train, but the overt violence of that couple's relationship has been repressed and their marriage is built around a pattern of interlocking gestures. The peremptoriness of the father (Charles Coburn) is met by the faintness and claim to 'heart trouble' of the mother, Martha (Beulah Bondi). Stevens expresses Peter and Francey's problem in his treatment of spaces in the Morgan home. There is no shot of its exterior, or of its ground-floor rooms, those that we might expect to be the proper place for an announcement of a marriage. Peter's confused idea of bringing Francey home as his bride is to prepare his bedroom as a connubial site – 'I want it to look very feminine' – to the understandable puzzlement of the family's maid.

Francey does not enter or even approach the Morgan house during the film. The spaces in which appetites can be acknowledged are located outside the home: the women's powder room at the Faculty club in which Martha and Francey share a cigarette and discuss silk stockings, the dark university boathouse which turns out to be full of courting couples, and Peter's biology laboratory and class-room, the site of continual sexual double entendre. The space in which Francey and Peter hope to be alone together represents a continuation of their difficulties: she has retreated to a hotel for women where her room contains an inefficient folding bed. The visual connection is with the train compartment, suggesting both a confined area and the unpredictable course of desire, which is echoed in the way the bed either suddenly emerges from the wall or stubbornly refuses to do so.

It is possible to see *Vivacious Lady* as centred on the problem of the man. Peter is like his father in temperament, with a tendency to bluster, and he expects to inherit the role of President of the University. His inability to break the news of his marriage to his father speaks in part of their closeness, of a desire not to hurt him and of a respect for his opinion. For the marriage to succeed, it will have to bring father and son together rather than drive them apart. As in the Astaire-Rogers cycle, the woman has very little direct contact with the older male figure associated with her lover, and it is not the film's project that Francey will reform Peter's father. (An exchange in which she announces that she is giving Peter up and returning to New York is the only moment in the film when Francey and Peter's father are alone together.)

Francey precipitates the crisis that unites father and son by destabilising the parents' marriage. With some help from Keith and in Peter's absence, she releases Martha's inhibitions by teaching her to dance. The result is that Martha, who is shown throughout as barely managing to contain her resentment at her husband's repressiveness, decides to leave him. Francey also decides to leave for New York,

Two estranged wives, Martha (Beulah Bondi) and Francey, on the train in Vivacious Lady, *with Willie Best.*

and the two women board the train. Stevens demonstrates through a series of gags and visual tableaux that they are now exactly alike in their situation.

This development now means that the two men want the same thing, or two versions of the same thing. It is Peter's role to assist his father, to help him put aside his insistence on power and position. To watch James Stewart and Charles Coburn play these last scenes of the film is to sense the importance of the affection between father and son. The two sacrifice the father's car, and, as they board the train, they have a conversation about relative values, about what a car and a wife are worth. Peter's father behaves like a child, pretending to have been hurt in the crash, so that Peter can find a space to behave like an adult in his final passionate embrace of Francey, and the film ends with the closed doors of their two compartments, with the implicit consummation of one marriage and revival of the other.

BACHELOR MOTHER (Garson Kanin, 1939)

In *Bachelor Mother*, the Rogers character again encounters a close bond between a son, David Merlin (David Niven), and his father, John B. Merlin, played by Charles Coburn in much the same peremptory manner that he adopted in *Vivacious Lady*. Here the Rogers character is directly dependent on the men through an obvious structure of class and power; the father and son own a department store, John B. Merlin & Son, in which Polly Parrish (Rogers) works as a salesgirl. The Merlins indulge in the fantasy that a corporation is like a family: Kanin begins his film with John B. Merlin's Christmas Eve address to his employees, a speech touching on loyalty, co-operation, the father and the son, and the seasonal celebration. These homilies are treated with some irony; Polly's first gesture in the film is to show another salesgirl her dismissal notice – she has a temporary, seasonal job – with the words 'Christmas Card'.

Left: David (David Niven) threatens to fire Polly (Rogers) for bad motherhood in Bachelor Mother.

Opposite: Cinderella goes to the ball – Polly and David on New Year's Eve.

The main plot device is that Polly chances on an abandoned baby which is then assumed to be hers; the transformation of her single girl's rooms into a simple family home portrays a successful form of domestic life that does not depend on riches. The baby's arrival produces an instant bond between Polly and her landlady, Mrs Weiss (Ferike Boros), the only actual mother we see in the film. Mrs Weiss's motherliness is associated, through her hesitant, accented English, with immigration, and hence Europe (and tradition) rather than America.

Kanin shows the ways in which a young woman in this situation can be thought of, and treated. From the perspective of the store, she can be seen as an emblem of their support for the institution of motherhood and so is re-employed. For David Merlin, she becomes an attractive image of maternal domesticity. As her employer, it is in his power to enter into parenthood and play father (there is a sequence in which he attempts to consult an instruction manual on feeding the baby), but to put this aside when it suits him. A New Year's Eve sequence explores David's positioning of Polly as Cinderella, tied by the presence of the baby to the domestic hearth until he arrives. Then the baby is left with the land-lady, clothes worthy of a princess are brought from the store, and Polly's position is magically disguised as bourgeois foreignness – she is introduced to Peter's classy friends as 'the daughter of a Swedish manufacturer'.

David and Polly find themselves acting the roles of a married couple in a setting without clear class associations: Sunday in the park. When John B. Merlin finds them here together with the baby, they are demonstrating their drift towards married status by quarrelling in public (an activity already understood as one of the prerogatives of the married in *Vivacious Lady* and, earlier still, in *It Happened One Night*). A little later there is a much more significant rift. Merlin has con-cluded that the baby is his grandson, and intends to use his power – his money or, given his name, wizardry – to claim him. David goes to Polly's apartment to

Real and fantasised relationships: J.B. Merlin (Charles Coburn) in Bachelor Mother *tracks down David, Polly and 'their' child.*

warn her of this. With his attention focused on his father's desires rather than his own, he offers a statement that comes out as a deadly insult: 'He even wants me to marry you, wants to set me up with a ready-made family, just so he can have a grandson'. Polly's response is to turn him out of her apartment and to prepare to flee the city.

Rogers's fine performance in this sequence successfully conveys Polly's authority, her achievement as creator of a simple, successful home for 'her' child and as a figure of desire. The apartment is photographed and framed here in such a way as to show it as unglamorous but functional; as the dialogue begins, she is standing at a stove, warming milk in a bottle. In her close-ups the very soft styling and lighting of Rogers's hair presents her as a desirable, if tough, version of the domestic woman, dismissing a man who is unable to see that the space in which they are standing contains a life that he might desire.

The sequence is part of the sombre note represented through the treatment of toys in the film. Kanin's opening shot announces it, an image of the Merlin skyscraper which, as the camera pulls back, turns out to be a model in the store window, a kind of doll's house. We might think that David, who overwinds and breaks the baby's Donald Duck toy, is treating Polly and her baby like playthings, and on the mantelpiece of Polly's apartment sits a doll, which we see at two significant points. The first is when David is about to dress his Cinderella for the New Year's Eve Ball, a hint writ larger a few moments later in the opening shot of the ball sequence, when an image of one of the Merlin store dummies dressed in a fur coat dissolves into Polly wearing the same coat. David's treatment of Polly as, in effect, a dummy could be because he is used to experiencing something similar at the hands of his father. The second shot of the doll appears when David is talking about his father's wish for him to marry Polly, indicating that he is little more than a pawn in his father's plans. Unlike *Vivacious Lady*, in which the problem is solved by father and son acting equally together, *Bachelor Mother* seems to be aware of the possible ineffectuality of the son, his unsureness of his own purposes.

This shift between *Vivacious Lady* and *Bachelor Mother* can be thought of in terms of destinations. In *Vivacious Lady*, Stevens has father and son pursue the women onto a train, and leaves them there, without making it clear exactly where they are heading. *Bachelor Mother* ends with a clearer but less radical destination: father and son pursue Polly to bring her and the baby back to the Merlin mansion. Significantly, just before the lovers' final embrace, Merlin has swept into the apartment and triumphantly carried the boy off, dismissing any importance the lovers might have: 'I don't care who the father is, I'm the grandfather'.

KITTY FOYLE (Sam Wood, 1940)

Kitty Foyle is, in my view, the key film in Rogers's early 'forties work, presenting us with a structure that will be crucial to several of the films that follow. It goes much further, though, in emphasising the negative associations of wealth and class, and contrasting them with the positive qualities embodied in an alternative, more democratic, lover. The rich family is shown as unreformable, and the relationship between the Rogers character and the son of that family is now a source of melodrama rather than comedy.

The source novel, *Kitty Foyle* (Liveright, 1939; film tie-in edition, from which page references are taken, Grosset & Dunlap), by the prolific and interesting minor American novelist Christopher Morley, was adapted for Rogers in Dalton Trumbo's script and Sam Wood's film. Morley's *Kitty Foyle* is a first-person narrative told by its eponymous heroine, the daughter of a working-class Irish family in Philadelphia. She falls in love with the son of an aristocratic banking dynasty, Wyn Strafford VI. Such a marriage could work only at the unacceptable cost of

Wyn (Dennis Morgan) introduces Kitty (Rogers) to his mother (Gladys Cooper) in Kitty Foyle.

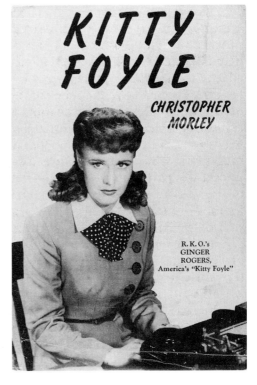

The movie tie-in edition of Kitty Foyle.

divorcing the son from his family, or of Kitty allowing herself to be totally absorbed by the Philadelphia aristocracy. (The word 'aristocracy' seems appropriate here in that the Strafford family trace their money and power back several generations and seem to think of themselves as an American equivalent of a European titled family.) The couple part, and Kitty moves to New York, but they continue intermittently to see each other, and she becomes pregnant. She is about to inform her lover when she reads of his engagement to a Philadephia debutante. Kitty has an abortion. Seven years pass, during which she meets Mark Eisen, a New York Jewish doctor specialising in childhood diseases. The novel ends with Kitty's contemplation of whether her feelings for Mark would justify her marrying him – it is implied, but significantly not stated, that she may do so.

Some of the changes made to this material for the film clearly relate to censorship considerations. The physical nature of Kitty's affair with Wyn (Morley makes it explicit that they are lovers from an early stage) was disguised, and the abortion episode rewritten so that Kitty and Wyn marry but quickly part, and their child, conceived in wedlock but due after their divorce, dies at birth. In the light of the Production Code, these are not surprising revisions, and the echo of Morley's original emphases are evident in the film, for example in a sequence in which Kitty (Rogers) and Wyn (Dennis Morgan) journey to the Strafford cabin in the Pocono mountains to 'see the sunset', which offers us the opportunity to conclude that they are lovers without the film needing to state it.

In the novel, Kitty's narrative places her affair with Wyn firmly in the past. She emphasises its passion and intensity, treating its collapse with regret. Her possible marriage to Mark is seen as patriotic – 'I'd be a better American if I married Mark than if I'd married Wyn' (Morley, p.280) – but the novel does not (quite) end with a marriage, and its whole structure might be regarded as Morley's way of dramatising Kitty's not entirely successful attempt to convince herself of her new choice. The film reorganises the material so that Kitty's choice between the two men is presented as a moment of decision between current alternatives, while contrasting the worlds associated with Wyn and Mark in such a way as to direct our preference towards Mark (doctor, democrat, wage-earner, potential husband) and away from Wyn (banker, aristocrat, private fortune, potential adulterer); the book's possibly contentious identification of Mark as Jewish is dropped. Wood begins with a proposal of marriage from Mark, immediately followed by the unexpected reappearance of Wyn in New York, announcing that he has left his wife and child and offering to take Kitty to South America as his mistress. Kitty's dilemma is presented through a dialogue with her image in a mirror, and her history with the two men is recounted in flashback. Her decision to opt for marriage and Mark emerges only in the final frames of the film.

Wyn's inability to offer Kitty marriage is a final twist with which the film ensures that he represents a negative version of Rogers's rich young lovers in previous films. The resonance of an American fortune has significantly changed, for here it is associated with the inflexible power of an old class order signified by Philadelphia and the banking business, as opposed to commerce or education. In the presentation of the family the figure of the reformable father (and thus the bond between father and son, central to *Vivacious Lady* and *Bachelor Mother*) has disappeared. Wyn's father, who is very briefly mentioned in the novel, does not appear in the film; the family is headed by Wyn's impassive, controlling mother

Left: Giono (Eduardo Cianelli) brings milk for the pregnant Kitty in Kitty Foyle. *Right: Kitty and Mark (James Craig).*

(Gladys Cooper). The repressive patriarch remains in the form of an image, which is also a reminder of the continuity of this family's power. This is the portrait of Wynnewood Strafford IV, in front of which Kitty takes her decision to cross a threshold in another direction, leaving the Strafford house and her brief marriage.

Linked with these figures is another father, also connected with the world represented by Philadelphia. Unlike the Rogers characters in *Vivacious Lady* and *Bachelor Mother*, Kitty has a living parent, Pop Foyle (Ernest Cossart). Pop, who introduces Wyn to Kitty (the occasion suggestively includes a sudden conflagration, and Kitty's being partly undressed) is associated with the values of Philadelphia; invalid and alcoholic, he is the complementary figure to the Strafford patriarchs, the powerless father at the other end of the social scale.

His death enables Kitty to sever her ties with Philadelphia, and with the move to New York, the presentation of her character changes. In Philadelphia her context is the family and her role as Pop's supportive daughter. She is never shown with other women, except in her indifference to the socialites who waste time in Wyn's office. The New York sequences (apart from those including Wyn) present her consistently as a typical white-collar girl, one in a group of women, whether of the workers at the perfume shop, the three girls sharing the apartment, or the occupants of the Pocahontas hotel for women. Kitty also replaces Pop Foyle with a strong mother figure associated with Europe: the successful businesswoman Delphine Detaille (Odette Myrtil). Delphine, who looks after Kitty when her child dies at birth, plays an analogous role to Mrs Weiss in *Bachelor Mother*, again as if the quality of motherliness has to be imported from an older society.

The contrast between Philadelphia and New York is implicit in the comedic prologue of *Kitty Foyle*. Here the shift from family member to worker is located as the history of the American woman. We see a turn-of-the-century world in which the woman moves smoothly from the porch of her father's bourgeois home to marriage, the parlour of her own home and the announcement of impending motherhood. This is replaced by modernity, a culture in which women have the vote and employment but have sacrificed any clear structure underpinning relations between the sexes. A rolling title locates the problem as the 'five thirty feeling', the difficulty encountered in the transition from work to life outside. The main narrative picks up the question, beginning with a shot not of a home but of a descending lift, looking at a group of women as they finish work and discuss marriage and men. Wood directs the sequence so that Rogers is firmly located in this context; she emerges out of invisibility at the back of the group only at the end of the conversation, and we hear her voice before we see her.

The difference in environments is used to make distinctions between Kitty's suitors. We see her with Wyn in homes – her own home with Pop, the Strafford mansion, the cabin in the Pocono mountains. With Mark, the spaces are city rooms (a slum living room and the cramped apartment that Kitty shares with two other girls) and various forms of transport (the back of a taxi in their first sequence together and later a New York bus). We can make a connection between these sequences and the opening (bus) and closing (train) settings of *Vivacious Lady*, which also celebrates the lovers' ability to feel at home in such places. *Kitty Foyle* can be read as a film which, by assigning qualities to two different men that are attractive to the Rogers character, attempts to resolve tensions left open in *Vivacious Lady*. As Kitty is driven away in the final sequence, she seems to know where she is going.

Despite this ending, the important quality of *Kitty Foyle* is its equivocation. Wood's film is crucial for Rogers in that it so precisely balances the move towards the embracing of a democratic, prosaic and implicitly modern America with a nostalgia for an aristocratic, glamorous America – a world much closer to that of the Astaire-Rogers musicals in that it offers, or might be imagined to offer, the conditions that operate in them. The key sequence here is Kitty's and Wyn's evening love scene in the Pocono mountain cabin. It begins with a moment that seems to be a deliberate prompt, an invocation of *The Gay Divorcée*: Kitty taps out a rhythm on Wyn's hand and invites him to identify 'Night and Day'. In the ensuing dialogue, Kitty claims that the education of woman is the proper business of man and asks Wyn to tell her about love. He replies with a version of the story of the Garden of Eden. Throughout the sequence, neither actor moves beyond a sitting position. Dennis Morgan is first lying, then sitting, on a sofa, bending over Rogers who sits on the floor in front of a fire, and Wood films the couple in increasingly tight close-up, ending in a single, ninety-second take of their faces. The scene invokes some of the qualities found in comparable moments of the Astaire-Rogers films, but accompanied by stillness. Instead of dance, there is a striking immobility.

TOM, DICK AND HARRY (Garson Kanin, 1941)

Tom, Dick and Harry extends the range, if not the depth, of exploration of themes covered in *Vivacious Lady*, *Bachelor Mother* and *Kitty Foyle*. It offers the Rogers character a choice between the three suitors of the title whose qualities recall those of the male characters in the earlier films of the group. Dick Hamilton (Alan Marshal) represents effortless glamour and the desirability of inherited wealth. Tom (George Murphy), an automobile salesman for whom marriage to Janie (Rogers) would be one of the rewards of his promotion, represents a myth of success and progress that is embodied most notoriously in the fiction of Horatio Alger (1834-99), in which dutiful conduct wins the girl. Harry (Burgess Meredith) plays Huck Finn to Tom's Tom Sawyer – what Harry has to offer Janie, exemplified in his promise to take her fishing every day, clearly contrasts with the

Small town family: Janie (Rogers) with Ma (Jane Seymour) and Pop (Joe Cunningham) in Tom, Dick and Harry.

measures of success that preoccupy Tom. Harry's indifference to his own lack of money and the fact that he is well known in a community (he greets everybody he meets) loosely link him to Mark in *Kitty Foyle*.

Part of the interest of these characters is that Kanin and screenplay writer Paul Jarrico have made them a source of mild satire on the various ideals of success held by American men. They are distinguished by their money and their various ambitions and are shown without any context (the suitor's family is now entirely absent, even in the case of Dick). When Janie imagines what a future life with any of them might hold, satirical intent seems to dominate. Tom's and Harry's proposals are followed by sequences in which Janie dreams about her future – as a housewife bound to a career-obsessed or feckless husband. (The final dream, after Janie's first encounter with Dick, is not mainly about the man, but about Janie's anxiety that she will be exposed as a fraud, and about her triumphant narcissism.)

Another echo of *Kitty Foyle* emerges when Janie's choice (of Harry) is made in the final frames of the film. Kanin offers the image of the couple strolling hand in hand as the visual keynote of Janie's relationship with Harry, as compared to Tom's and Dick's courtships, which are associated with the technologies of flashy car and plane respectively, hinting, perhaps, that of the three suitors it is Harry who most resembles Astaire. In the absence of dance, this cannot quite emerge, and Kanin substitutes a device, a piece of outrageous, comic cinematic prompting,

*Above: the proprietor (Gus Glassmire) disapproves as Janie and Harry
(Burgess Meredith) dance in the music store in* Tom, Dick and Harry.
Below: Janie's dream of married life with Harry.

to confirm our knowledge that Harry is the right suitor. When Janie and Harry kiss they (and we, but not the other characters in the film) hear the ringing of bells on the soundtrack. Kanin can thereby claim that Janie is being directed by desire while reducing the matter to a gag.

Our attitude to Janie's choice is also informed by knowledge of her situation. The distinction made at the beginning of *Kitty Foyle*, that marriage has a different meaning for the working woman and for her domestic sister, is collapsed here: Janie is both a worker (a telephone operator) and the marriageable daughter of a benign, small-town family. Both Tom's and Harry's proposals of marriage are accepted on the family porch, and Janie's decision is announced in the living room at a family breakfast. These circumstances seem to reduce the sense of rescue, or of risk, attached to her choice of husband.

Possibly *Tom, Dick and Harry* is a film that knows its own lightness and understands itself as an adolescent dream about the married lives that might emerge from a context of family security. It begins with a consideration of what we want from an evening at the movies, and specifically what a generic romance might offer a wartime audience. The sequence takes place in a cinema, with Janie and Tom enjoying the end of a film that evokes a revised version of *Kitty Foyle*, one in which the aristocratic lover offers marriage and the heroine leaves for South America, not as mistress but as bride. As it ends, Tom says to Janie, 'We already seen the newsreel. Do you want to stay and see it again?' She grimly declines, and, as they leave, there is an enthusiastic exchange with her usherette friend Paula (Vicki Lester), who has seen the film twelve times. Kanin's point seems to be that the pleasure given by versions of the Cinderella story is all the sharper in the light of current events – the newsreel playing as the couple walk out is of Hitler's rallying call to arms.

ROXIE HART (William Wellman, 1942)

Roxie Hart was Rogers's first film with 20th-Century Fox, marking the end of an unbroken run of twenty films with RKO, from *The Gay Divorcée* to *Tom, Dick and Harry*. The film is based on the play *Chicago* by Maurine Watkins, and Rogers plays Roxie, a girl with show-business ambitions who allows herself to be imprisoned and tried for shooting an admirer, because the publicity will further her career and the city has never been known to convict a pretty woman. (Her husband is the guilty party, a fact that is ignored for almost the whole of the film.)

All the romances examined so far in this chapter depict Rogers as a working woman in the city. In *Roxie Hart*, the American city is now conceived entirely in terms of satire, as a world of excess and manic energy dominated by advertising, photography and performance, in other words, newsworthiness. (Such a harsh critique can be assigned comfortably only to a past era, here to the American city in the 'twenties.) It is conceived not simply as a trap, or prison, but as a society that has no use for the world beyond its boundaries. In this comedy, there is (with one limited exception) no possibility of retreat into what Northrop Frye termed the 'green world' (*A Natural Perspective*, Harcourt Brace, p.142). This is an indoor world: before Roxie's acquittal, the camera ventures outside only twice, once in the opening shot of a bleak street in drenching rain, and once in a brief moment of violence, a gas-station shoot-out. *Roxie Hart* could be compared

Newsworthiness: Homer (George Montgomery), Babe (Phil Silvers), Amos (George Chandler), Benham (Nigel Bruce), Jake (Lynne Overman), Roxie (Rogers) and Murdock (Charles D. Brown) in Roxie Hart.

to another, slightly earlier, film dealing with the city, crime and the press, Howard Hawks's *His Girl Friday* (1940). The difference is that Hawks's film, while set in what Stanley Cavell has likened to an environment drawn from Jonsonian comedy, offers us 'an adventure in love' for its two major characters (*see* Cavell, 1981, pp.169-170, and Frye pp.14-33). *Roxie Hart* is distinct from the other films considered so far in this chapter in that it is not built around a romance. Indeed, such a thing as romance cannot be entertained, or even imagined, by its characters.

Wellman and the writer of the screenplay, Nunnally Johnson, make the point by showing how the potential lover is ignored, or invisible, to the extent that for Roxie he has no significance as an individual. This figure is Homer Howard (George Montgomery), a young reporter who sees Roxie when she is being arrested – one of the many occasions in the film that are assembled into a pose for a newspaper photograph by Babe (Phil Silvers). When Homer says, looking at Roxie, 'But she's just a girl, like me', part of what he means to say is that she is, in his eyes, young like him. (The opening image of the film's framing narrative has shown another youngster, a first-time reporter being sickened at the sight of a corpse.) The main, flashback narrative is marked by the complete exclusion, not just of children, but of anyone (other than Homer) who would wish to claim youth or innocence. Roxie's response to his attentions never moves beyond a bright, conceited interest that exudes the self-regarding energy of which the film is full.

Apart from fast talk, the main forms of energetic expression in *Roxie Hart* are fighting and dancing, and there are two extended examples of each. One of the first events in the film is the protracted fight between Roxie and the reporter Jake Callahan (Lynne Overman) in her bedroom, and the jail sequences open with another fight, this time between Roxie and a fellow prisoner, Velma (Helene Reynolds). There is no sense on either occasion that there is anything unusual or traumatic for the participants or onlookers in these fights. These are apparently routine ways of behaving, unrestrained by ideas of what is appropriate to a particular time or owed to a specific person.

The two dance numbers both take place in the jail, and again part of the point is that there is no sense of particular standards of behaviour being appropriate to specific locations. As the assembled reporters urge Roxie to show off the way she dances the Black Bottom, she expresses a doubt to Jake. Here Wellman poses him alone, at the head of a long table – a man delivering a careful judgement (the whole sequence has the quality of a rehearsal for the trial to come):

Roxie: You don't think it might be – what you'd call – out of place?
Jake: Certainly not. Do you think we'd ask you, if it would be?

The hesitation in Roxie's line brings into question whether it is even possible to pose such a question here, to formulate the concept of the inappropriate.

The second dance is Roxie's tap number, performed on the prison stairs. The two dances both express liveliness and fun, and the romantic couple is not at their centre. In the Black Bottom, men and women dance as individuals, rather than as couples. The exception is Roxie, who dances with Homer, but there is no intense connection – he is just treated as an available young male. The prompt for this dance is that Roxie has just kissed Homer, but again there is no sense that his interest in her has any effect other than stimulating her exuberant physical energy and skill as she seizes the moment for a solo. (The idea of Roxie's unstillable energy is felt throughout the film in her incessant chewing of gum, which may sometimes be a reflex movement making her look as though she is chewing gum; this is especially obvious in the Black Bottom number, in the climax of the courtroom sequence, and when she chooses between suitors. It may also be a way of expressing the character's limitations – she sees no one of these occasions as more important than any other.)

In presenting figures who are, or might be, in the position of a father to Roxie while not being blood relatives – offering to educate her (the form this takes is friendly, or professional, advice) and acknowledging her sexual attractiveness without being themselves aroused by it – *Roxie Hart* follows the earlier romances covered in this chapter. This is where Wellman starts, with the double act of Jake and the 'theatrical agent', E. Clay Benham (Nigel Bruce), masters of slightly different kinds of ceremony. (The subject of impersonal sexual allure runs through the film and is emblematised by Roxie's legs. They are the first part of Roxie's body that we see, and a few minutes later Jake carefully helps Roxie to extricate her leg from a broken door panel: 'you don't want to damage your defence'.)

A more complex instance, in which the limits of a father figure's position are explored, is that of Billy Flynn (Adolphe Menjou), the ingenious lawyer who is to ensure Roxie's acquittal. The film introduces Flynn at the moment when, via a gag, it is disposing of the matter of Roxie's literal parents. Roxie's husband Amos (George Chandler) appeals by telephone to her parents for help, but he is unsuccessful; when told that Roxie is to hang, her mother says, 'What did I tell you?'. The parents do not appear again.

Flynn now takes on the role of Roxie's father or saviour, and sequences in various public settings comically explore his professional virtuosity. But against the various trials and rehearsals, Wellman poses another set of exchanges between Flynn and Roxie. There are four of these scenes, one in the gaol and three in the ante-room to the court, and they are identifiable by a striking element of the *mise en scène* – literally foregrounded in two cases – the presence of masses of flowers. In each scene, the couple are in effect alone and have escaped into as near an approximation of Frye's 'green world' as this film can allow itself to import into its guarded spaces.

In the first sequence in jail, Flynn's role as father to Roxie is established through a familiar device of romance, his recounting the story of her life to her. (He is supplying her with a biography for the newspapers.) In the second, immediately before the trial begins, he gives her last-minute coaching. This dense sequence is full of visual and verbal gags, as Menjou and Rogers mug their way through a series of fake emotional states. Flynn looks in the mirror to check that his hair is in just enough disarray. Responding to Roxie's threat to 'crown' the prosecutor, he reminds her that 'always you're frightened, and helpless, and demure'. On the last word, Roxie obligingly pulls her skirt slightly above the knee.

Flynn: Demure, I said.
[Roxie pulls the skirt still higher]
Flynn: Don't you know what demure means?
Roxie [aggressively, loudly]: Certainly.
Flynn: What?
Roxie: [hesitates] What?
Flynn: Demure means shy, timid, modest *[he makes a gesture which we understand to be jerking the skirt down, but the camera remains on his face.]*

This is important and touching, because it expresses the limits of Flynn's education of (and thus his fulfilment of the role of father to) Roxie. A few seconds later, Roxie and Flynn prepare to enter the courtroom, and the pointed irony is that the image is reminiscent of a father about to give away his daughter in marriage, as Roxie excitedly spins around under his gaze. (This situation is destabilising enough to induce a parapraxis – Flynn gives Roxie his law book, while he clasps her bouquet.)

There can be no question of giving in marriage here. A few seconds later, Flynn violently pushes aside Homer, who is trying to wish Roxie luck. The later two scenes in the ante-room contain further expressions of the limitations of Roxie's and Flynn's closeness. The third springs from the possibility of actual disaster: they are facing the fact that the one man who could clear Roxie is dead, but are interrupted by Homer. The fourth scene is the shortest, containing only one intimate gesture, or fatherly act – Flynn takes the chewing gum out of Roxie's open mouth. After this, he will address only one word to her ('Quiet!') in the remaining part of the trial, and he is not seen with her after the verdict is announced.

Watched by Homer and Billy Flynn (Adolphe Menjou), Roxie fakes pregnancy in Roxie Hart.

'Describe it to the audience . . . er, to the jury': Billy questions Roxie in court.

Roxie Hart can be read as the last in the group of films that begins with *Vivacious Lady*. The figures representative of a father and son arc still present, but the world that contains them has darkened to a point where there are no forms of contact with the Rogers character other than momentary or vestigial ones, of which nothing can come in terms of human relations. Wellman acknowledges this when he chooses to turn his camera away from situations in which emotion might be manifest, or its absence horrifying – for example, the moment of Roxie's acquittal, which is handled as a sequence of newspaper headlines. This is a film which involves two marriages, but shows no proposal.

It is possible to see the 'happy ending' of the film in this light, as a gag, a parodic reprise of Rogers's roles as versions of Cinderella. She spurns Homer, preferring the wealth of O'Malley (William Frawley), the foreman of the jury, but the passage of time and the Wall Street Crash see her established with Homer in the final frames. Wellman does not, however, show the couple at home. He ends the film in the family car, where numerous children tumble over their parents and each other. Cinderella has become the Old Woman Who Lived in a Shoe.

2. THE MELODY LINGERS ON

In an early sequence of *Vivacious Lady*, Peter, wooing Francey, asks her if she thinks things out carefully. She replies, 'If they're small things, I never do. But if they're important things, I never do, either.' One feature that links the films discussed so far is the ease with which the Rogers characters approach romance. This has to do with her toughness and assurance, the sense of not requiring rescue, and further, with a kind of optimism that believes that it is not always wise to submit marriage, and the concomitant issues of sexual fulfilment, of intimacy or of loneliness, to close examination. (This is taken to an extreme in *Tom, Dick and Harry*, in the impulse to accept all the suitors who propose marriage and to be disappointed that a choice has to be made between them.)

The next group of films invokes another, seemingly opposite, form of behaviour in the face of marriage. This involves strategies of averting the pressure of sexual attentions by appearing to be someone to whom such approaches are not (yet, at least) thinkable or proper. In the previous group of films, the men wish to disguise Rogers (as variously a student, a foreigner, a submissive wife, a virtuous woman), but here it is Rogers who chooses to disguise herself (as a kind of gold-digger, as a child, as an unmarried sister travelling with her brother). Pretending to be a child is the most obvious version of this, and occurs in *Primrose Path* (Gregory La Cava, 1940) and, centrally, in *The Major and the Minor* (Billy Wilder, 1942), but I will start with another, less drastic disguise in *Fifth Avenue Girl*, the film released immediately after *Bachelor Mother*.

FIFTH AVENUE GIRL (Gregory La Cava, 1939)

Fifth Avenue Girl might be thought to belong to my earlier grouping. It bears evident similarities to *Bachelor Mother* and *Vivacious Lady*, repeating the close tie between a father and a son, a romantic attraction between this son and the Rogers character and sharp differences relating to money and power – the solitary girl

Fairytale meeting: Mary (Rogers) encounters millionaire Timothy Borden (Walter Connolly) on a park bench in Fifth Avenue Girl.

and the family of millionaires. But here the initial relationship of the Rogers character to the family is through the father, rather than the son. The family home is the central site of the film, the place which it is the Rogers character's work to reform, rather than being an eventual, or a possible, destination for her. (The figure who enters and reforms an American home was a subject of recurrent interest to La Cava, who had previously explored it in *She Married Her Boss*, 1935, and *My Man Godfrey*, 1936)

We first see the interior of the Fifth Avenue mansion as millionaire Timothy Borden (Walter Connolly) – the surname presumably a gag about parents who have poor relationships with their children – wanders alone through its vast, pretentious open space, which is dominated by a grand, straight, central staircase reminiscent of a stage set for a Ziegfeld musical, disconsolately whistling 'Happy Birthday to You'. The house represents a failure of intimacy – Timothy's empty marriage to his wife Martha (Verree Teasdale), who is beginning to contemplate taking a lover, and his estrangement from his children. When Timothy's daughter brings a party of friends home, one of them enquires, 'Do people really live here?'

As part of a wider project to sort out his life, Timothy suggests to Mary Grey (Rogers), a young woman he has encountered in Central Park, that she stay in his house. Her impact there is such that she is even able to find some spaces to treat as homely, places for domestic activities. To address the impersonality of the central living space is beyond her, but, after her arrival, the roof of the mansion becomes a place to revive Timothy's boyhood hobby of pigeon racing,

'Just what is your racket?' Tim (Tim Holt) reacts ambiguously to Mary in Fifth Avenue Girl.

and the kitchen is twice the scene of sexual reconciliation. The first of these is when Mary stages a little melodrama with a kitchen knife in order to drive the film's minor romantic couple, Timothy's daughter Katherine (Kathryn Adams) and her bombastic, inarticulate lover Michael (James Ellison), into each other's arms. This performance causes the cook to resign, so that the owners of the house have the kitchen to themselves. Their marriage is now revived over a meal consisting of Timothy's favourite dish prepared by Martha.

Timothy's own plans for the retrieval of his marriage are not dealt with in detail in the film, but involve pretending to be a reveller – every evening, he goes out of the house with Mary – so as to appear less the staid business man and more like Martha's recent escorts. It is never clear how long a reconciliation formed on this basis would have lasted, given Timothy's enduring aversion to socialising, but this question is avoided. It is rather the couple's shared history, celebrated in the re-enactment of their youthful domesticity (beef stew in the kitchen) and confirmed by the ritual of looking through images of their lives in a photograph album that rejuvenates the marriage. The blessing of the minor romance (the marriage of Michael and Katherine) is a footnote to it, springing from the same source. The dialogue makes it explicit that this young couple are repeating an earlier stage in the lives of Timothy and Martha, an American narrative in which eventual success emerges from homespun beginnings. Perhaps the family was never truly in need of reform, but just required the catalyst of Mary to turn its attention to its own history.

Mary's function in the Borden home is as an actress, playing her various roles with some adeptness (a hysterical woman in Michael's and Katherine's presence, a grasping woman in Martha's). What is striking about her (and makes Mary different from Rogers's related characters in *Bachelor Mother* and *Vivacious Lady*) is that apart from these roles she has no context: no apparent home, no job and apparently no social life whatever. Allan Scott named the character Mary Grey, and at one point in the film she calls herself Miss America – so she can be taken to be both undefinable and representative, but without a fixed identity.

In, say, *Bachelor Mother*, the Rogers figure knows when she is in disguise (as the daughter of a Swedish manufacturer) and when she is out of it (mothering a child, selling toys), but matters are by no means as clear here. The result is that her romance with Timothy's son Tim (Tim Holt) is dogged by her sense of confusion, anxiety and distrust: why should Tim wish to make love to her if he thinks she is a gold digger? (This is perfectly met by Tim Holt's embodiment of sexual interest working against an almost impermeable primness, an act which Orson Welles was shortly to use to wonderful effect in *The Magnificent Ambersons*, 1942.)

The confusions in the romance are exactly those that can be rendered irrelevant, at least temporarily, by a dance number in a musical, and Scott and La Cava know this. They offer a sequence which is suggestive of the degree to which the possibility of dance has receded, although it has not entirely disappeared. Tim and Mary take an evening walk in Central Park, and La Cava makes a point out of their strolling past a mute chorus of courting couples. In this American Eden, Mary buys an apple for Tim's dinner, and they find a park bench which is continually occupied and vacated by pairs of lovers, culminating in the embodiment of the spirit of the place, a sailor and his girl. The sailor – played with imperturbable good humour by Jack Carson – entertains the occupants of the bench with bawdy songs, adding to the discomfort of Mary and Tim, and a fight is narrowly avoided. Finally Tim kisses Mary. She shows no pleasure at this, but runs away and the sequence ends.

In the next sequence showing the couple together, Mary is sitting on the steps outside the Borden house, as if she can neither stay inside it nor leave it entirely. Tim sits beside her, and their quarrel continues in terms that perversely invoke Rogers's fame as a dancer:

Tim: Don't you ever do anything but sit?
Mary: I like to sit.

Perhaps this exchange can be read as indicating that Rogers's character likes to be in a position from which she can be lifted up, swept off her feet – and that she is aware of the dangers and melancholy of this position, in which the risk is that if

'Would you mind going to the opening with my son?'
Timothy, Mary and Tim in Fifth Avenue Girl.

you sit (literally, metaphorically), you abandon the possibility of initiating the action. Mary is prepared to sit in these different, mundane places until someone, so to speak, lifts her up. Tim's uneasiness springs from his not knowing exactly how to do it, but they are both waiting for him to find out; this much is clear from the end of the sequence, when Mary brushes aside a passing policeman's inquiry as to whether she needs help. The final sequence of the film finds them on these steps again, and at last Tim finds a substitute for dance. His way of sweeping Mary off her feet is to pick her up bodily and carry her back into the house. If he cannot be Astaire, at least he can be Tarzan, and the rightness of the moment for the couple is confirmed by Mary's, and the film's, final line ('Why don't you mind your own business?'), a further reminder to the patrolling police-man that this action is outside his jurisdiction.

PRIMROSE PATH (Gregory La Cava, 1940)

Primrose Path begins with a title quote from Menander, 'We live not as we wish to, but as we can', and a landscape in which dogs root around in rubbish for scraps as a little girl runs home to a shack, carrying some stolen food. The poverty shown here is considerable, and there is little indication in the film of anywhere within reach where people have money and live differently. The characters who emerge out of this poverty include a shrew, a drunk, variously loose or available women and a thieving child obsessed with receiving gifts. Rogers plays Ellie May Adams, the elder sister of the thieving child. As soon as she appears on screen, it is evi-dent that she is disguising herself as a protection against lascivious interest and possible exploitation. The opening conversation with her grandmother (Queenie Vassar) reveals that her plaited hair is a deliberate strategy to make herself look like a (younger) child. (For a contemporary audience, the fact that Rogers had dyed her hair brunette for the part – she tells in her autobiography of carefully concealing the fact until the film had been released – would have heightened the sense of disguise).

Innocence: Ellie May (Rogers) in plaits, with Ed (Joel McCrea) in Primrose Path.

Ellie introduces Ed to her mother (Marjorie Rambeau).

Taken as a literal strategy, plaiting your hair as a protection against sexual advances is absurd, but Ellie's belief in it helps to define the character that Rogers is portraying, a girl who counteracts the seaminess surrounding her by seeing magical, or fairy-tale, possibilities. Her suitor Ed Wallace (Joel McCrea), when he appears, is not so very different: he is young, poor and naïve. When she first attempts to seduce him, she imitates her mother's sexual allure and, when this fails, behaves as if she were acting in a fairy tale, or perhaps in a musical. The sequence finds the couple alone, on a deserted jetty. Earlier Ed had kissed her, and she now refers to this kiss as an enchantment. Elaborating on the mood, she disowns her family and her old life. Ed rejects her, and after making him kiss her twice more, she moves towards the edge of the jetty, as if to throw herself into the water. When he moves towards her, she falls, in a faint, into his arms. The composition of this shot, with which the sequence ends – Ed bending over the prone Ellie, Rogers's back arched in a pose of surrender or abandon – resembles the end of a dance number. It is as if by her behaviour Ellie has created the conditions of the musical for a moment, and in doing so has successfully brought about the transformation that is enacted in such sequences and she so desires, for in the next scene the two are married.

In a harsh world, however, this is a dangerous strategy. The short time for which the enchantment lasts is caught in the scene in which Ed chases Ellie around his boat and pins her to the ground, another moment when physical contact – lovers fighting, or pretending to fight – stands in for something that might have been presented in dance. The sequence is striking for both its eroticism and its sense of youth. The couple are quite unequipped to deal with the business of integrating their feeling for each other into the film's larger social world, where questions of proper and improper forms of masculinity and femininity draw on estimates of how much money a character possesses and how that money was acquired.

This is explored in the central sequences, in which the attempt to bring the marriage back into the ambit of Ellie's family results in disaster. Ed and Ellie are invited to dinner with the family, and Ed discovers that Ellie's father Homer

Under the tutelage of Thelma (Vivienne Osborne), Ellie is costumed for her role as a 'companion' to older men in Primrose Path.

(Miles Mander) is an alcoholic. Supposing that he is being set up to support these feckless in-laws, he deserts Ellie and quits the house. His friends now tell him of the dubious reputation of Mamie (Marjorie Rambeau), Ellie's mother. At the same time Homer, in a confused and drunken rage, shoots Mamie. La Cava cuts the two acts of male destructiveness together, framing Ed's sadistic attitude towards Ellie (in which he invites her to kill herself) with the act and then the aftermath of Homer's fatal shooting of her mother. The link is male paranoia and humiliation, a suggestion that Ed is acting in a way not unlike the obviously defeated Homer.

The temporary end of the marriage takes place on the same set as its beginning, the jetty at night. Ellie collapses into a sitting position and Ed does not raise her to her feet. She tells him, 'I wish you hadn't said them things in there. I wish you'd just hit me instead', indicating that the lack of any kind of touch is an unbearable contrast to the nature of their former encounter here. When Ellie leaves, he has still not touched her. A bar-girl now enters and he pushes her away, at least (subconsciously?) aware of the significance of physical contact in this place.

Versions of the group of women and of the Rogers character's older woman friend appear in the final sequences. After the death of Mamie, Ellie reluctantly accepts that she must make use of her sexual appeal to keep the family from starving. She contacts her mother's friend Thelma (Vivienne Osborne), who sets her up as an available female companion for older men. One might suppose this to be merely a way of disguising the business of prostitution so as to meet the requirements of the Production Code, but the effect is more complex. The fact that the precise nature of the favours bestowed by women like Mamie and Thelma on men like Mr Hawkins (Gene Morgan) is never made explicit is part of a strategy to treat them positively, which goes almost as far as to suggest that this is by no means the worst form of sexual relationship. In line with this is the happy ending of the film, in which the couple are reunited and Ed is installed as head of the family. This ending is brought about by Mr Hawkins, once Mamie's 'friend', and the character to whom Thelma has offered Ellie, rather than by the – to Ed – much more obviously benign father figure of Gramp (Henry Travers).

This reading of *Fifth Avenue Girl* and *Primrose Path* suggests that part of what La Cava is doing can be thought of as exploring what musicals might become if there were no dancing partner, no Astaire to dance with the Rogers character. (I have already mentioned that both films were written by Allan Scott, the principal writer of the Astaire-Rogers musicals.) Dance is replaced with cruder, more forceful physical contact. On repeated viewing of *Primrose Path* this seems pervasive. Characters wrestle, raise or throw stones, threaten with knife or stove-handle, assert their masculinity in front of women by waving a gun or misbehaving on a motorcycle and sidecar. But even more central to this reading is the presentation of Rogers. The only options that the Rogers character will exercise are those of sitting down or being somehow swept off her feet – outside these possibilities she will accept no mundane existence and create no context for herself. To take this position is to insist on being treated in ways that are more often encountered in musicals.

Happy ending? Ellie and Ed with Grandma (Queenie Vassar) and Honeybell (Joan Carroll) in the delapidated family home.

LUCKY PARTNERS (Lewis Milestone, 1940)

Lucky Partners is the final film in this group and Rogers's eleventh and last film to be written or co-written by Allan Scott. (This count includes Scott's uncredited contribution to the script of *The Gay Divorcée*.) Its French original, *Bonne Chance* (Fernand Rivers, 1935), was written by and starred Sacha Guitry, and part of its difference from the two Scott/La Cava films that precede it is expressed in the casting of Rogers's co-star, Ronald Colman, in the Guitry role. The choice of Colman seems to suggest something of a continuation of the impulses of the Astaire-Rogers musicals – Rogers encountering a man of known assurance and grace. (Colman might be thought of as an equivalent for Hollywood of Guitry in projecting these qualities – the personae of both actors depend in part on their distinctly modulated voices.)

Colman's persona at this time was not a simple one, and his work in the late 'thirties is an important context here. In Frank Capra's *Lost Horizon* (1937), Robert Conway (Colman) is both a pragmatist, tipped to become the next English Foreign Secretary, and a visionary, named by the founder of the utopian experiment of Shangri-la as his successor. Capra described Colman as 'responsive both to poetic visions and hard intellect' (Capra, *The Name Above the Title*, Macmillan, New York, 1971, p.193). Another recent part had presented him not as an aristocrat, but as an English gentleman able to take on, without difficulty or hesitation, the manners of a monarch. This was *The Prisoner of Zenda*, (John Cromwell, 1937), in which Colman played both the weak monarch and the much larger role of Von Rassendael, the double who impersonates him. The film offered American audiences the attractive proposition that a man without rank might – for a suitably brief period – be able not only to play a monarch but to be more powerfully diplomatic and more erotic than the man born to the title. Obviously closely related to this is *If I Were King* (Frank Lloyd, 1938, scripted by Preston Sturges), in which Colman plays François Villon encountering another bad monarch, Louis XI. The Colman film immediately preceding *Lucky Partners* is William Wellman's 1938 version of Rudyard Kipling's 1891 novel *The Light That Failed*. Here the visionary quality is represented by the eye of a painter. Dick Heldor (Colman) is a war artist whose active service has left him with a concealed head injury. He creates a painting that is possibly a masterpiece while struggling against this legacy from the other, violent world, and the injury renders him blind just as the painting is completed.

The common quality in Colman's roles is that he portrays a man of vision whose life is nevertheless firmly determined by the exigencies of the social world, a visionary with his feet, for better or worse, on the ground. In one context, it is evidently for worse – a recurrent subject in the films is his difficulty in achieving a satisfactory relationship with a woman. In *Lost Horizon*, Conway's lover cannot leave Shangri-la, in *The Prisoner of Zenda*, Von Rassendael gives up his love so that Princess Flavia (Madeleine Carroll) can do her political duty as a member of the nobility and marry the king, and *The Light That Failed* traces the disintegration of Heldor's relationships with his childhood sweetheart Masie (Muriel Angelus) and with an energetic working-class figure, Bessie Broke (Ida Lupino). So while in charm and grace Colman might be compared to Astaire or Guitry, his persona also carries negative elements.

In *Lucky Partners*, Paul Knight Somerset (Colman) is again an artist, evidently of some talent and reputation, who is in hiding after a scandal and has adopted the pseudonym David Grant. That such a man might be a kind of successor to Astaire is suggested by some visual prompting in the opening scene: a first encounter between the two stars as strangers on a Manhattan street. Jean Newton (Rogers) is walking past a 'Dine and Dance' sign, when David impulsively wishes her 'Good Luck', and they pause on the street. On the doors of the 'Dine and Dance' building a notice has mysteriously appeared (it does not seem to be in an earlier shot) announcing that the establishment is closed. After a seductive conversation they part, backing gently away from each other. The sequence involves four shots showing David as he retreats past the 'Dine and Dance' sign, although they do not show his linear progress past it, for Milestone wants to draw our attention to an unusual quality in his movement. Rather than thinking of this as a continuity error, we could regard it as having the effect of emphasising Jean's seduction – as if she sees him, and this dance-like movement takes place, in a space and time different from that of the ordinary street they were in a moment ago.

From this beginning, Milestone and Scott develop a comedy of repression. Jean can acknowledge her desire for David only through the conceit that being together brings them luck, and a series of scenes derive their comedy from her insistent denial that anything else is going on. When she is given a ball gown by a perfect stranger, she associates this event with the good-luck wish from David, even executing a miniature version of their backwards movement as she ponders the connection. The subsequent attempt to explain these events to her Aunt Lucy (Spring Byington) contains the idea that Lucy's interpretation of the story as a romance, while in fact quite wrong, represents Jean's feelings correctly. The background is completed by the introduction of Jean's steady, insurance engineer fiancé Freddie (Jack Carson). David and Freddie might almost be defined by the respective resonances of 'Good Luck' and 'insurance'. The dim prospect of connubial happiness with Freddie echoes the imminent marriage of Professor Huxley and Miss Swallow at the beginning of *Bringing Up Baby* – we are told that there is to be no honeymoon and that the couple will settle down in Poughkeepsie after the wedding. (Perhaps a trace of *Bringing Up Baby* can also be identified in the pseudonym David Grant, which conflates the names of star and role: Professor David Huxley/Cary Grant.)

David's understanding of his own desire is also problematic. Jean proposes to David that they should test their luck by entering the sweepstake together. He replies that if they win, the money should be spent on a 'honeymoon', which he defines as a trip in which they would travel as brother and sister before her marriage to Freddie – elsewhere he calls this 'a journey into the absurd'. We might read this as his wanting some part of the experience of marriage outside the context of a social world – the honeymoon absorbing Jean into his insistence on privacy or anonymity. The events leading up to the trip also reflect the way in which the impeccable manners of Colman's persona act as a force limiting his relationships with women. Despite his evident attraction to Jean, he characterises himself to her as 'purely impersonal, like a guide, or a scientist making an experiment'. Only in the face of Aunt Lucy's unabashed desire for a romance between David and Jean can he privately admit, 'I've been stupid – I am stupid.'

Buying the sweepstake ticket in Lucky Partners. *Freddie (Jack Carson), David (Ronald Colman) and Jean (Rogers) with Leon Belasco and Edward Conrad.*

The trip takes place not as a result of their ticket winning the sweepstake, but because the provident Freddie has discounted the risk by selling off a part of it – the film's acknowledgement of his value. The couple follow tradition in 'honeymooning' at Niagara Falls, and begin to fall in love. There is an ambiguous suggestion that David might be slowly approaching the public world (or possibly just drawing Jean into his conspiracy to turn his back on it). The prominently signed Paul Knight Somerset painting that he loans to her can be read as a hint, an attempt to reveal his true identity. But just as we never quite see any other detail of the painting, his motive here is unclear. The romance develops in a midnight conversation on the telephone (with a cinematic image of intimacy, a

Strange invitation: David and Jean meet Alice (Cecilia Loftus) and Alvah (Brandon Tynan).

split screen in which the couple almost appear to be sharing the same bed), and they decide to meet on the dance floor.

What follows and what replaces a full-scale production number (think, say, of the newly intimate couple taking to the floor in *The Gay Divorcée*) is the film's investigation of the circumstances in which desire and marriage exist. After their dance, David and Jean are approached by an elderly couple, Alvah Sylvester (Brandon Tynan) and his wife Alice (Cecilia Loftus), who ask them to share a mysterious journey, to come into something that they variously claim is, and is not, a garden. It emerges that this couple are 'Peter Possum' and 'Jenny Wren', writers of bedtime stories and fairy tales, and the place to which they transport David and Jean is reached by a bridge, in Jean's words 'to whatever you want on the other side'. Across the bridge lies a wishing well, where you can wish that your marriage will last forever. Peter Possum and Jenny Wren made their wish fifty years ago; now they offer the same opportunity to this apparently perfect young couple.

This sounds like difficult, arch or kitsch material. Milestone and Scott take care to establish an attitude towards it: from the moment that the couple approach David and Jean, the tone is set by including in the performance the idea that this fey pair are taxing to the patience of the young. David is more reluctant to participate than Jean, but recognises it as good manners to do so, and his final response to these rituals is precisely in line with the division of Colman's persona between the visionary and his sense of the pressures of the social world. When it is explained to him that he must carry Jean across the bridge, he is happy

Honeymoon behaviour: David and Jean at the Niagara Falls hotel.

Freddie, Jean and David meet in court in Lucky Partners.

to do so, and the erotic moment climaxes in their only kiss, but at the wishing well, he turns away, and shortly afterwards flees from the hotel, leaving Jean a note explaining that he cannot expect her to share his bohemian life.

This sequence seems to have been conceived by Scott; it has no equivalent in the Guitry film. Both in the sense in which it stands in place of a musical number and in its partial drift into fantasy, it seems to refer us to the musical by creating an action that will climax in a perfect embrace but then raises the problem of relating this to married life, an ordinary existence that would necessarily include places like Poughskeepsie. By this point, the elderly couple stand as a clear expression of the limits of any impulse towards such fantasy, so that it is located in the marginalised worlds of the elderly and of children, and the difference between David's and Jean's responses effectively draws a line under the possibility of retrieving a world analogous to that of Rogers's 'thirties musicals.

The comedy ends with a return to the mundane by a different route. The proposition is that only the law, which is understood to have caused David's bitterness and aversion, can achieve a reinsertion of the couple into the social world. The principal characters are accused of misdemeanours and brought to trial in front of a kindly judge played by Harry Davenport. The judge's apology from the bench dissolves David's antagonism, and the end of the sequence suggests a wedding ceremony.

3. STICKING HITLER ON THE FUNNY PAGE

The distance between the fact of the world war and the existence of a world in which comedy and romance are possibilities is famously addressed at the point in *His Girl Friday* (Howard Hawks, 1940) when Walter Burns (Cary Grant) gives the instruction to stick Hitler on the funny page. The public occasion is the paper being reset to carry a big new story; the private occasion is the celebration of Walter's winning back of Hildy (Rosalind Russell). I take this as a subtle reminder, from a newspaper editor, that subjects relate to each other, and that this fact can be expressed (or confirmed, or distorted) through their positions in a newspaper. It also maintains the film's insistence that the larger social world cannot ultimately be dismissed: Hitler is still in the newspaper, even if, for the moment, stuck on the funny page. Rogers's work has already touched on this subject in the opening sequence of *Tom, Dick and Harry*, which acts as a reminder that the fictional feature film and the newsreel occupy adjacent spaces in the cinema programme. That film proclaims that comedy can elbow Hitler out of the headlines: when Janie is dreaming of her marriage to Dick, we see a newspaper in which the headline, 'Janie Gets Married', has displaced another piece of wish fulfilment: 'Adolf Hitler Assassinated'.

The three films which conclude this chapter directly address the idea of fighting for democracy. This is part literal – in two cases, the hero is a soldier; in the third, an American anti-fascist journalist. They are all in different ways romances, and a sense that romance might need redefining, or differently emphasising, for a world in a state of war is central to them. Questions relating to the intelligibility of marriage in wartime are raised in all three films, but possibly only Leo McCarey in *Once upon a Honeymoon* engages with this in a way that asks not only what marriage is, but what we are doing watching a Hollywood comedy of this sort, something like a funny page into which Hitler has been stuck.

THE MAJOR AND THE MINOR (Billy Wilder, 1942)

The Major and the Minor was written by Billy Wilder and Charles Brackett with Rogers specifically in mind. The film involves a long central sequence in which the Rogers character pretends to be a twelve-year-old girl, a role possibly prompted by her brief scenes as a child in *Kitty Foyle*, and her opening sequences in *Primrose Path*. But *The Major and the Minor* relates more extensively than this to Rogers's preceding films.

The film is structured as a journey, taking the Rogers character through four main milieux, with further travel implied at its end. The first of these is New York, with Rogers playing a variation on her roles as a working girl in the city. The next setting is a train heading towards an implicitly older, rural America; the third is a place that is alien to such a woman – an educational institution steeped in its own traditions. This might appear to have something in common with *Vivacious Lady*, and the fact that the Rogers character finds herself surrounded by the traditions of an older America might make a connection with *Kitty Foyle*. But the film now departs from these models: when the Rogers character flees, she returns, not to the city, but to an American utopia. Wilder's final setting is the porch of the character's maternal home in Iowa, with a brief coda at a railway station, ending as the couple board the train – again *Vivacious Lady* provides a point of comparison.

What links these different milieux is the sense that the assumptions about the Rogers character depend entirely on the context in which she is seen. The opening New York sequences are striking for Wilder's insistence on Susan Applegate (Rogers) as the subject not so much of the gaze as of multiple glances. As she goes up to the apartment suite of Mr Osborne (Robert Benchley), where she has an appointment to give him a scalp massage (using the 'revigora system'), she is treated to a series of glances and looks, culminating in the supercilious attitude of the lift-boy, all of which seem to indicate curiosity about the kind of titillation that such girls might offer.

Susan (Rogers) dismisses the attentions of Mr Osborne (Robert Benchley) in The Major and the Minor.

The apartment sequence establishes the main subjects of the film. There is the idea that identity is supplied by context (Osborne's hope is that because she works for a scalp massage business, Susan might be to some degree sexually complaisant) and the sense of uncertainty about how the rules work in this situation. Allied to this is a comedy of male sexual insecurity (the nervousness with which Osborne approaches Susan and the implicit anxiety over his baldness). Finally, there is the awareness that the background to this behaviour, and these anxieties, is a time of war (*Osborne:* 'I regret that I have but one wife to give to my country'). Echoing an earlier role, Linda Keene in *Shall We Dance*, Susan announces her boredom at being pawed and her intention of going home and marrying a boring suitor – Will Duffy (Richard Kiske), feed and grain merchant, who occupies the place of the equally hapless Jim Montgomery in the earlier film.

'Twelve, next week': Susan as Zuzu on the Chicago train.

Wilder now moves into the sequences in which Susan disguises herself as Zuzu, a twelve-year-old girl. This is presented not as an enchantment, or a spell, which might have a complementary affect on those who see her, but as a straightforwardly practical, or pragmatic, strategy. Wilder shows us the process of transformation as a matter of face-scrubbing and cutting up clothes. At the plot level it simply involves paying half fare on trains when you do not have enough money for the full fare. The disguise has been prompted by the sight of a little girl and by some overheard dialogue about the girl's brother wanting an upper bunk so that he can play Tarzan. The assertion here is less that nobody will see through the disguise (which is quickly proved untrue) as that the world can be made to connive in a kind of foolishness, or play, a typical expression of the optimism that is so often to be found in Rogers's roles. It contains the idea of starting over, as if it were possible to repeat the journey through adolescence, or at least to feel again what it was like to be twelve. It is a temporary reprieve from adulthood, but it does not erase the character's sexuality. Marina Warner, describing the disguised heroines of fairy tales, comments that 'the figure of the fugitive girl in animal disguise stood not for the rejection of sexuality but for the condition of it' (Warner, p.358), and Susan's disguise is analogous, not denying her femininity but provoking a particular response to it.

After some comedy involving suspicious porters and guards, Zuzu stumbles into the one private space in the film, the train compartment occupied by Major Philip Kirby (Ray Milland), the only character who has a literal reason for not seeing past Susan's disguise – he has defective vision. At the core of the sequence is the moment when Philip and Zuzu, sleeping in separate bunks, are both awakened by a thunderstorm. Here Philip is faintly reminiscent of the little boy who wanted to play Tarzan. He bangs his head, fails to fix a broken window blind, and, telling Zuzu that 'every time there was a storm at night I used to crawl in with my Aunt Jenny', holds her in his arms while insisting on explaining the nature of thunder and lightning in fairy-tale terms and ignoring her offer of a scientific explanation. In its intimacy and licence, this echoes an Astaire-Rogers sequence, in particular, the explanation of thunderstorms given by Jerry to Dale in the opening of the bandstand sequence in *Top Hat*, which leads in to 'Isn't it a Lovely Day (to Be Caught in the Rain)'. For Zuzu's benefit, Philip spins out his fairy tale, and, while both of these adults know that this is fantasy, for a few moments they allow themselves the closeness of seeming to share a belief in it.

The film now moves to the Wallace Military Institute, where Philip triumphantly introduces Zuzu to the senior faculty to prove to them and to his fiancée Pamela (Rita Johnson) that nothing improper went on aboard the train. Five men and one woman believe that they are seeing a twelve-year-old girl. If this is wildly improbable, it can be interpreted in terms of the nature of the place, and Wilder helps us with a line exactly at this point about the 'chalky deposit' that prevents the commanding officer from bending down to retrieve Pamela's and Philip's wedding invitations. The Institute is rigidly divided between the faculty, who define themselves as old men without sexual energy (or partners – we never see faculty wives), and the boys, young men whose energies are supposedly subsumed into their training and discipline. It is characteristic of Wilder that in his first American film as a director he creates a world where everybody is masquerading: everybody is in some kind of uniform, pretending to be wise elders,

or young soldiers, and Zuzu is assigned a position – temporary companion for the young officers – that is rigidly defined and impossible to penetrate from the viewpoint of the Institute. Alongside this is the symbolism of an institution that is both a training ground and a home for semi-retired soldiers; it is full of impressive phallic symbols, swords and cannon, that both suggest military power and are museum pieces.

The women at the Institute are deceived by Susan's disguise exactly to the extent that they are part of its rigidity. When Pamela first encounters Zuzu in Philip's compartment on the train, she instantly assumes that she is seeing a good-time girl whom he has somehow picked up. Once back at Wallace, she conforms to its view, accepting that Zuzu is twelve until the testimony of an outsider forces her to admit that this is not the case. However, Pamela's younger sister Lucy (Diana Lynn), who keeps her distance from the Institute and its rituals, is the one person at Wallace not deceived by Zuzu, immediately recognising her body as that of an older woman.

In the context of the Institute, Philip appears to be in an anomalous position, being younger than the rest of the faculty and having a potential sexual partner in Pamela. However, we learn that Pamela has been plotting (stressing the seriousness of Philip's disability to his superiors), and her ambition is that they should marry and he should remain permanently as a teacher at the academy – in Philip's phrase, a job 'a man of eighty could do'. Pamela is the commanding officer's daughter and the marriage would thus not involve her separation from her father.

The atmosphere of the Institute is reflected in a repressive domestic world. Wilder takes us inside only one home, which is nominally that of Pamela's father, whom we never see there. The only family feeling that is revealed is bad:

Opposite: Philip (Ray Milland) introduces Zuzu to Pamela (Rita Johnson) and the officers of the Wallace Institute in The Major and the Minor.

Right: Zuzu with young scientist Lucy (Diana Lynn).

the antagonism between Pamela and Lucy. As Pamela's plot to tie Philip to the place and to expose Zuzu as a fraud comes to a head, Wilder's photography becomes increasingly suggestive of *film noir*.

Philip's desire to gain a posting away from the school is clearly sincere, but he simultaneously responds to his disability (and sense of impotence, his inability to gain an active service posting) by thinking of himself as a non-combatant, both militarily and sexually. There is nothing in the film to suggest that he has any strong desire for Pamela. At the school, he is carefully paternal in his attitude towards Zuzu – the masquerade he is playing is complementary to hers, the part of a man older than he really is. There is no repressive father figure in *The Major and the Minor*; rather, the figures of father and son in some of the earlier films have become internalised in the debate between Philip's forms of behaviour as old, or disabled, as soldier and as young lover.

In a characteristically self-reliant variant of the Cinderella role, Susan arranges to meet Philip and dresses in a ball gown that she has bought herself – 'if you model them you can buy them for thirty dollars at the end of the season'. By now, her disguise has been penetrated, and she flees the Institute in order to protect Philip's reputation, leaving him to Pamela. The comparable flight in defeat from a repressive, aristocratic world is in *Kitty Foyle*, where Kitty escapes to New York, but here Susan returns to her mother and her origins, to where she belongs, or thinks she belongs: Stevenson, Iowa. By the time of *Roxie Hart*, Rogers's lack of a mother had taken on the quality of a familiar, caustic gag, epitomised in the rejection of the daughter by the mother in a single line. Perhaps to emphasise the significance of the contrast, Wilder cast Lela Rogers – Ginger's actual mother – in the part of Mrs Applegate.

Maternal advice: Susan, masquerading as her own mother, discusses wartime marriages with Philip in The Major and the Minor.

The opening of the Iowa sequence shows it as a tedious utopia. While Mrs Applegate sorts fruit, and Will Duffy, the feed and grain merchant, sits patiently on the steps, Susan lies in a hammock, a picture of boredom, but aware that a marriage to him is not what she wants. Philip now arrives in Stevenson, on his way to active service but also (though he has not acknowledged this to himself) in pursuit of Susan. One of his first questions to Zuzu in the train compartment had been 'Where do you belong?', and she had replied with this address, to which he has come to make sure that it is where she truly belongs.

Now he finds her – as if to show him a version of herself at yet another stage in her life – masquerading as her own mother. Two things have to happen. He has to recognise that he wants this woman (these women) – a task with which he will need some help. And then he has to propose marriage of a very different kind from that offered by Will Duffy, and find out if such a proposal is acceptable.

The couple talk through what his offer of marriage would consist of, with Philip ostensibly alluding to another couple, young people who will marry 'in an hour . . . then she'll take him to the troopship, and a goodbye kiss at the dock, wet handkerchief, then a letter from him every two weeks maybe – no, that's too much to ask of any woman'. Susan replies, 'I think you underestimate us, Major Kirby. Perhaps all a woman wants is to be a photograph a soldier tacks over his bunk, or a stupid lock of hair in the back of his watch.'

Perhaps there is more here than simply an expression of female abnegation convenient to the purposes of the times. Susan appears to be defending an idea that a woman might be allowed her own definition of marriage, which would not necessarily, or at all times, turn on the presence of the man, or a shared place called home, or even the possibility of a sexual act. Rather, what is stressed is a recurrent concern of the film, the importance of how a woman is represented to the imagination in a visual image (photograph) or a symbolic object (a lock of hair). To consider this moment is to be reminded of another 1942 film and the debate contained in the final scene between Bette Davis and Paul Henried in *Now, Voyager* (Irving Rapper) on the subject of 'some man who'll make you happy' and what can be asked of women and what they want.

Philip sees that the woman is Susan only in the final scene of the film, which echoes the sequence after their night together on the train when we first saw him giving his eye muscles a 'ten-minute workout' (following the tip of a pencil as he moves it towards his face). On the station platform at Stevenson, the pencil tip is replaced by Susan's finger and then her face as she moves in to kiss him, offering herself as the object that will exercise his eye.

ONCE UPON A HONEYMOON (Leo McCarey, 1943)

The subject of *Once upon a Honeymoon* is Hitler's progressive invasion of Europe and the Nazi persecution of European Jews. Some elements of the film, however, have parallels with *Kitty Foyle*. The common ground concerns the Rogers character's relations with two men, one an aristocrat with private money – Wyn in *Kitty Foyle*, Baron Von Luber (Walter Slezak) in *Once upon a Honeymoon* – and the other a wage-earner – doctor Mark in *Kitty Foyle* and newspaperman Patrick O'Toole (Cary Grant) here. The Rogers character, Katie O'Hara, is again

'. . . no wallet, no passport, nothing – but O'Hara.' Katie (Rogers) and Patrick (Cary Grant) amidst the ruins of Warsaw in Once upon a Honeymoon.

139

The aristocratic male: Katie with Baron von Luber (Walter Slezak) in Once upon a Honeymoon.

an American from a working-class immigrant Irish family whose surviving parent appears only at the beginning of the film. Again her progress upwards in terms of class is confirmed by her marriage to the aristocratic figure, but her insight into the nature of his world causes the collapse of the marriage.

The parallels are not only matters of broad outline. In both films, the Rogers character's attachment to the wage-earner is accompanied by a move from one city to another, part of a wider association of the two men with different kinds of space. The distinction between the wealthy (Philadelphia) home and the ordinary (New York) apartment in *Kitty Foyle* becomes the distinction between the swanky suite in the (Vienna, later Warsaw) hotel where Katie lives with Von Luber, and the balcony of the little (Paris) pension where she dines with Patrick. McCarey consistently associates Von Luber with lush interiors and Patrick with spaces that are either marginal (the cellar to which he and Katie retreat during the bombing of Warsaw) or out-of-doors. The occasion of Katie's shift of allegiance from one man to the other is expressed in these terms: the aristocratic order is shown in a state of collapse when Patrick finds her alone in the bomb-wrecked remains of her once-luxurious hotel suite; a little later they flee the baron and make for Patrick's hotel, only to find that the bombing has destroyed it entirely. Grant's line here makes explicit the connection between the two elements of his situation, being homeless and being in love: 'You're looking at a ruined man. I'm wiped out, no money, no wallet, no passport, nothing – but O'Hara'.

A further connection between the two films concerns either literal or metaphorical sons and daughters. In *Kitty Foyle*, an early sequence (evidently written

Katie and her Jewish maid Anna (Natasha Lytess) read the headlines.

for the film as it has no equivalent in Christopher Morley's novel) shows Mark proposing marriage as Kitty holds a baby that he has just delivered. The child's parents do not appear in the sequence, emphasising the image of a family composed of Mark, Kitty and a baby, as opposed to Wyn, Kitty and their dead child. In *Once upon a Honeymoon*, there are figures with a similar role but who are not exclusively children. Von Kleinoch (John Banner), a naive young Nazi diplomat, shows Katie a photograph of his fiancée and talks of his hopes for life after the war. In the next sequence, he is shot dead, casually sacrificed to disguise the involvement of the Nazis in Von Luber's assassination of one of his political opponents. This murderous treatment of the young can be contrasted with Katie's giving away her passport to rescue her Jewish maid Anna (Natasha Lytess) and Anna's two children from Nazi persecution. (The photograph of Anna is attached with an emblematic American product, chewing gum.) McCarey links the diplomat and maid by juxtaposition, Anna's first appearance immediately following the sequence of Von Kleinoch's death. McCarey's film might be thought of as taking the domestic politics of *Kitty Foyle* and translating them into the international politics of the time. This has the effect of making explicit subjects that had been lost in the adaptation of the material for the earlier film. Morley's novel had touched on the unaristocratic figure being the better American, and on Jewishness, subjects omitted from *Kitty Foyle* but present in *Once upon a Honeymoon*. Robin Wood has advanced the argument that *Once upon a Honeymoon* is a film about anti-fascist commitment as follows: 'In terms of "reflection" its plot can be reduced to a skeletal allegory: Katie O'Hara (Rogers) represents

America (at a crucial point she actually impersonates the Statue of Liberty) progressing from total unconcern to total commitment, from wilfully ignorant liaison with Nazi Germany to (literally) pushing it overboard.'

Wood lays out this position in detail in his valuable reading of the film (*Film Comment*, January/February 1976). My focus is somewhat different. I wish to concentrate not on this allegory, but on the terms in which it is delivered, and the reaction it invites in the audience, a change of mode from *Kitty Foyle* as well as a reinflection of subject matter into an explicitly anti-fascist film. Three sources, or genealogies, form contexts for the film:

1) Cary Grant, whose immediately previous films are *The Philadelphia Story* (George Cukor, 1940), *Penny Serenade* (George Stevens, 1941), *Suspicion* (Alfred Hitchcock, 1941) and *The Talk of the Town* (George Stevens, 1942).

2) Leo McCarey, whose previous four films as director are *The Milky Way* (1936, with Harold Lloyd), *Make Way for Tomorrow* (1937), *The Awful Truth* (with Cary Grant, 1937) and *Love Affair* (with Charles Boyer and Irene Dunne, 1939).

3) Two films which share with *Once upon a Honeymoon* the appearance of Adolf Hitler: *The Great Dictator* (Charles Chaplin, 1940) and *To Be or Not to Be* (Ernst Lubitsch, 1942).

And of course there is a final genealogy which scarcely needs restating: Rogers's previous work and specifically the Astaire-Rogers musicals.

These groupings include romances focused around a couple (*Love Affair, Penny Serenade*, the Astaire-Rogers musicals), the great Hollywood comedies of re-marriage (*The Awful Truth, The Philadelphia Story*) and clowns (Harold Lloyd and Chaplin; earlier in his career McCarey had worked with Laurel and Hardy). In the opening sequences of *Once upon a Honeymoon*, McCarey seems to want to evoke these connections. The title and Robert Emmett Dolan's romantic melody played over the opening credits lead us to expect another *Love Affair*, the opening situation (Patrick discovering Katie on the eve of her marriage) invokes the remarriage comedies, and we are soon offered satisfying pieces of clowning (Patrick attempting to take Katie's measurements, and later his sitting down, forgetting that he has stuffed a framed photograph of Von Luber into the back of his trousers).

My argument is that these are not incidental gestures, but important prompts as to how the film is intended to function. The question here is what a director such as McCarey, and stars such as Rogers and Grant are doing in a film about the war in Europe, what effect on the film their presence might (or possibly is bound to) have. The film does not address this matter and then put it aside: it is something to which, by a number of strategies, the audience is caused continually to return.

There is the device of having the principal characters repeatedly deliver lines which make sense at two levels. These function as dialogue within a specific current narrative (sometimes only marginally), but they also work as asides, relating to the tone, serious or comic, that the film's material might be supposed to demand. The most overt examples are probably Patrick's lines in the Warsaw cellar sequence. Two Nazi officers enter and, after one of them has stumbled

Patrick and Katie are categorised as Jewish in Once upon a Honeymoon.

twice on some loose masonry and is being dressed down by his superior officer, Patrick says 'Stop that, that isn't funny'. At the end of the same sequence, Katie is discovered in possession of a passport (actually her maid's) which seems to prove that she is a Jew: Patrick's line is 'Now he thinks we're Jewish, this could be serious'. In terms of their situation, the lines make sense, though the first one seems at the very least pointless or odd. But they can also be read as asking a question: is introducing Nazis through physical comedy tasteless? Does the fact of being arrested in Warsaw on suspicion of being Jewish require a shift of tone to seriousness? Other lines with a similar quality are Rogers (in the measurements scene): 'This is getting a little ridiculous', Grant (after the measurements routine): 'I do feel a little silly about that', Rogers (after a routine about pronouncing her name): 'This utter nonsense is at an end', and Patrick (when Von Luber has been pushed overboard at the end of the film) repeating a line: 'This could be serious'.

Alongside this we can put McCarey's interest in confronting us with America's present in the form of other contemporary popular cultural products. Von Luber's line to Patrick, 'You might even write a book called 'Inside' something', is a flip reference to John Gunther's then well-known series of popular political surveys which began with *Inside Europe* in 1936. Opportunities to quote film titles appear in the script: Patrick chances on *Shop around the Corner* (Ernst Lubitsch, 1940), and a quotation that Katie offers to Patrick (Polonius's advice to Laertes in *Hamlet*), which might appear only to evoke Shakespeare, had a contemporary American context in the shape of Anatole Litvak's *This Above All*, a solemn war melodrama produced in the same year as *Once upon a Honeymoon*. Its climax is the reading of the lines that Katie quotes.

Intimacy, fun and delight: Patrick and Katie in the measurements sequence of
Once upon a Honeymoon.

There are three references that are even closer to home, all specifically to
Rogers's work. The mildest is the response to Katie's Shakespeare/Litvak lines,
where Patrick quotes the lyrics of 'Don't Wait Too Long' to her, and names its
composer, Irving Berlin. The most startling, because it breaks cinematic convention, takes place at the end of the opening (Vienna) segment of the film. Patrick
stands in front of Katie so that he can tell her that he wants to remember her
'just the way you look tonight' – there is no point or excuse for the moment
beyond the opportunity to say this line. Rogers's response to this sudden evocation of *Swing Time* – it seems proper to attribute it to the actress rather than the
role – is to turn with a look of appeal, directed behind her into off-screen space
which we know to be (in terms of the plot) empty. Perhaps she is looking at
McCarey. She now turns back to Grant, who corrects himself ' . . . today'. For a

second, his rueful expression acknowledges that this is a gag, and then the actors recover themselves. The final reference, at the end of the film, is framed as a question. Patrick is railing at the double agent Gaston Leblanc (Albert Dekker), who has put Katie into a dangerous situation. Patrick's line is: 'I'd like to know, what man was ever hero enough to say, "I have but one wife to give for my country", I'd like to know that.' The answer would have been readily available to a 1942 audience, as the line is borrowed from Robert Benchley's dialogue at the beginning of *The Major and the Minor*.

Finally, there is an early scene in the film, the measurements sequence, in which Patrick and Katie meet for the first time. Intent on obtaining a story on Von Luber, Patrick has gained entry to Katie's apartment by masquerading as a tailor's cutter there to take measurements for her bridal wardrobe. He proceeds to measure her with a retracting metal tape measure. The scene, and its more or less blatant visual fun with a phallic object (*see* Wood, 1976) has obvious connections with earlier comedy, situations in which the man, meeting the woman, both annoys and pleases her. The man is getting the measure of the woman, or a process of mutual measuring and exchange is taking place. But a metal tape measure? Cannot Katie draw the obvious conclusion, that of course this man is no cutter? This does not seem to matter. Or, rather, we can understand how it matters (to Patrick and Katie, to Grant and Rogers, to McCarey), if we assume that the object of the sequence is to remind us where exactly this world is, to locate it both as a Vienna hotel room and as a Hollywood sound stage.

McCarey could be offering the scene as a commentary on his own situation. If we think of a man approaching a task by using an instrument which might appear to be largely inappropriate but being saved from foolishness by finding a way to generate an unexpected pleasure, we have something like a metaphor for McCarey's strategy for a Grant-Rogers romance involving Hitler. Like Patrick faced by Von Luber, his approach could seem wildly ill-judged, or inappropriate, but it is not. (I am a little encouraged in thinking that McCarey might have intended some part of this reading of the scene by the appearance of the words 'angle' and 'cutter', small gestures to the medium of film, and by the thought that a metal tape measure is unlikely as an implement for a tailor, but is an unsurprising item to find on a film set).

There is another way in which the sequence directs its reading. Parts of the dialogue are close to nonsense, as is the treatment of language and accent. Patrick's voice, in particular, varies from pretences to speak English like a Frenchman, or a German, to purely American tones. The following is representative:

Katie [in her 'Philadelphia' accent]: Might we get on with it?
Patrick [lost in thought, in American]: Hm? What? *[he fumbles with her]*
Entschuldige *[He tries to measure her waist with the steel tape]* . . . *[in French accent]* I cannot get it like zis, mam'selle. *[He tries again, but cannot see the numbers on the tape from his position]* . . . *[in American]* What's it say, come on . . .
Katie [the Philadelphia accent, emphatically]: I can tell you, it's twenty-four, it's been twenty-four for a long time.
Patrick: [no trace of anything but American]: Lucky girl!

Only repeated viewing can give the sense of this mood of fun, of not exactly being in role, in the whole of the Vienna segment of the film. It culminates in three defining moments. In order of occurrence they are:

1) A conversation between Von Luber and Katie about their marriage which includes some outrageous (and hilarious) performance by Rogers. Her massively sonorous delivery of the line: 'Are you cancelling our marriage, too?' prompts one of the film's self-conscious cracks a few moments later from Von Luber (or Slezak?): 'That might be over-doing it'.

2) A dialogue gag, with insufficient plot to excuse it:

Patrick: Hitler is here.
Katie: Well, I can't see him now, I'm dressing.

3) The most explicit moment of all, the 'The Way you Look Tonight' joke that I discussed earlier.

This clowning exists in the same film as something that might be thought of as its opposite, the five instances of newsreel footage that are scattered through the narrative. Three are of German troops in the streets of European cities, and two are images of Hitler with the troops, one announcing the invasion of Poland and the other containing in the frame Hitler and the Eiffel tower. The function of these instances is carefully addressed by the credits sequence, which seems to conclude normally enough with McCarey's director's credit, but is then followed by something presented as another credit, the words 'Timetable by A. Hitler', and its emblematic equivalent, a clock with a swastika for hands. The newsreel image of the German army in Vienna is the opening shot of McCarey's film.

All this might remind us that a movie can include figures who are recognisable (our ability to identify them from a brief glimpse is one quality of their presence) and who are both everything (the action of the movie could not exist without them) and nothing (in that they are not characters and cannot interact with the actors in the film). Typically, such a figure passes across a set, strolls down a corridor, almost but not quite bumping into the hero, as if to emphasise the degree to which he or she is both present and remote. The most obvious example of this is, of course, Hitchcock's appearances in his own movies. McCarey's inclusion of the duly credited figure of Hitler has a similar function, as if to make the point that Hitler can be thought of as a different kind of director, here appearing in a cameo. This underlines the film's understanding of reality as inclusive. It contains Leo McCarey and Hitler, as well as actors named Cary Grant and Ginger Rogers, and the roles that these actors play in the film (which are themselves multiple). The film offers these realities together, does not confuse them, but proposes that they are not to be absolutely distinguished as 'reality' or 'illusion'. If all of this is reality (or all equally an 'illusion of reality'), it contains Hitler's will and progressive possession of Europe as well as the characters' and the actors' intimacy, fun and delight, and the roles in which they do not – in which McCarey has not let them – quite submerge themselves.

In a sequence that sums up McCarey's approach, the couple spend their one evening in Paris, drinking champagne and talking of their future. The sequence has a number of the generic qualities of a domestic interlude in a war film – the sense of a time of calm in the face of not quite specifiable impending danger (though it is the woman rather than the man who will leave the next morning to face that danger), the hope and anxiety involved in the imagining of a future, and the importance of written words, a form of letter from one lover to the other.

The climax of the sequence exemplifies McCarey's depth. Literally what happens is that Patrick has written what he calls a poem. Katie reads out his words and preserves the paper on which they are written. This is the couple's commitment to each other, a marriage service in motif, even down to the obvious prompt of including the words 'till death do us part', and McCarey films it as an unbroken two-and-a-half minute take of Grant and Rogers in two-shot. The take ends with the simplest of studio devices. As Katie speaks the line, '. . . our only night in Paris, nothing must spoil it', rain begins to fall. Katie's response is: 'We mustn't let it, because nothing in this world can keep us from supposing, because we're supposed to be supposing, darling.'

The force of this moment depends on the density of meaning compressed into 'supposing'. At one level, Katie is talking about imagination, the right in any circumstances to imagine a utopian, or at least a better, world. I also believe Rogers to be talking about acting, as what she and Cary Grant are employed to do – they are supposed to be supposing. And the word here has an erotic edge, generated by an earlier exchange (*Patrick*: It's awfully hard just to go on supposing. *Katie*: Let's suppose, like everything, Pat, just for tonight. Suppose I've just come back from Reno), which clearly takes us as far as it was possible to go under the Production Code to imply that the couple would spend this night together. They now kiss, and these meanings inform the final line of the sequence, and the end of the take, Patrick's 'That's mighty nice supposing, Miss O.'

TENDER COMRADE (Edward Dmytryk, 1943)

That *Tender Comrade* can also be approached in terms of what it has in common with *Kitty Foyle* is not surprising in that both films were written by Dalton Trumbo. The film begins with the Rogers character now married to the young American worker – here he is Chris Jones (Robert Ryan), a serviceman who has been given a single night's leave to visit his wife before going on active duty. After their night together, Jo Jones (Rogers) accompanies Chris to the railroad station, and the view of ordinary American lives and prospects embodied in this couple is spelt out in their conversation. They imagine leaving Los Angeles for a 'little place on the edge of town', a world of barbecues, neighbours, sleeping late on Sunday mornings and a 'big back yard' where they will keep chickens and where their future children can play.

Tender Comrade again poses this imagined modern life against an older, more high-toned America. The variation on the terms of *Kitty Foyle* and *Once upon a Honeymoon* is that the aristocratic lover has disappeared, although the subject remains embodied in the film. The female group is now one of war workers in the Douglas aircraft plant, four women with husbands in the services. All four are living in what Jo calls 'rat-holes', and she proposes that they pool their resources to rent a substantial house. This capacious place, initially defined in size and type by one establishing exterior shot and some dim interiors, is the physical remnant of the high bourgeois world, shown not so much as unoccupied as almost abandoned, in need of thorough cleaning and the extermination of the mice

Almost a family: Doris (Kim Hunter), Helen (Patricia Collinge), Jo (Rogers) and Barbara (Ruth Hussey) in Tender Comrade.

that infest its attic. Nothing personal of this America remains, no landlord or landlady, and although the house is furnished, there are no portraits on the walls. As the women settle in for their first night, they place photographs of their husbands at their respective bedsides.

The social positions of the women are expressed in their responses to this version of domesticity. The two who find it least problematic are the evidently upper-class Helen (Patricia Collinge) and the youngest wife, the gauche Doris (Kim Hunter). The clearly uncomfortable figure is Barbara (Ruth Hussey). Her husband, Pete, is defined as a worker, described as more at home with a monkey wrench in his hand than a chequebook, whereas Helen is the wife and the mother of officers. Jo's position is between Barbara's and Helen's; she is aware that this form of living has to be negotiated. When the group find the house impossible to clean (significantly announced by Barbara's falling over her mop and pail), it is Jo who proposes that to make it manageable they must hire a housekeeper. This is Manya (Mady Christians), who is associated with European culture and motherliness – 'I have kept house for my father in Dresden, he had eight little ones.' The relation of mistresses and servant is carefully avoided by the five women now sharing out their disposable income equally.

A long sequence follows in which Dmytryk shows us attempts at various kinds of regulation – of sexual activity in Barbara, who intends to date another man while her husband is overseas, of the organisation of the domestic (Manya is upset that the butcher is breaking rationing laws in their favour) and comedically of consumer appetite, in the 127 lipsticks in Doris's collection. It is Barbara who finds herself expressing the connection between these various regulations and the idea of a home itself: '. . . bacon, men, lipsticks, gab, gab, gab, moral, moral, moral, you'd think we were running a home for *[she searches for a word]*. . . a home!' I take this to be a discovery that the value of the house is constituted not by what is actually allowed or disallowed but by its being a place where such issues can be spoken of, where quarrelling is not disastrous. To this extent, it hovers on the edge of being a home, as opposed to a 'home for' these solitary women.

The film seems to conclude that the group of women cannot quite revivify the house or constitute a family. The nearest approach that Dmytryk can make to their successful bonding is a brief interval built around the subject of motherhood. It is night, and Jo has returned to the house after giving birth to Chris's baby, which is being looked after by Manya. The baby cries, and Dmytryk links the four women through shots of them waking to the sound, hearing Manya singing to the baby, and resuming their slumbers. Manya is singing '*Gute Nacht, gute Nacht, mit Rosen bedacht*' to the baby. Again, this nurture can be thought of as something associated with Europe, something these women can feel but from which they remain at a slight distance. The women stay alone in their rooms, and Dmytryk shows us neither Manya nor the baby.

The unexpected arrival of Doris's husband, Mike (Richard Martin), allows the tensions within the house to be inflected as comedy, a wedding meal in which each woman insists on cooking her husband's favourite dish, food which Mike is unable to eat and throws into the fire. This is the last appearance of the rest of the cast in the film – the focus now narrows to Jo as she goes to her bedroom carrying the telegram with the news of Chris's death.

The film avoids the conclusion that the death of its representative fighter for democracy is a disaster by addressing it not only through the birth of a child, but in the very marked and insistent establishment of a relationship between all fathers and sons in which the adult contains the figure of the child, and the child implies the figure of the adult. This subject is introduced in an earlier sequence, shortly after Jo has arrived home from hospital with her son. Helen receives a

Flashback: Jo amd Chris (Robert Ryan) before the war.

149

Jo admires the photograph of Doris's husband in Tender Comrade.

letter, and Jo's line – 'Everybody gets mail around here but me' – is the first intimation of the death of Chris. The two women share the reading of the letter, in which Helen's husband recollects the childhood and young manhood of their son Ted, concluding with the insistence that although Ted is now a newly promoted major, his father's feeling towards him is still the desire to protect their 'little son'. Minor notes stressing that adults can be loved as if they were children are sounded earlier by Doris, whose photograph of her husband was taken when he was about ten years old, and by Barbara, whose final comment on her husband in the film is 'he's just a little twerp, you know'.

These moments inform the final sequence of *Tender Comrade*, in which Jo responds to the news of Chris's death. Waking her sleeping son with the identical gesture and line with which she had awakened his father at the opening of the film, she speaks of what is to come – 'Just by being brought up with him I know everything that's going to happen to you' – and recollects her past with Chris as if describing, or claiming it, as her son's future. Part of this insistence on the parallel lives of father and son has to do with class, with the rejection of the aristocratic – 'no million dollars, or country clubs, or long shiny cars for you, little guy' in favour of the ordinary American's dream of space and nature, now heard in the disembodied voice-over of the dead father, 'a big back yard with a vegetable patch, and a place for him to play'. The earlier letter from Helen's husband, with its uneasy wish to treat the adult as a child – 'strange to think he'd resent it' – is both echoed and corrected here in the treatment of the child's life as both a

150

repetition and an ideal continuation of the father's. Thus the Rogers character's relationship to the good American is both fulfilled (in her marriage and the birth of the couple's child) and brought to its conclusion (in the death of the husband in the service of the ideal of American democracy).

It may now be possible to stand back a little from these films and see the changing possibilities and energies which they record. It is instructive to follow the treatment of a single recurrent figure: the young, usually high-toned woman who is evidently the rival of the Rogers character. There is a shift from her being physically fought with – Helen (Frances Mercer) in *Vivacious Lady*, and briefly Velma in *Roxie Hart* – to the verbal dressing down given to Pamela in *The Major and the Minor*. By *Once upon a Honeymoon*, the figure is both comedic and internalised, represented in 'Katherine Butte-Smith', the identity that Katie O'Hara uses in Von Luber's circle and finally abandons. By *Tender Comrade* either no trace of the figure remains or it has dwindled into one element of the inoffensive Doris.

The trajectory of this figure is part of a larger picture to which I have pointed at intervals, the gradual disintegration and rejection of a world of glamour and money as opposed to simpler American working lives. Here we begin with *Vivacious Lady*, *Bachelor Mother* and *Fifth Avenue Girl*, all of which show Rogers marrying young men whose riches, we are to understand, will not stand in the way of her happiness. *Lucky Partners* takes another young man in retreat from his own money and world, only to have an (albeit judicial) father figure restore it to him at the end of the film.

Kitty Foyle is the pivotal film, in which the loss of the person associated with glamour has to be faced and accepted at the same time as his seductiveness is acknowledged. The possibility of another kind of grace, attached to a man who

Doris with Jo after the birth of Jo's baby.

might express it in the way he walks you along the street, is now hinted at in the character played by Burgess Meredith in *Tom, Dick and Harry*. Both *Roxie Hart* and *The Major and the Minor* address the subject by constructing worlds in which wealth and power are seen only negatively. The shift is complete in *Once upon a Honeymoon*, where the seductiveness of the young man who proclaims himself to have nothing is embodied in no less a star than Cary Grant. The change of emphasis between *Kitty Foyle* and *Once upon a Honeymoon* is clear if we match the roles against each other: Dennis Morgan's role becomes Walter Slezak's, and James Craig's role becomes Grant's, but the erotic charge in the films' two major sequences of romance shifts from the figure associated with several generations of money and power to the self-made man, from Morgan and the Pocono mountain cabin to Grant and the Paris balcony. The movement is concluded in *Tender Comrade*, where the figures of the inheriting son and the rich father have disappeared completely – there is a striking absence of older men of any kind in the film, even in minor parts. (This is not to say that the structure disappears from Hollywood cinema. A later instance of it – and one full of references to Cinderella – that was offered to Rogers at an early stage in pre-production is Max Ophuls's *Caught*, 1949, a further version of the plot in which the characterisation of both male figures is taken to extremes. The millionaire Smith Ohlrig, Robert Ryan, is presented as effectively psychotic, and the good worker, Dr Quinada, James Mason, as undeviatingly benign.)

The attitudes of the films towards these subjects can be seen in their treatment of a place, essentially the grand house, which in the earlier films is the destination of the Rogers character and in *Kitty Foyle* is rejected. The later films end with the couple in the interior of an automobile (*Roxie Hart*), on a station platform (*The Major and the Minor*) and on board ship (*Once upon a Honeymoon*). *Tender Comrade* represents a point at which the older American order now remains only as a ghost, in the form of an almost Gothic house, in which a family cannot quite be at home. (Beyond it lies the recollection of a benign but remote order, which runs through several of the films.) The house is now nothing more than a set, understood as a stage appropriate for the defining moments in the characters' lives. This is most explicitly stated at the centre of the film's narrative: a furious row between the women is reaching a climax when the shocking news of the possible death of Barbara's husband is heard on the radio. Dmytryk shows Barbara receiving the news in a striking shot, caught half-way up the staircase of the house: 'Ever since I was a kid, I always wanted to be an actress. I guess I've been building my whole life to this moment . . . I never expected the timing to be so good – and on a staircase, too.'

In these interlinked trajectories, from rivalry with the high-toned girl to her disappearance, from seductive millionaires to plain-talking workers, and from hallowed family mansion to Gothic house, a progression in Rogers's work comes to its conclusion. *Tender Comrade* recalls a previous ending in the elements it shares with *The Story of Vernon and Irene Castle*. Both films give us the history of a good marriage in which the husband, who is identified as an ordinary American and a patriot on active service for his country, is killed in action. What further links them is that the final memories of the two widows are clearly benign. When I return to Rogers's work of the later 'forties in Chapter 5, we will see her roles linked again to memories of the past, but to much darker moments in her characters' histories.

CHAPTER FOUR

CHANGING THE STEPS
FRED ASTAIRE FROM 1938 TO 1943

In the period between the completion of *The Story of Vernon and Irene Castle* in early 1939 and that of *Tender Comrade* in late 1943, Fred Astaire made six films, while Ginger Rogers made eleven. His were exclusively musicals, whereas hers include none that can properly be described as such. It was an Oscar-winning period for Rogers, but for Astaire it was less uniformly successful, and critical treatment of Astaire has tended to view these films as an interlude between the Astaire-Rogers cycle and the Arthur Freed musicals of the late 'forties and 'fifties.

For Astaire, the period starts with *Broadway Melody of 1940* (Norman Taurog, 1940) and *Second Chorus* (H.C. Potter, 1940) both of which initiate a new pattern by associating Astaire with a male partner who shares his profession; a later film with another male star in an analogous role was *Holiday Inn* (Mark Sandrich, 1942). Two of the films made in this period co-star Rita Hayworth: *You'll Never Get Rich* (Sidney Lanfield, 1941) and *You Were Never Lovelier* (William A. Seiter, 1942). Finally, there is a film which offers both the promise of a return to an earlier manner and a continuation of some of the concerns of the films with Hayworth, *The Sky's the Limit* (Edward H. Griffith, 1943), Astaire's final film with RKO and his last musical to be shot in black and white. This chapter follows the chronological order of production except for *Holiday Inn*, which was made between the two films with Hayworth. Astaire writes in his autobiography, *Steps in Time*, that the three projects were proposed to him simultaneously, and the exact order seems to have depended on matters of his convenience – he was able to 'fit the Crosby epic in' between the two other films.

BROADWAY MELODY OF 1940 (Norman Taurog, 1940)

The film opens with a wedding that makes marriage appear as an everyday event alongside the sales of furniture and dance-hall tickets. In the opening shot, the camera follows Astaire as he walks, or rather processes, along a New York street. He is wearing top hat and tails, and on his arm is a woman in a bridal gown whom we do not recognise. A small crowd accompanies them. The next shots in the sequence show the pair turning to enter Dawnland, a dance hall, and the plot becomes clear, or at least clearer. It is 'wedding night' at Dawnland, and Johnny Brett (Astaire) is doing a job of work: one of his duties as an employee is to collect the evening's bride, walk her to the dance hall and deliver her into the arms of her future husband (here the uncredited George Chandler, who will later play

Roxie's first husband in *Roxie Hart*). The couple giggle and grin, while Johnny's face conveys his distance from this marriage. As the wedding march plays, he spots his own partner in another part of the room.

The sequence that follows lays out this partnership as a professional one – Johnny and King Shaw (George Murphy) are a song-and-dance team. We learn that they have come to the city hoping to crash Broadway with their 'specialty act'; after five years, they are undiscovered, broke and getting older. The sequence explores the possibility that the partnership might be dissolved, but they pull themselves together and perform the film's first number 'Please Don't Monkey with Broadway'. Cole Porter's lyric – 'Think what stars used to stroll along it all day . . .' – is about making Broadway an exception to the endless modernisation of the city. The song embodies the position held by Johnny and King, whose act is in the vaudeville/revue-based tradition of entertainment, exemplified in the second (dance) half of the number. The action now moves to a location which represents the contemporary style: we see Johnny in the audience of a current Broadway show, *Gangway Please*, starring Clare Bennett (Eleanor Powell).

The implication is clear: the past, represented by Johnny's and King's act, is being superseded by the book-based musical. The way forward for Johnny or for King involves the dissolution of their partnership and the forming of a new and different one. This is realised in one of them becoming Clare's new partner in a musical built around their dancing.

This could be viewed as a version of the development from the vaudeville sketch involving two men to a heterosexual dance couple that was seen previously in *The Story of Vernon and Irene Castle*. The repetition of this progression in *Broadway Melody of 1940* is marked by an entirely different conception of the woman of the couple, and her dance. Consider the scenes in the two films where we see Astaire watching Rogers and Powell dance. Where the point of the 'Yama Yama Man' number was its amateurishness (*see* pp.91-92), Clare's first number, 'I Am the Captain', in *Gangway Please* shows her skill and grace as she dances without a partner but with a male chorus. The sequence establishes clearly that she does not need the ideal partner to make her dancing blossom; she is a competent, confident professional, in charge of what she does. The contrast to Rogers's solos in the RKO cycle could not be sharper. From its opening (Powell slides down a ship's mast) through its subsequent high kicks, splits and the tossing of Powell between the members of the chorus, this dance has an athleticism which underlines its distance from Rogers's dance. Thus there will be an essentially different relationship between Astaire and his female partner, as has already been hinted in a line delivered before we see Powell. When King asks Johnny where he goes every night after their act, he describes watching Powell with the words, 'I take dancing lessons'. Nothing in the earlier films would have allowed Astaire to describe seeing Rogers in this way.

In the sequence after the 'I Am the Captain' number, Taurog and his writers characterise the values of Broadway in a way which contrasts them with those of the Dawnland ballroom. The setting is Clare's luxurious dressing room, and we see two couples: Clare with the show's director, Bert Matthews (Ian Hunter), and its producer Bob Casey (Frank Morgan) with his girl of the evening, Pearl de Longe (Ann Morriss). It becomes clear in conversation that Clare and Bert have reinvented themselves for their current context. Clare was once plain Brigit

'Is this your partner?' King (George Murphy) introduces Clare (Eleanor Powell) to Johnny (Astaire) in Broadway Melody of 1940.

Callahan, and Bert was 'nothing but a great big baritone' until he told Casey how to fix the second act of Casey's then current show. Bert proposes to Clare (we learn that this is a routine act for him), but her response confirms that, for her, marriage is subordinated to professional duty: she traps him into exposing an anxiety that she might leave the show, and then tells him 'I'm just trying to prove that the theatre is your real love and I guess the same thing goes for me.' The way in which Casey relates to Pearl initiates a running gag showing another attitude to women that leads nowhere: Casey takes out a different girl each night, using as a lure an ermine coat which he literally snatches off their backs at the end of the evening.

The new style of Broadway show is associated with something formal, elaborate and expensive, and with professional commitment to 'the theatre'. While Dawnland shows us marriage and the male double act, which conforms to older traditions of entertainment, Broadway combines the refusal of marriage bond with the presentation of the couple on stage, but only as spectacle.

By a plot device involving Casey and a case of mistaken identity, King comes to be considered as Clare's dancing partner for a projected new show, and he triumphs in his audition duet, 'Between You and Me'. The central scenes of the film characterise Broadway (represented by Bert) as interested in punctuality and what it considers adult behaviour, insistent on physical dexterity and poise and brusquely dismissive of those seen as unimportant (as when Bert ignores Pearl in the dressing room sequence and again when he ignores Johnny after

First night: Johnny wishes Clare 'all the luck in the world' in Broadway Melody of 1940.

King's audition). This Broadway orderliness is continually interrupted, and Bert is exasperated, by a force which is presented in part as anarchic comedy, but also as ordinary or spontaneous and sometimes as clumsy. This can be writ large, as in the terrible vaudeville acts (a comic chanteuse and a unicyclist) which Casey forces on Bert's attention and which interrupt rehearsals. Sometimes the styles of Broadway and vaudeville collide, as in the sequence in which Clare and Johnny first meet. Johnny and a juggler (Trixie Firschke) are fooling around in Bert's outer office, which Bert and Clare enter just as the horseplay is reaching a climax. Bert's admonitory line to Johnny, 'You're a big boy now', indicates his attitude to such child's play. Sometimes the point can be as delicate as when, shortly afterwards, in his nervousness at his first interview with Bert and Clare, King knocks over the water bottle on Bert's desk. (A cruder, more strained version is the repeated gag with the statuette that Johnny upsets when he sees Clare.) As Johnny applauds Clare in 'I Am the Captain', he is involved in a little comic routine in which a pompous ass has his top hat ruined. This vignette is a kind of vaudeville sketch, set up in contrast to what is happening the other side of the footlights, on the modern Broadway stage.

As rehearsals for the new King Shaw-Clare Bennett show, *Swing Song*, move into their final stages, King comes to exemplify the stress associated with a form of success he can neither control nor quite fathom. He is conscious that the show depends on him but unsure of his qualities as a dancer. Also, he cannot separate his role as a new Broadway star from a belief that he must necessarily love Clare, and that she must love him. Both areas bring him sharply up against the limitations of his skill, or experience, and his response is to begin drinking heavily. After scenes in which we see him antagonising Bert, Clare and Johnny, King walks out of the theatre, leaving Johnny and Clare effectively alone.

In the romantic solo that follows, 'I've Got My Eyes On You', Johnny repositions a number which we understand to be a big romantic duet from *Swing*

Song, taking it out of its commercial setting by dancing with a photograph of Clare and using the props from the show that are scattered around the set. This brings in the quality of disorderliness, or chance, alluded to in Clare's reply to Johnny's claim that he changed the steps 'by accident': 'I like it better by accident'.

One might have taken this as a pointer that Clare would now move away from her commitment to Broadway towards the world of Dawnland and marriage, a rediscovery of herself as Brigit Callahan. But this is not the case. The next sequences are crucial, considering the available possibilities in order to redefine Broadway and include Johnny in it.

Clare and Johnny go off together for lunch and encounter a choleric silhouette artist played by Herman Bing, who displays a combination of precision in a creative activity and destabilising emotional intensity. He could be thought of as a kind of warning, a suggestively unhappy mixture of obsessive professional and man of feeling. In what follows, romance for the couple is hinted at and put aside:

Johnny: I was thinking . . .
The Silhouette Artist [as a Parthian shot]: He don't like your nose. *[He curls his lip and leaves.]*
Johnny: No, I was thinking a . . . *[hesitates]* about that dance you do in the second act.

The dance that follows is thus positioned as a professional rather than a romantic occasion, an exhilarating exhibition of skill, but one that does not change the way the dancers relate to each other. Strikingly, there are no other diners in the restaurant, as if to emphasise that the couple have not moved into the context of ordinary American folk – this is just another rehearsal stage. They end up, not

Johnny and Clare encounter the silhouette artist (Herman Bing).

157

The dance routine in the Italian café in Broadway Melody of 1940.

collapsing into chairs or sitting on the ground, but facing each other, both laughing nervously. Johnny says a few words that seem to indicate embarrassment, or lack of point – 'Well, I don't know' – and they stroll off in a way that expresses the uncertainty of what can be made of a dance that is neither romantic duet nor public performance. When they arrive back at the theatre a few minutes later, the proceedings are interrupted by the film's final gesture to vaudeville, one notable for its farcical violence, the unicyclist who crashes into the orchestra pit.

Johnny is now brought into the show via a plot involving King's collapse. It

Final sequence: King joins Clare and Johnny onstage.

would seem that the film has abandoned its earlier critique. There is really nothing much wrong with Broadway – it just needed somebody tougher and more skilled than King. Johnny's and Clare's two subsequent duets in the film repeat rather than extend the image of the perfect professional ensemble that was seen in the restaurant dance sequence, underlining this quality in their relationship. In both cases, Johnny acts professionally, stepping in to save public performances of *Swing Song*, first from the disaster of King's being too drunk to go on ('I Concentrate on You') and then from King's pretence of drunkenness as he cedes his position as Clare's dancing partner to Johnny ('Begin the Beguine'). To say this is not, of course, to attack the quality of these performances, but to argue that they offer themselves as fine sequences of professional dance rather than of dance articulating the expression of emotional intensity. A comparison of 'Begin the Beguine' to, say, 'Never Gonna Dance' expresses the difference clearly – in this film, quite simply, the show must go on.

Certainly the film observes convention in asserting Johnny and Clare as its romantic couple, but the sequence that mainly does this is interestingly awkward and crude. Appropriately, it is set in Dawnland and positioned between the two final numbers. Clare has gone to search for Johnny, who has returned to the ballroom where the film began. There is now another version of the opening wedding sequence, so that the sight of what she thinks is Johnny's marriage can enable Clare to realise that she is in love with him. We see the couple's understanding purchased at the cost of the humiliation of the plain, ordinary bride on Johnny's arm. This time, there is no receiving groom, and Taurog shows her standing alone amid general laughter, as Johnny runs to Clare with the line, 'This isn't mine'.

The design of the film's closing minute expresses its preference for the figure of the professional entertainer, but includes a minimal gesture in the direction of the romantic couple. After King's latest drunkenness has been exposed as a polished piece of performance mounted to save the show – Bert's line is 'he's as good an actor off as he is on' – Johnny and Clare drag King on stage, and the threesome perform a tap reprise of 'I've Got My Eyes on You' to end the film. The dancers are treated equally by the camera, and Clare, at the centre of the trio, divides her glances between both men. Only in the film's very last frames does she turn clearly towards Johnny.

The major innovation of *Broadway Melody of 1940* is not the introduction of a male dance partner for Astaire, but the change in the way both the leading men relate to the leading woman. The shift of attention, achieved with a measure of difficulty, or sacrifice, that is registered here in the quality of Astaire's solo number, is a turning away from the couple, or the triangle, and the issue of how desire is contained or expressed (as marriage or as loss) to embrace instead a world of highly professional entertainment, which is seen as a form of modernity. In the light of this, it is not surprising to find that Stanley Green, in his *Starring Fred Astaire* (Dodd, Mead, 1973), lists as unused in the film two Cole Porter numbers that might perhaps have invoked the charged, personal world of desire: 'I Happen to Be in Love' and 'I'm So in Love with You'.

SECOND CHORUS (H.C. Potter, 1940)

Second Chorus can perhaps best be thought of as a footnote, or appendix, to *Broadway Melody of 1940*, but shifts from a mode close to melodrama to one that has more in common with farce. The film is similarly centred on a male double act, and retains the convention (but little more than that) of the Astaire character's winning the leading lady, here Paulette Goddard. It repeats the structure in which the two men have exercised their skills for some years (here seven) in a context which they perceive as provincial or at least far from the peak of their profession. In *Second Chorus*, this changes when they become rivals for a new position that unquestionably represents success. Danny O'Neill (Astaire) and Hank Taylor

Light comedy: Danny (Astaire) and Hank (Burgess Meredith) flirt with Ellen (Paulette Goddard) in Second Chorus.

(Burgess Meredith) are trumpeters with a college band, the 'University Perennials', and the spot they both seek is a place with Artie Shaw's Jazz Band.

Broadway Melody of 1940 explored how an entertainer's relations with professional partners is affected by his assessment of his own skills. In *Second Chorus*, this is put aside, and the film makes no distinction between the trumpet-playing ability of the two men or their attitudes to their skill. While the move from the Perennials to Artie Shaw's band provides the plot with its structure, nothing much turns on it beyond straightforward professional advancement. It is neither a move from simple failure to success (we are told that the Perennials make 'a very good living') nor from an outdated practice to a contemporary one.

The function of Ellen Miller (Paulette Goddard) in the film is also peripheral. She is a secretary in a debt agency who serves a summons on Danny. Danny and Hank pursue her, dupe her boss into sacking her, and employ her as their manager. It is in this role, as the streetwise city girl, that Ellen dances with Danny in a simple, impromptu duet on the subject of learning to dance: 'I Ain't Hep to That Step but I'll Dig It'. Shortly after this number, she is spotted by Shaw, who offers her a job in New York as his manager; she becomes just a functionary, and her dancing never reappears in the film, even as a possibility. Her role, as the focus of the comedic rivalry between the two men, generates wit and banter but nothing much of substance seems to depend on it – the triangle has similarities to that of Bing Crosby, Bob Hope and Dorothy Lamour in the first of the 'Road' movies, *The Road to Singapore* (Victor Schertzinger), also released by Paramount in 1940, and some of the slapstick scenes are comparable to the physical comedy of the Road film.

In *Steps in Time*, Astaire writes of *Second Chorus*, 'My main reason for doing this one, however, was that I had an idea for a solo number in which I would dance-conduct Artie Shaw's band' (Astaire, p.242). The sequence is filmed as a number in a Shaw concert in which Danny, apparently finding himself unexpectedly in charge of the band, breaks into a performance that treats conducting as an extension of solo dance, as if to enhance and underline the dominance of the soloist, who both controls the music and enacts the dance. In the light of *Broadway Melody of 1940*, this can be seen as a further extension of its treatment of dance as professional skill rather than as an expression of a couple's romance. Ellen, watching admiringly from the wings, is entirely absent from the dance except as part of the audience.

HOLIDAY INN (Mark Sandrich, 1942)

Holiday Inn gives the strategy of pairing Astaire with another male player a different dimension through the use of an unambiguously major star: Bing Crosby. The established personas of the two stars seem to underpin an apparently clear set of differences between them, laid out in the film's opening scenes. It is the eve of a marriage, a last night on Broadway. Jim Hardy (Crosby) and Ted Hanover (Astaire) are about to perform a threesome number with Lila Dixon (Virginia Dale). Lila has promised to marry Jim, who is quitting show business to live on a farm, but she does not wish to give up her career. She thinks she is in love with Ted, who is apparently offering her 'diamonds, sables, your own little penthouse', and cannot face telling the enamoured Jim. After their show, which is a gag number about the differences between two suitors, Jim playing a singer and Ted a dancer, Jim learns the truth. He retires to his farm, leaving Lila and Ted together.

For the next twenty minutes or so, the film contrasts the two men's ways of life. Jim is attached to the country, the creation of a home and a family life with the possibility of children, a benign relationship to the processes of nature, songwriting (a form of creativity that can be carried out in a domestic context) and solo, or at most duet performances requiring little or no aid from technology. He imagines a relationship with a woman primarily as marriage rather than stage partnership. He has an image of himself as a man with ideas about living, and particularly work, a view that most work is wasted life. He wants what he will later call 'a simple little layout'. Ted is a creature of Broadway, and his creativity lies in dancing in the technologically sophisticated world of the New York stage. He imagines a relationship with a woman primarily as a partnership on stage, only incidentally, or as an afterthought, as marriage. As for working – he does not think of what he does as work.

Jim's preferred existence is summed up in the image which follows his discovery that Lila is staying with Ted. As he leaves the New York room, he talks about rejoining the human race, and sings the opening line of a number, 'Lazy',

Creatures of Broadway: Ted (Astaire) and Lila (Virginia Dale) in Holiday Inn.

that extolls the virtues of country life. We now see him emerging from a doorway. He is carrying lumber into his farmhouse, but his load obscures his view and he tumbles over. This is a man who believes in a simple, practical life, represented by his gathering fuel for an open fire (the hearth will be an important motif in the movie), but he is also evidently a dreamer, a man who cannot see where he is going. Ted, on the other hand, belongs among the sets on which he dances, which use props to mimic, or signify the outside world, to invoke it with a kind of superciliousness, as if the distinction between what is inside and outside were an inconsiderable one. This notion will come to be important, and more complicated, later on. Jim's belief in his own sincerity is linked with a propensity for self-delusion. Ted is defined by his self-knowledge, part of which is his knowledge of his own duplicity, or insincerity.

Thus *Holiday Inn* shares with *Broadway Melody of 1940* and *Second Chorus* a structure which contrasts the ordinary, quotidian and domestic with the polished, professional and assured. But it departs from the earlier films in placing the male leads on opposite sides of this contrast and in having a different narrative trajectory. Rather than beginning out of town and ending on Broadway, it begins with Broadway and moves away from it. Jim comes up with what he thinks of as an ideal setting for entertainment: he will turn his farm into a kind of roadhouse, to be called Holiday Inn, that will put on shows only during holidays. This will address the defects that were visible in the montage over the singing of 'Lazy', the laboriousness of the country life, and also its loneliness. (Once Jim has left Broadway, the film is structured around nine episodes that take place on major holidays: New Year's Eve, Lincoln's Birthday, St. Valentine's Day, Washington's Birthday, Easter Sunday, Independence Day, Thanksgiving, Christmas Eve, New Year's Eve.)

The film now introduces its female lead, aspiring singer and dancer Linda Mason (Marjorie Reynolds), who is part of the audience for Ted and Lila's Broadway show, where their number, 'You're Easy to Dance With' expresses the couple's easy compatibility on the dance floor but implies, as even the title might indicate, that this is a connection of no great depth, and Lila subsequently disappears for much of the film. Linda travels to Holiday Inn and falls, or is knocked, into the snow. Wearing a bathrobe while her clothes dry, she sits alone with Jim in front of the roaring fire. Jim claims to be auditioning her for the soon-to-be-opened inn. He sings 'White Christmas' to her, and by the end of the number, they are singing in harmony.

This is the twenty-third minute of the film. As its determining moment of mutual seduction, 'White Christmas' is comparable with 'Night and Day' in *The Gay Divorcée* or 'Isn't This a Lovely Day (To Be Caught in the Rain)' in *Top Hat*. It is the only number in *Holiday Inn* delivered in a setting where a couple is safely

Who you are and what you live for: Jim (Bing Crosby) and Linda (Marjorie Reynolds) in Holiday Inn *in the lead-in to 'White Christmas'.*

alone. We might be tempted to take it as a moment when the central values of the film are definitively and uncomplicatedly asserted: the domestic couple by the hearth, the seamless connection of past to future implicit in the famous lyric. Despite the force given to the sequence by the song's staggering commercial success over the next decade, it is possible to see that Sandrich is showing us these values not simply as nobly embattled, but in conflict with other imperatives in the culture, as in this part of the conversation that acts as the song's prologue:

Linda: Fifteen holidays a year – you're a lazy fellow.
Jim: Not especially, just have my own ideas about living.
Linda: My father was like you, just a man with a family. Never amounted to much, didn't care, but as long as he was alive we always had plenty to eat and clothes to keep us warm.
Jim: Were you happy?
Linda: Yes.
Jim: Then your father was a very successful man. I hope I can do as well.

So having your own ideas about living – about where you live and what you live for – defines success and happiness formed around the family and the figure of the father as provider in a way that stands uneasily against what is understood as success, and acknowledged in the form of money. (We already know that the inn is effectively broke.) Worldly success, which has no interest in the father-figure or the family but involves glamour, money and movement, is represented by Ted, and by part of Linda's ambitions for herself: what Jim, much later in the film, will call 'illusions of glory'.

Sandrich expresses the limitations and contrariety of ideas of success in American culture through Jim's and Ted's treatment of Linda. Jim's problem is his inability to separate his desire for Linda from his sense of failure, a feeling of not being the father-figure who can feed and clothe a (potential) family. The Lincoln's Birthday segment of the film is introduced by a sequence in Linda's room at the inn. Jim proposes to her and she wants to throw her arms around him, but he replies: 'better save that till you see the bank book'. As he speaks he is blacking up her face. His strategy for avoiding the need to compete with the qualities embodied by Ted is to disguise Linda's beauty, to turn her into a kind of invisible woman. There is an implied link here with the woman at the inn who is socially invisible, the other woman to whom Jim is close – the black housekeeper Mamie (Louise Beavers).

Ted fails to achieve with Linda something which has been possible for Jim and Linda in the 'White Christmas' number, a moment of privacy, which here stands for the possibility of intimacy. In their first duet, in the New Year's Eve segment, Ted is completely drunk. The effect (as well as giving Astaire, ably partnered by Reynolds, a wonderful opportunity to exercise his invention, to incorporate the idea of a man's intoxication into dance) is to deprive the meeting on the dance floor of consequence, as if it were a dream sequence. Afterwards Ted has no recollection of dancing.

The second duet is in the St Valentine's Day sequence. The setting is again a public one, a rehearsal. Jim gives Linda a valentine, which turns out to be sheet music – they are photographed in two-shot as he sings the opening verse of 'Be Careful, It's My Heart' to her. As the verse ends, Ted appears, and he and Linda

Ted with Linda and Jim at the end of the 'Drunk Dance' sequence in Holiday Inn.

move into a spontaneous duet, and the camera now concentrates on the couple, excluding Jim visually, although his presence continues for the first part of the dance to be registered in his singing voice.

The meaning of this sequence is in part determined by its evocation of the Astaire-Rogers dance style, effectively for the first time since the cycle ended. It is difficult to define the connection entirely, but it is expressed in the choreography, in the opening movement from Reynolds (arms lifted, palms outwards) which recollects 'Cheek to Cheek', in the lifts, in the couple's elegant stroll in dance across the floor and in the final pose. In contrast with his numbers in the previous two films, here Astaire returns to the mode of enhanced ballroom dance, while Reynolds's black gown recalls those worn by Rogers in several final numbers

(*Roberta, Shall We Dance, Carefree*). Even the prominent heart-and-arrow brooch worn by Linda for Valentine's Day seems to carry a visual hint, recalling Rogers's heart-and-arrows dress in *Carefree*. Sandrich had directed five films in the Astaire-Rogers cycle (*The Gay Divorcée, Top Hat, Follow the Fleet, Shall We Dance, Carefree*), and it seems to me that in recalling their image he, and possibly Astaire, wants us to appreciate what this couple could be, but also to recollect the increasing sense of frustration that became associated with the dancing as the cycle drew to a close. The evocation of *Carefree* is especially important. *Holiday Inn* can be thought of as a continuation of the logic of *Carefree*, to the point where the Astaire character is defeated and the other suitor wins the girl.

Shortly afterwards, Linda is asked for the first time to choose between her suitors. This is the film's only sequence in which Ted and Linda are together in private. It begins with a striking shot of Linda looking into a mirror as Ted comes into her room, so that she sees an image of the two of them as a couple. Ted offers her the world, the 'pick of engagements' – she counters with her 'promise' to Jim. (Nominally this promise is to work at the inn for the season, but it also involves the possibility of marriage. In the scene she uses the word three times.) Ted's two responses to this situation encapsulate the way that Astaire's role in the film relates to his previous two movies. First, he speaks of love: 'Linda, from the very first moment we danced together, I knew you were to be the one girl in my life.' We do not see Ted's face in the shot, but Astaire's vocal delivery renders clear the patent insincerity of this pitch. When Linda responds negatively, he, too, seems to dismiss it, as if this fiction doesn't matter now that she is not going to share it. His second plea is this: 'Think of yourself. Here's your chance to do the one thing you like best, not only for fifteen days a year, but always.' This is the important, sincere plea, made, one dancer to another, in the name not of love but of art.

Linda will finally choose love and the inn over a dance career with Ted. The Easter Sunday sequence is the last 'private' duet in the film – Jim sings 'Easter Parade' to Linda as they ride home to the inn from church. Now Ted arrives, and the next number is very different. For the American national festival, Independence Day, a stage is constructed outside the inn, offering the opportunity for a production number ('Say It With Firecrackers') which retains almost no trace of the domestic setting that was part of the previous numbers and concludes with a solo performance by Ted. (This continues the change of emphasis in Astaire's solo dance that was evident in the difference between *Broadway Melody of 1940* and *Second Chorus*, from the expression of romantic yearning to professional spectacle. Here it is a bravura improvisation mounted because Linda has failed to appear.) Suddenly technology has arrived at the inn, and film is included in the show, a montage of the American war effort projected to accompany Jim's patriotic song.

The effect is to tie the invocation of American freedom intimately to the technology of both warfare and Hollywood cinema. The Hollywood producer Parker (John Gallaudet) and director Dunbar (James Bell), who have been watching the act, turn out to be interested in making a film based on the idea of the inn and using Ted and Linda. Linda responds positively to the opportunity and leaves for Hollywood to dance with Ted. We see this in a second montage sequence, in which the dancing couple are shown repeatedly superimposed over images of cameras and technicians. In the Thanksgiving segment which follows,

Jim looks suspicious as Ted offers to share their 'simple pleasures' in Holiday Inn.

the inn has closed as a site of entertainment and returned to its earlier, purely domestic function. Jim, despondent at the loss of Linda, mopes until Mamie gives him a talking-to. She functions as the film's only parent figure, a substitute mother for Linda – 'I know her like I knows my own kids' – and implicitly for Jim. Spurred on by these maternal strictures, he travels to Hollywood to win her back. He surprises her on the set of the movie, where they fall into each other's arms. A coda shows the reopened inn and the singing couple (Jim and Linda) in harmony with the dancing couple (Ted and the returned Lila).

This could appear to be a narrative in which the appropriation of the inn by Hollywood moguls and dance professionals like Ted is finally defeated by the integrity of Jim, who can now take Linda away from all this falsity. Such a reading might be sustainable if the confrontation between Jim and Linda were set in an office, or a dressing room in Hollywood, but this is not the case. The film now introduces a place which is visually the inn, but is not the one in Connecticut. In terms of the literals of the plot, it is Holiday Inn rebuilt on a sound stage.

The revealing of the inn as a set is consciously theatrical – we see a huge door being pulled back. Sandrich wants to remind us that the inn can be understood as situated not just in Connecticut, but also in Hollywood – it was always an 'idea of living' as opposed to a specific place. The fact that the set is 'one of the most authentic reproduction jobs we've ever done', as Dunbar tells Jim, is to claim it and by extension the emotions that can be expressed in it, as a triumph, an example of what Hollywood can create.

It is in this Hollywood Connecticut rather than the film's Connecticut, that Linda can express her desire for Jim and the couple can be reunited. Jim arrives and looks over the set as if he is an interested amateur just before the 'White Christmas' number is to be shot. He makes two tiny adjustments, moving the Christmas tree next to the piano and surreptitiously leaving his pipe close to its keyboard. We now see the shooting of a sequence of Dunbar's movie:

1) The melody of 'White Christmas' begins, cued on the studio sound system. The shot shows Dunbar and crew on a crane, photographing Linda arriving at Holiday Inn. In the latter part of the shot Sandrich pans right and excludes the crew, framing Linda in a sledge. As the sledge stops, he cuts to

2) Linda and the inn's doormen. Sandrich's camera pans, following Linda as she walks up the steps of the inn. Dissolve to

3) Linda, in the background, moving across the living room of the inn. In the foreground is the crane, Dunbar and nine other technicians, moving in parallel with her walk across the set. Cut to

4) Medium shot of the fireplace at the inn. Linda walks into shot, puts down her bag, touches the mantelpiece. Cut to

5) Slightly closer shot of Linda, as she touches the fireside chair. The camera (which is now both Sandrich's and implicitly Dunbar's) follows her as she sits at the piano, framed by the chair and the Christmas tree. She begins to sing 'White Christmas'. At the end of the second line of the song, cut to

6) Close-up of Linda, which shows a teardrop on her cheek. After a few more words of the song, cut to

7) Linda's hand picking up Jim's pipe. Camera follows as she strikes five of the Christmas tree bells. Cut to

8) Medium shot of Linda, her singing faltering. Cut to

9) Close-up of Jim, whistling in counterpoint to 'White Christmas'.

Had the film simply offered the plot that Dunbar seems to be shooting – if Linda had fled Hollywood, come back to the Connecticut inn, started to sing 'White Christmas' and been joined in chorus by Jim – this would have reprised their opening performance, expressing a satisfying harmony. But here, there is something more: the awareness of Linda's performance as something not spontaneous but deliberate, the professional, imaginative assumption of a mood by the actress. There is a strong sense of Linda singing in public for an audience, both ourselves and the film professionals: shots which stress the presence of Dunbar and his crew (1, 3) are juxtaposed with shots which offer us the achieved performance, as if we were watching Dunbar's movie (4, 5, 6).

The paradox is that Linda's finding of the pipe (shot 7) suggests the limits of her self-possession. In that Dunbar's film involves no pipe, we have to assume that her action in striking the bells with it is involuntary, a kind of physical memory. Hence the pipe becomes expressive of the breakdown of the measured

The two couples on the stage of the inn at the end of Holiday Inn.

performance, the overwhelming of the character, opening a door into another, remembered or imagined, world. (We might feel that this prefigures another famous scene involving Christmas tree bells and a character who is overwhelmed, the closing seconds of Frank Capra's *It's a Wonderful Life* (1946), in which George Bailey (James Stewart) finds the inscribed copy of *The Adventures of Tom Sawyer*. Another connection between Capra's film and Sandrich's is that they both use models to express access to imaginative freedom. The model ship, which Jim examines as he tries to conceal his knowledge of Linda's whereabouts from Ted, can be compared to the models on George Bailey's work table in *It's a Wonderful Life*. A very helpful discussion of the these subjects, which considers states of 'imaginative limitation and release' in American film and painting, is given by Raymond Carney in his book on Capra (*American Vision: The Films of Frank Capra*, Cambridge University Press, 1986, pp.439-449.)

Holiday Inn appears at first to be tracing a shift from the natural, low-tech world of an earlier America (Linda arrives at the Connecticut inn in a horse-drawn sledge, for example) to the modernising of the countryside (as in Jim's arrival at the inn in an automobile, which he refers to as the coming of the 'machine age'). However, by the end of the film, we are being asked to see this differently, to understand that oppositions (such as mechanised/natural, modern/old fashioned, even outside/inside) are not fixed and can be interrogated, reinflected or even collapsed. The latter (Hollywood) part of the film insists on drawing attention to its own artifice – an example is the elaborate fairy-tale sledge, a piece of Hollywood hokum, in which Linda arrives at the reconstructed inn in Dunbar's version.

It is therefore appropriate that the final shot refers us back to the act of filming, which it does by reproducing the view of the exterior of the inn set just as Jim first saw it and as it appeared in the sequence of Dunbar's filming. The shot begins just outside the window, somewhere that the the film has established as the Connecticut inn, not the Hollywood one, but we also, of course, know that these two places are one and the same. Snow is falling as the camera, in a crane shot, pulls back past the trunks of the trees and the cars caught in the drifts to show us a couple of extras flapping their arms to keep warm – or to indicate to us that it is cold. We see the values implicit in this contrast – the warmth and joy within measured against the cold outside – in the light of our awareness of the technology that is operating here: the outside is only more inside, the snow only fake flakes falling from the snow machine. Earlier, *Holiday Inn* celebrated the triumph of its domestic couple, but we comprehend their setting only as an image of utopia – a utopia on a sound stage, a utopian moment performed.

RITA HAYWORTH IN 1941

In Astaire's two films with Rita Hayworth, *You'll Never Get Rich* and *You Were Never Lovelier*, the other main male role does not resemble those played by George Murphy, Burgess Meredith and Bing Crosby – a stage partner, a bachelor of roughly the Astaire character's age and a plausible, or serious, rival in love. Here the supporting role returns to being taken by a character who cannot be a suitor (because he is already married or is the girl's father) like those played in *You'll Never Get Rich* by Robert Benchley and in *You Were Never Lovelier* by Adolphe Menjou. The possibility of the woman's marriage to someone other than Astaire is posed by positioning a lesser or comic figure in the role, one analogous to Beddini in *Top Hat* or Jim Montgomery in *Shall We Dance*. In *You'll Never Get Rich*, the role is filled by a pleasant, uninteresting army officer, Tom Barton (John Hubbard), and in *You Were Never Lovelier*, it will disappear entirely, the blockage to the romance being the woman's father and the woman herself. The films conform to the model of the romances in the Astaire-Rogers cycle. Astaire encounters, or notices, Hayworth for the first time, dances with her, pursues her and after the resolution of sufficient misunderstandings, the couple dance together at the end of the movie. *You'll Never Get Rich* echoes *The Gay Divorcée* or *Top Hat* in that this final dance takes the form of a big production number with the couple at its centre ('Wedding Cake Walk'), although here this cannot quite be the end of the film.

The similarities to the Astaire-Rogers cycle foreground the contrast between the personas of Ginger Rogers and Rita Hayworth as she was in 1941, well before *Gilda* (Charles Vidor, 1946) and *The Lady from Shanghai* (Orson Welles, 1948). A discussion of Hayworth's later persona is to be found in Richard Dyer's 'Resistance through charisma: Rita Hayworth and *Gilda*', in *Women in Film Noir*, edited by E. Ann Kaplan (British Film Institute, 1980), which has assisted my own thinking about Hayworth.

Hayworth's first sequence in *You'll Never Get Rich* takes place on a Broadway stage where a musical is in rehearsal. Its director, Robert Curtis (Astaire), is called to the telephone. We see a line of figures, but first Robert's body and then the body of an extra obscure our view so that we have only the tiniest glimpse of one of the women in the row. When the camera moves back, we see that this is Hayworth playing a chorus-girl, Sheila Winthrop. In a medium shot in which

Robert (Astaire) dances 'The Boogie Barcarolle' with Sheila (Rita Hayworth) and chorus in You'll Never Get Rich.

they are facing each other, Robert tells Sheila that she is a beat off, and, for the last half of his speech, there is a cut to a head and shoulders shot of Hayworth. After she has delivered her couple of lines, we cut back to the first set-up of the couple, and they go into a precise, skilled tap routine: 'The Boogie Barcarolle'.

For the dance and the rest of the sequence, the lighting is even, relatively high-key and without significant shadows. The shot that stands out from the others is the establishing head-and-shoulders shot of Hayworth. It suddenly presents her in chiaroscuro: a line of shadow falls strikingly and symmetrically across the folds of her blouse, and her renowned hair, distinctive both in its shape and beauty, is lit with highlights. So the sequence as a whole tells us that Hayworth is a precise, practised dancer and that she is perceived as extraordinarily – exceptionally – beautiful. The unlikely shadows in which she stands for a moment express something about this beauty and the response it produces. In this context, it is relevant to look back at the Hayworth films that led up to *You'll Never Get Rich* and marked her rise from featured player to star.

In *Susan and God* (George Cukor, 1940), she plays Leonora, a young ex-actress bored by her marriage to an amiable bumbler played by Nigel Bruce and strongly attracted to a young actor. In this small role, she represents, along with another couple, the threat of sexual disorderliness which is the context for the film's main subject, the marriage of its principals, Susan and Barry Trexel, played by Joan Crawford and Frederic March. Leonora's physical attractiveness is such that it seems to require immediate acknowledgement when she is seen for the first time, as in Susan's 'Oh my dear, you're too lovely' and Barry's 'who's this lovely . . . you're an awfully pretty woman'. (A pointed contrast is made with the looks of the Crawford character. When her daughter tells her, 'you look so divine', Susan replies, 'I work like a Trojan at it'.)

Angels over Broadway, written, directed and produced by Ben Hecht in 1940, is a parable of lives saved from the destructiveness of the *noir* city. Nina Berona (Hayworth) and Bill O'Brien (Douglas Fairbanks Jr) dwell in a world of seedy hotels and clubs, and are on the brink of submitting to the corruption of such places. The keynote of the relation between them is Bill's confused attempt to insist to himself that Nina is already corrupt – 'you're just what you've always been' – while also seeing her as a 'dream girl' and protecting her from the predatory male: 'You ain't no buzzard's dish, neither, not while I'm around.' Hayworth represents the beautiful girl whose freshness or innocence in this environment is an extraordinary anomaly, or fantastic chance, hardly to be believed and under constant threat. One of her lines is: 'I never knew anyone who wanted to die – except myself'.

In *The Strawberry Blonde* (Raoul Walsh, 1941), Hayworth plays Virginia Brush, the blonde of the title, a role that, according to Walsh, had been intended for Ann Sheridan. Virginia, a woman whose beauty affects all men, rejects the aspiring young professional Biff (James Cagney), choosing to marry the best hope for worldly success, Hugo (Jack Carson). The latter part of the film strongly contrasts its two married couples, the good (poor, but honest and devoted) Biff and Amy (Olivia de Havilland) with the bad (rich, but corrupt and quarrelsome) Virginia and Hugo. Hayworth's role becomes that of a disappointed narcissist, successful only in worldly terms and enraged at her husband's physical deterioration in comparison to the pugnacious Cagney. A second contrast concerns fertility: the film ends with the announcement of Amy's pregnancy, and an earlier sequence hints at the childless Virginia's sexual rapaciousness. I have been unable to see *Affectionately Yours* (Lloyd Bacon 1941), in which Hayworth was cast as a threat to the marriage of Dennis Morgan and Merle Oberon.

The film which immediately precedes *You'll Never Get Rich* is Rouben Mamoulian's *Blood and Sand*, made in May 1941, which follows the career of bullfighter Juan Gallardo (Tyrone Power). Linda Darnell is Carmen, the bullfighter's devoted, virtuous wife, and Hayworth is Doña Sol, the beautiful, cosmopolitan woman who takes him as her latest lover but has no desire for marriage. This might seem like an obvious opposition of good and evil, but Mamoulian's film is relatively sympathetic to Doña Sol. It is implied that her considerable sexual experience resembles the career of the bullfighter in its serial and finally unsatisfying qualities. Don José (Pedro de Cordoba), one of the film's father-figures, tells Juan that he pities Doña Sol – 'There's nothing in the world that she can hold on to for long, nothing.' She tells Juan, 'If I were a man, I'd try bullfighting', and we see their sexual play taking the form of a game in which he plays the bull and she the matador.

Doña Sol's role is treated as a typical element in the rise and fall of a bullfighter's career. Juan's progress is traced from childhood to the flush of stardom in which he is seduced by her, to his decline and her moving on to the next rising star, Manolo (Anthony Quinn). That such serial loyalties are inherent in bullfighting is stressed in the explicit parallel between Doña Sol and the critic Curro (Laird Cregar), who similarly first lionises Juan and then passes on to Manolo.

In her films of this period, then, Hayworth is cast as a woman whose beauty is great but always somehow problematic: the physical response to it may be strong and immediate but does not lead to a life that fulfils the promise suggested by such beauty. The films that show her sensual life indicate lack of satisfaction – sexual frustration in *Susan and God* and *The Strawberry Blonde*, boredom with diverse sexual experience in *Blood and Sand* – while Hecht's presentation of her as a young girl suggests that her looks are as much curse as blessing. In 1940-41, Hayworth is not a *femme fatale*: her only lover to die is Juan in *Blood and Sand*, and his death belongs to the trajectory of the bullfighter's life. She exists under a shadow: the damage that her beauty does is to herself and to her relationships with men.

YOU'LL NEVER GET RICH (Sidney Lanfield, 1941)

Almost the first thing that those who meet Sheila Winthrop in *You'll Never Get Rich* feel they must speak of is her physical beauty – lines to this effect are given to the characters played by Robert Benchley, Frieda Inescort and Osa Massen. The opening offers ways in which the Hayworth figure is ignored or devalued, showing how her beauty operates to define and limit the way she can relate to other people. In the first sequence we see Martin Courtland (Robert Benchley), a theatrical producer and inveterate pursuer of beautiful girls, in a Fifth Avenue jeweller's shop. He is buying a diamond bracelet with which he hopes to purchase his latest lovely, but he cannot remember Sheila's name and has to telephone the theatre to ask for it. Sheila is attracted to the one man in this place not overwhelmed by her looks, a man 'up to his neck in pretty girls' – Robert Curtis (Astaire). She resorts to a professional trick (pretending to make mistakes) to attract his attention and cause him to dance with her.

When Martin attempts to give her the diamond bracelet, Sheila seems bored rather than insulted; it is clearly not the first time a man has made her such an offer. Here Benchley's persona (affable, nervous, impotent) is as crucial to the lack of any sense of real threat as it is in the comparable situation in *The Major and the Minor*, where the woman is played by Rogers. Sheila turns him down and returns the bracelet to his pocket, where it is found by his wife Julia (Frieda Inescort). Now, as a way of confounding Julia and unaware that Sheila has already seen the bracelet, Robert agrees to pretend that the gift was his and to give it to Sheila in Julia's presence at a smart night spot.

The effect on Sheila of this piece of theatre is to make her feel that she is of no consequence, that she can be thought of (as apparently evidenced by the derisive and disbelieving gaze of Julia) as no more than a body to be bought and a counter to be used to show Robert's loyalty to Martin. After some angry taunting of Robert, she quickly makes an excuse and leaves. The expression on Hayworth's face as she strides off past the camera finely conveys her hurt and rage. Nevertheless, the newspapers report the couple's 'engagement', causing a further row, and they part in mutual hostility.

The film now introduces a topical subject for the America of late 1941 – Robert receives his call-up papers and is drafted into the army. In Robert's army physical,

Martin (Robert Benchley) passes the diamond bracelet to Robert in the presence of Sheila and Julia (Frieda Inescort) in You'll Never Get Rich.

his dancing skills count for nothing. Stripped to his underwear, he is five pounds underweight and has to con his way into a service that requires a different kind of body. Joining the army is figured here as leaving not only skills and profession but also women. Although the Broadway company we have previously seen is a mixed one, only the girls of the chorus come to see Robert off at the station. The Cole Porter production number, 'Shootin' the Works for Uncle Sam', is leave-taking writ large, and Lanfield edits a glimpse of another, more homely farewell into it.

Camp Weston may be governed by regulations and military discipline (Stanley Green tells us that Lanfield researched the background at an actual camp), but it is also a place of nonsense and clowning, represented in the routines of Swivel Tongue (Cliff Nazarro) and Kewpie (Guinn Williams). Sheila literally becomes a dream, her next appearance being in a dream sequence as Robert sleeps at camp. His dance is confined to the place where the military contains what it cannot allow: the guardhouse. The Delta Rhythm Boys (in the role of black American soldiers sent to the guardhouse for some unexplained reason) sing and play 'Since I Kissed My Baby Goodbye', which inspires Astaire to dance in a spontaneous solo performance which seems to conjure up Sheila. She stands, close but

Robert and Sheila dance to 'So Near and Yet So Far' in You'll Never Get Rich.

inaccessible, in the shadows thrown by the bars of the guardhouse window and reminds us of her opening shadowed head-and-shoulders shot by effectively re-prising the line that accompanied it: 'Hey, Soldier, you're a beat off'.

Sheila never enters the guardhouse in the film. She can be wooed only in places that are somehow outside the discipline of the army and which allow for various forms of play-acting, or dressing up. At first, this is illegitimate and only partly effective, as when Robert, to impress Sheila, dresses in Captain's uniform and visits her at a nearby farm where she is staying with her fiancé's mother, a place that has in common with Sheila's New York apartment the possibility of interruption by a rival suitor.

A more satisfactory context for Robert is the musical. The plot has Martin offering to produce a show for the army in order to promote Sonya (Osa Massen), the subject of his latest romantic pursuit. The show is a setting that Robert creates rather than one in which he is confined or over which he has no control: the first rehearsal sequence opens with him calling for props – a house, a tree – and then '. . . hey boys, bring in the ocean, will you?' Robert now appears in the

Astaire signature costume of white tie and tails for his one romantic duet with Sheila; the title of Porter's lyric, 'So Near and Yet So Far', alludes to the key image of the film, the physical closeness of a woman divided from a man by an impassable barrier – such as a barred guardhouse window.

The film moves through a series of reconciliations and misunderstandings built around some intricate plotting concerning the bracelet, its inscription, and Martin's schemes. The final twist demonstrates Robert's belief that what happens (or is created) on the stage can be a reality. Their last number together is a wedding dance – 'Wedding Cake Walk' – that is part of the performance staged for the draftees. Sheila is about to marry the boring army officer Tom, but Robert forestalls this by substituting a real Justice of the Peace for the actor in the number, and so a 'genuine' marriage takes place on stage (a nice reversal of the plotting of the conclusion to *Top Hat*).

It might have been possible to end the movie here, with Sheila realising the rightness of her choice and dancing off in Robert's arms, but the final sequence addresses the qualities of Hayworth's persona – for Sheila the choices involved in marriage are not easy ones. Robert is back in the guardhouse, and it is a time of night and shadow. Sheila has had a conversation with Martin which has cleared away her misapprehensions and she comes, still in her wedding dress from the

Production number: Robert and Sheila dance the 'Wedding Cake Walk'.

show but without her veil, to visit her new husband at the barred window. The shadows of the bars are seen on both speakers as they have this conversation:

Sheila: Mrs Curtis calling on her husband.
Robert: The last I heard, the Curtises don't live here any more. They broke up, I heard.
Sheila: I heard she might be coming back to him.
Robert: You did?
Sheila: Mm. But it's rather awkward, with the bridegroom behind bars.
Robert: Awkward? It's awful.
Sheila: I could pitch a tent out here, and we could look at each other *[for a moment they do just that]*.

At this point, their conversation is interrupted by Colonel Shiller (Boyd Davis), who has come to release Robert and let the honeymoon take its course. There is no final clinch, and we do not see the couple united either inside or outside the guardhouse, only a last wordless shot of Hayworth through the bars.

We should note that Sheila did not seek entry to the guardhouse in order to face Robert. She chose to have this conversation through the bars, wishing, perhaps, to acknowledge that something still divides them – something 'rather awkward', whether it is his being in the army or the difficulty she has in trusting, or believing what he says or does (the film raises this several times), or the question of what they want of each other. Her claim in her final line is that this barrier is a bearable one, a place from which to start a life together.

This is not quite the last word. Northrop Frye has described buffoon figures (like Swivel Tongue and Kewpie) as having affinities with 'the master of revels' and being a 'development of what in Aristophanic comedy is represented by the Chorus' (Frye, *Anatomy of Criticism*, Princeton University Press, 1957, p.175). After the departure of the couple, the two buffoons burst through the floor of the jail at the feet of Colonel Shiller, and their lines about being lost in the fog and Swivel Tongue's nonsense speech occupy the place that would be filled by the concluding speech of a classical chorus and end the film on a note of not knowing exactly where things are headed.

YOU WERE NEVER LOVELIER (William A. Seiter, 1942)

The movement from Broadway to Camp Weston in *You'll Never Get Rich* is also a move from a place where Astaire's professional dance is admired and validated to one where it is embattled and has to find a space, to create a context for itself. The movement in *Holiday Inn* (made between the two films with Hayworth) from Broadway to Connecticut, from a dance stage to somewhere initially given over to song, is not unrelated. *You Were Never Lovelier* offers a further variation along these lines.

Astaire plays Robert Davis, a Broadway song-and-dance man, but no part of the film is set in Broadway. It begins with a few establishing shots of Buenos Aires and a brief sequence which makes it clear that Robert has lost all his money at the racetrack – a prince of professional entertainers is shipwrecked, as it were, on a foreign shore. The entire action takes place in Buenos Aires, in a hotel owned by an imperious paterfamilias, Eduardo Acuña (Adolphe Menjou), and in his family

Fairytale princess: Maria (Rita Hayworth) momentarily framed between her father Eduardo (Adolphe Menjou) and Robert (Astaire) in You Were Never Lovelier.

mansion and its garden, the Acuña family's little kingdom. The film is a comedy following a classical model, its presiding topic being erotic fulfilment. The Acuñas have four daughters, and Robert's arrival coincides with the marriage of the eldest, Julia (Catherine Craig). The two younger daughters, Cecy (Leslie Brooks) and Lita (Adele Mara), have lovers to whom they are unofficially betrothed, but they cannot be married until a suitable husband has been found for Maria, the second daughter. This is the part played by Hayworth, and the plot involves what Northrop Frye describes as 'a kind of comic Oedipus situation' (Frye, 1957, p.181). To awaken Maria's desires, her father anonymously sends her orchids and romantic notes. Robert is misidentified as the unknown suitor and becomes a reluctant actor in the father's scheming. He falls in love with Maria, loses her when his connivance with the father is revealed and finally wins her back.

The film posits particular places as being appropriate for different kinds of dance. The space dedicated to professional entertainment is the Sky Room, the night spot of the Acuña hotel, which is presided over by Xavier Cugat and his band, who play themselves. Cugat's presence signifies a meeting point between Latin American and North American entertainment cultures – Cugat's band was highly successful at the Waldorf-Astoria in New York – but Eduardo will not

The antagonism between Robert and Eduardo in You Were Never Lovelier. *Xavier Cugat and his band look on.*

consider employing Robert to dance here. Although he owns the hotel, Eduardo claims never to go to the Sky Room ('my cover charge is too high') and treats Cugat with disdain ('remind me to give Cugat back to the Waldorf').

The first part of the film is not to do with the couple, but is devoted to a series of gags about Robert's professional standing, his difficulty with audiences in this alien setting. When he tries to announce his business to Acuña's secretary Fernando (Gus Schilling) with a single tap of the foot, as if this slight gesture were enough to make it clear, Fernando has no idea what he means. When Eduardo gives him the brush-off, he insists that he is 'an important guy', and in the Sky Room he automatically rises to take a bow in response to applause which is not meant for him. What makes others lose their indifference to the Astaire character is inevitably his dancing, and finally Robert forces Eduardo to watch the first substantial dance number of the film, an exhibition of skill utilising the tables and chairs of his office. Eduardo is not seduced; he bellows 'Excellent! Beautiful! But I don't want it!'. (The recollection of Menjou's various roles as a theatrical or film producer provides a background here.)

It may be noted that this is perhaps the first time in Astaire's roles that his solo dance can be understood to have failed in the purpose assigned to it. It is as if his professional role, lost and then found again in *You'll Never Get Rich*, might be deserting him – once more he needs to find his place as a dancer. This he does in his dance with Maria.

You Were Never Lovelier could be described in terms of its fairy-tale elements, as the story of four royal daughters and the difficult position of one of them. No noble suitor in the kingdom can tempt her, but her interest is awakened by the charms of a stranger, who might seem to be a peasant (he will claim this), but who is actually a prince in disguise. (There seems to be no single fairy-tale to which this narrative conforms, but the film includes such fairy-tale elements as awakening and disguise.)

Maria's beauty is such that she is instantly courted by almost all men – at Julia's wedding, she is suddenly surrounded by a chorus of adoring males in a scene very similar to one early in *The Strawberry Blonde*. In fairy-tale terms, she is under an enchantment (the metaphor that the film uses for this enchantment is the idea of being frozen, turned to stone or otherwise made inanimate, here given a neat modern twist by Hollywood – 'a personality like the inside of a refrigerator'). She seems to be barely awake. She dreams through Robert's singing 'Dearly Beloved' and is unable to respond to him in their first conversation, when she seems hardly to hear what he is saying. Later, she will have some difficulty in recalling where she has seen him before. But 'Dearly Beloved' has the force to pass from character to character, undoing this spell. Eduardo unconsciously picks on these two words as the opening motif of the anonymous love notes accompanying the orchids that he sends to Maria, and her response to them

Fun in a doorway: Robert and Maria in the final moments of the dance to 'I'm Old Fashioned'.

culminates in the sequence in which she dances a simple solo waltz across her room as (dubbed by the suitably luxuriant voice of Nan Wynn) she reprises the song, which we were unaware that she had truly heard.

The romance blossoms in a private Eden, the garden of the Acuña mansion in the late evening. The crucial ingredient of Robert's pitch is his claim to ordinariness. Nominally, it is part of his scheming with Eduardo – he has promised to disenchant Maria by stressing his lowly status. He tells her that he is a 'plain, ordinary guy from Omaha, Nebraska', which was Astaire's actual birthplace. In a sense, he is associating this ordinariness with being Fred Astaire. Maria responds by singing Johnny Mercer's lyrics to 'I'm Old Fashioned', and the couple slowly move into a dance duet. The mood, of looking backwards in time towards some imagined simplicity or innocence, is echoed in the relatively simple choreography of the dance. It ends with a couple of gags – the two figures gently colliding as they pass through a doorway and the flick of their feet with which the doors are closed – which recall such games in Astaire-Rogers numbers.

A second duet seems complementary to the first. In the Sky Room the next day, Maria finds Robert rehearsing 'Shorty George', a number with lyrics about Harlem, and they turn this into a modern dance duet. If the point of the first number was its privacy and 'old-fashioned' qualities, this public number seems to indicate the possibility of the modernisation and Americanisation of Maria. What it does not quite imply is the re-establishment of dance in a professional context. The number is offered as spontaneous fun rather than as a rehearsal for a performance, and there is no audience, no applause at its end.

The film still needs to chasten the presumptuous Eduardo for thinking that he understands women, and when the scheme is exposed Maria must forgive Robert for his part in it so that all the couples can be united. The action now returns to the house and garden of the family mansion, where it remains for the rest of the film. It is the occasion of a further celebration of marriage, in the form of the Acuñas' twenty-fifth wedding anniversary party. What now occupies the film is the problem of Maria's future – how to turn Robert's interest into a marriage proposal – which is resolved in a way that is determined by Hayworth's screen persona, so not easily or straightforwardly.

First, Maria humiliates herself and gambles with her own happiness by announcing to the assembled family that she and Robert are not in love, because 'everybody's trying to push him into marrying me'. This anxiety is about to be resolved when Robert takes her out into the garden, evidently in order to propose.

We see a medium shot of Robert and Maria strolling in the garden, their backs to camera. As they turn to face each other, Robert speaks: 'I just wanted to say . . .' He hesitates, and Seiter cuts to a medium close-up of Hayworth with the shadows of leaves falling on her bust. Finally Robert continues: '. . . gee, you're beautiful'. Was this what she wanted to hear, or what he originally intended to say before being overcome? Maria does not smile – her unchanged expression indicates that this response to her body is part of their problem. Robert quickly finds a way of acknowledging that at least he understands this. He asks her to turn away, explaining that he cannot concentrate when 'you look at me like that'. She turns to camera and smiles. When she turns back, Robert sings the title song which, of course, praises Maria's beauty. As the song ends, he faces her again but is still struck dumb, and she has to help him – she declares that she loves him and kisses

The humiliation of Maria in You Were Never Lovelier. *The company assemble in Eduardo's study.*

him. The last part of the sequence is a reprise and answer to the end of the 'I'm Old Fashioned' dance number, when he had failed to kiss her. One difference between the two is that the deep shadows that surrounded Maria in the earlier scene have now dissolved.

However, a more serious humiliation of Maria is still to come. The revelation that the notes and orchids were sent by her father takes place in front of the whole family. The sequence takes place in a room full of weapons, and the atmosphere is one of anger, when Eduardo's best friend, labouring under a misapprehension, supposes himself to have been cuckolded and wants to shoot him. To prevent this happening, Robert now explains the truth about the notes and his role. Maria's awareness of her body's power to arrest the gaze has turned into a lacerating sense of being publicly exposed to pitying looks: '. . . everybody knows now. I guess nobody had any way of knowing I'd make such a complete fool of myself.' Her costuming for these sequences underlines the idea of her as the subject of different kinds of look. She wears a gown (by Irene) quite unlike those worn by her sisters; the upper part of the front and the whole of the back is sheer net. The visual effect embodies the paradox of material that ought to offer at least a degree of concealment and protection having the effect of increasing a sense of nudity, of transparency and exposure. (There is much more to be said about this vital aspect of the presentation of Hayworth, the way in which her situation is expressed through her gowns and the lights and shadows that fall on them.)

The coda to the narrative is its happy ending. Robert courts Maria, showering her with orchids, but to no avail. Of course not – they are condemned as her father's tokens. Perhaps the orchid, always beautifully encased in its square, transparent box, is an image of Maria's entrapment, or enchantment, in the Acuña

Portrait of Hayworth in the final Irene gown for You Were Never Lovelier

household, so that Eduardo's choice was unwittingly pertinent. The final re-course is again to fairy-tale, to the figure of Lochinvar. Robert arrives in full armour, on his white horse. He makes to dismount and falls off. As he stands up, the carapace of metal falls perfectly away, revealing him in white tie and tails. The fairy-tale motif of a disguise at last magically dissolved is combined with elements that are part of Astaire's persona: falling to the ground, being prepared to look like a fool and, of course, the costume of white tie and tails.

Maria's costume at this point is equally expressive, a white net Irene gown in which the shadows of leaves that appeared in earlier images of her are now transfigured into embroidery. It is as if, in wearing such a gown, she triumphs over the shadows, or at least subdues them. As she comes to him and they go into the closing dance, she tosses him a finally unboxed orchid.

Alongside the problematic nature of Hayworth's persona, there is an uncertainty in the Astaire character in *You Were Never Lovelier*. His professional dance can find no context and falls away, and even the informal, spontaneous dance disappears in the latter part of the film. Song remains crucial, but after 'Shorty George' the role of dance is substantially over, apart from a brief social waltz at the party and the couple's triumphal dance at the very end, which lasts barely one minute. The uncertainty is also expressed in Robert's vacillation, his striking inability to stand up to Eduardo's pressure for him to abandon Maria. In the wedding anniversary sequence, he accepts Eduardo's arguments on this subject no fewer than three times. It is as if he is himself unsure of being worthy of Maria's love and is easily persuaded that there must be a better man for her. I have suggested that the male rival for the girl's hand in marriage has disappeared in this film or has been superseded by the Hayworth character's own problem with the response to her beauty. At the same time, the Astaire character experiences a growing sense of uncertainty as to both the relevance of his professional skill and his romantic role.

Robert, an apologetic Lochinvar.

THE SKY'S THE LIMIT (Edward H. Griffith, 1943)

When *The Sky's the Limit* was released in July 1943, there may have been an expectation that it would resemble Astaire's films of the 'thirties. It was a return to RKO, his first film with the studio since *The Story of Vernon and Irene Castle*, and contract players from the Astaire-Rogers cycle, Clarence Kolb and Eric Blore, appear in small roles. Unsurprisingly, the return brings with it credits that are links to Rogers. The producer was David Hempstead, who had been responsible for *Kitty Foyle* in 1940 and would make *Tender Comrade* with Rogers later in 1943. Both the 1943 films are photographed by Russell Metty and feature Robert Ryan as an American serviceman.

There was also a big shift in the casting of the leading woman. Joan Leslie might have been thought a lot closer to Rogers, another optimistic, uncomplicated young woman of the American city. Leslie's association with Americanness and her extreme youth are two points of similarity with Rogers of the 'thirties and contrast with Hayworth. The names of their respective roles are eloquent. As opposed to the casting of Hayworth, which explicitly or implicitly invokes foreignness (Nina Berona, Doña Sol, Maria Acuña), Leslie had starred as the American woman in prominent films celebrating the nation's culture and achievement – as Marcie Williams in *Sergeant York* (Howard Hawks) and as Mary in *Yankee Doodle Dandy* (Michael Curtiz), which won the Best Picture Oscars in 1941 and 1942 respectively. In 1942, she had played a teenage role in *The Male Animal* (Elliott Nugent), a comedy on the subject of freedom of speech in American academe. When Leslie made *The Sky's the Limit*, she was seventeen – an audience that had seen her earlier roles as a child would have had an idea, even if they did not know exactly, how young she was. Could her role in this film have been anticipated as that of a 'new' Ginger Rogers in the sense of a clear assertion of freshness, as if a young co-star could retrieve the mood of fun and streetwise confidence projected by Rogers in the 'thirties?

Such thoughts are prompted in part by James Agee's review of the film (*The Nation*, 4th September 1943, reprinted in *Agee on Film*, Grosset & Dunlap, 1969, vol.1, p.51) in which he writes of the 'charm and flow' of the first half hour, as a result of which 'I quite expected another *Top Hat*'. He goes on, 'I didn't get it', and the overall tone of the review is one of slightly puzzled disappointment. Bosley Crowther's *New York Times* review, which piqued Astaire sufficiently for it to be quoted in *Steps in Time*, is similarly reserved. Crowther writes that Astaire 'does one solo which is good, but a bit woe-begone and the rest of the time he acts foolish – and rather looks it – in his quick-fitting clothes'. Astaire's own comment in *Steps in Time* is that the film 'did not develop as a strong picture. It wasn't bad but it didn't come off as hoped for, receiving a very mixed press.'

The Sky's the Limit is a 'domestic front' war movie, a furlough romance, in which a love affair takes place in the shadow of the man's imminent departure on active service. Other examples are *The Shopworn Angel* (H.C. Potter, 1938) and *Waterloo Bridge* (Mervyn LeRoy, 1940), and the most famous is *The Clock* (Vincente Minnelli, 1945). Another stars Rogers: *I'll Be Seeing You* (William Dieterle, 1944), based on the radio play 'Double Furlough' by Charles Martin.

In *I'll Be Seeing You*, the narrative is constructed around a secret, unspoken shame – Rogers plays a convicted criminal on a Christmas furlough from prison, a fact that she fails to tell the young soldier played by Joseph Cotten at the point when they are casual acquaintances and becomes unable to tell him after they fall in love. The film ends with the disclosure of the secret and the survival of the bond. In representing the woman's situation as a form of imprisonment that is survivable, a sentence with an ending, the film is offering a metaphor for the situation of the wives of servicemen in wartime.

The Sky's the Limit is based around a whole series of secrets or deceptions. Fred Atwell (Astaire) is an aviator on furlough and in civilian clothes; he sees Joan Manion (Leslie), follows her into a night spot and then walks her home. He does not at first think of consequences; asked to explain himself, he will quote Cole Porter: 'It was just one of those things'. He does not tell her that he is a 'flying tiger'. Thus he knows, and she does not, that their time together is limited to a few days, a problem that can perhaps be addressed, but crucially he also knows that his departure will be for active service. His treatment of her has to take into account the strong possibility that he will die or be seriously maimed in action, a fact that can barely be borne, or addressed.

Joan assumes that Fred is not in the armed services, but never directly asks him why, perhaps imagining some shameful reason. Because none of this is articulated by the characters, the film seems unresolved – which may account for the puzzlement with which it was received. (A comparison here is with the clarity of *The Shopworn Angel*, in which the possible death of the soldier played by James Stewart is never disguised; the unspoken questions circulate around the woman.) *The Sky's the Limit* makes sense only if its unspoken understandings are adequately conveyed; some discussions of it as a minor, not particularly interesting film seem unaware of the unspoken aspects of its narrative.

Two sets of sequences show the development of the romance, and both culminate in a dance duet. Both are followed by sequences in which the possibility of Fred's death is implied, after the second of which comes the climax of the film, Astaire's solo dance, 'One for My Baby (and One More for the Road)'. The film ends with a coda which addresses but does not imply a resolution to the enigma at the centre of a furlough film, the couple's unknown future.

At the start of the romance, we see Fred's consciousness of time, of the shortness of his furlough, only as a kind of energy, a desire to speed up the progress of the seduction. When he has walked Joan home, he talks the suspicious landlady, Mrs Fisher (Elizabeth Patterson), into giving him a room in the same building. When Mrs Fisher advises him, 'try planning your life a day ahead sometime', he replies, 'No point in it. I may not be here. You may not be here, who knows?' – he is claiming his life to be no more and no less uncertain than Mrs Fisher's. In his desire to speed things up, he breaks into Joan's kitchen and prepares eggs and coffee for her; then there is a conversation with an older family man, a dock foreman, in which he claims that Joan is his wife and that the cause of her odd behaviour is pregnancy – the man advises him to give her a 'good bust on the nose'. (The use of the word 'screwball' here by the foreman and then by Joan may alert us to how much of this echoes *It Happened One Night*.)

After more play of this kind – a scene in a darkroom, a tussle with a recalcitrant apron – the seduction turns on what Fred can or should do in order to earn a living. Their bargain is that she will let him feed her that evening on the condition that he will apply to her boss for a job the next day. Joan's assumption that for

some unstated reason Fred cannot fight for his country is reinforced when for their evening out she takes him to the servicemen's canteen, and he gets in as her helpmate and as a civilian. The subject of what he can do continues. Speaking of Joan, the hostess of the club asks him 'Could you do anything with her?' and he replies 'Could I!' It is a prompt – the film now goes into the first dance duet, 'A Lot in Common with You'. This fine dance, which can be compared most obviously to 'I'll Be Hard to Handle' in *Roberta* and 'They All Laughed' in *Shall We Dance*, dramatises their relationship, starting with the couple sitting on the dance-floor steps and developing with her discovery of Fred's skill through the fun he gets from mixing 'mistakes' and perfect movements. At the end of the sung part of the number, doubt vanishes, and the rightness of the couple is expressed in the confident, synchronised tap routine that concludes it. (The film's awareness of what Hollywood stars were doing in wartime – entertaining servicemen – can be seen in its giving the couple their own first names and referring to their recent film partners in a gag about Cagney and Hayworth that is worked into the lyrics.) It seems plausible to assume that up to this point, about thirty-five minutes into the film, James Agee could have expected another *Top Hat*.

When the number is over, Fred is accosted by two men in uniform, his fellow aviators, Reg Fenton (Robert Ryan) and Dick Merlin (Richard Davies), whose smart patter contrasts with the mood of the preceding duet and brings with it the threat of exposing him as a fellow 'flying tiger'. Elements of the sequence suggest darker notes. The snake dance – Fred's solo on their small table, which is the price of Reg's silence – is presented as an exercise of power and a reminder of the threat

Opposite:
Wartime courtship.
Fred (Astaire) and
Joan (Joan Leslie) in
the darkroom of
Eyeful magazine in
The Sky's the Limit.

Right: Watched by
Reg (Robert Ryan),
an MP puts an end
to Fred's snake dance.

of height rather than as entertainment. As he climbs reluctantly on to the table, Fred the aviator says, 'It's dangerous up here.' The implication is faint and is modified by the way in which Fred takes over the dance and ends by enjoying himself, but it is followed by a much more direct image, of Fred putting his money on the table in an attempt to bribe Reg to leave him alone. Reg's reply contains several of the film's subjects – food, death, payment and time: 'Ah, what's money – just lettuce. We've got a date in the Pacific next week, and the Japs don't eat lettuce'. I have not emphasised enough how *The Sky's the Limit* works around the significance of money, both earnings and payment. This scene must be read against the times in the early part of the film when Fred uses cash to advance his plans (payment for the hamburger that is Joan's supper and for his week's rent to the suddenly friendly Mrs Fisher). It looks forward to the scene where he throws his money on the table at the end of 'One for My Baby (and One More for the Road)'.

In this sequence, Fred has been reminded of what he is and what his future may hold. His wooing of Joan falters or, rather, becomes confused. At the end of their evening together the couple discuss the possibility of happiness personified by Joan's other suitor, her boss Phil Harriman (Robert Benchley). When they part, there is a physical sign of this shift in Fred's intentions: he surprises Joan, who is waiting to be kissed on the lips, by kissing her cheek. The following morning he learns that his furlough is cancelled, and he must report for duty in 48 hours' time. This seems to clarify Fred's intentions, and in the next scenes he is clearly attempting to assist Harriman in his wooing of Joan.

These scenes are striking in that the two men are not competing for Joan, but both want her to have what she wants. (Again *The Shopworn Angel* is a reference point: The Astaire/Benchley/Leslie triangle here resembles that of James Stewart/Walter Pidgeon/Margaret Sullavan in the earlier film, the difference being that the events in that plot – Stewart marries Sullavan immediately before embarkation and dies on active service – have become fantasy or supposition rather than actuality.) Joan realises that she is in love with Fred, and the second half of the film begins, following the same trajectory as the first but now with Joan in pursuit and Harriman playing the enabling role. She proposes to Fred – still not understanding who he is or what he does – and they reprise in dance 'My Shining Hour', which Joan (dubbed by Sally Sweetland) had sung at the opening of the film. The difference between this dance and 'A Lot in Common with You' is caught in Joan's words, 'This is the kind of night that doesn't belong to your life. You could just do anything and it wouldn't count'. The number offers a private harmony and order that depend on the sense of temporary isolation from the social world.

Directly after this sequence comes a return to the social, a dinner honouring aircraft financier Harvey Sloan (Clarence Kolb). This is the equivalent of the snake-dance sequence in the first half of the film. It includes a comic Benchley routine – a speech introducing Sloan and his business, the point of which is a little unclear. Perhaps its function is to indicate that, since this kind of statistical reality is irrelevant to the hopes and fears of its audience, nobody appears to mind hearing it reduced to good-hearted gobbledegook. It throws into contrast

the character whose function in the narrative parallels that of the two aviators in the earlier sequence, but this time seems an even more unavoidable *memento mori*: the war widow who dedicates a plane to her husband's memory. Thus the movement between the two halves of the film is from Fred's awareness of the threat of his own death, to his being aware of Joan's possible suffering if he cannot make her abandon him.

This is the background to the conclusion of the sequence, in which Fred engages in a careful and deliberate impersonation of a self-obsessed neurotic. He tells Sloan (the only person in the film who asks why he is not in the forces) that he has been assessed as 'emotionally unstable' and insists to Joan that he has no character, throwing in for good measure an implication that he has a drinking problem. His impersonation is not perfect – it slips as he grows eloquent in telling Sloan the faults of his warplanes and in his coded response to Sloan's sarcastic comment, 'just when are you coming down to earth, young man?' (Fred replies, 'When it's all over, I hope', but Sloan does not pick up the implication.) The scene between Fred and Joan is unusual for Astaire in that he is portraying a man who despises himself. The problem with it is that (except insofar as this reading makes sense of the film), it finds no way of clarifying for us that the character is faking for Joan's sake. As she walks out of the dinner, we can read the confusion in Fred's face as reflecting his feeling of loss, but it could equally be read as part of the hopelessness of the character he is impersonating.

That all this was an act becomes a little clearer in the next sequence, in which Harriman and Fred have retreated to a bar. Harriman has discovered Fred's

Harriman (Robert Benchley) discloses his knowledge of Fred's identity as a 'flying tiger' in The Sky's the Limit.

identity, and this elicits from Fred an image that indicates how close his situation is to those encountered in *film noir*: 'I'm just walking a tightrope between some-where and somewhere else and I've got to walk it alone, understand? I got myself in over my head and I had to get out, that's all.' (Frank Fenton, one of the writers of this film, was later to be a contributor to the script of the quintessentially *noir Out of the Past*, Jacques Tourneur, 1947.) As Fred speaks these words, the Harold Arlen melody of 'One For My Baby' begins on the soundtrack.

The importance of 'One For My Baby (And One More For the Road)' is absolute. It acts as both reprise and summary. In the sung part of the number, Fred moves through the bar in which he bought Joan her hamburger to the swanky joint which was the setting of their first meeting and of their final parting. (This may be the chance result of RKO's small budget for sets, but it has its effect.) The number moves through despair (smashing a single glass, hurling his hat on the floor) to memory (a few bars of 'Shining Hour' and a few steps of dance with an imagined Joan), and this memory is a stepping stone to triumph. Finally the motif of height returns, as Fred answers his earlier dance on the canteen table by tap dancing on the empty bar, his bravura movement domin-ating this surface of classy glamour. He smashes the ordered, piled glasses – an image not of despair but of control, of dictating the point, perfectly included in the rhythm of music and dance here, at which violence is enacted and danger faced. The climax, on an exact musical cue, is the smashing of the bar mirror with a stool, an evocation of the brio of a hundred saloon fights in Westerns. We may say that dances like 'A Needle in a Haystack' in *The Gay Divorcée* and 'No

Strings' in *Top Hat* implied a future. Reversing the movement from solo to duet 'One for My Baby (and One More for the Road)' finds a role for solo dance which can express both an acknowledgement of the past – of the couple's duet – and a triumph over the present, over the possibility of loss.

There is only a little to be said about the film's coda. After unsuccessfully trying to comfort Joan, Harriman is confirmed as the enabler of the romance, sending her off to find Fred and allow the deception to be dissolved. There is a reminder that money is 'just lettuce' for these aviators (the scramble to pay the bill in the canteen), but almost the last significant scene in the film indicates that money can have value other than purchasing power. The importance of luck has been established earlier, through the symbol of the penny that Fred spotted on the pavement during his first walk with Joan which expressed his luck in meeting her on his leave: 'I couldn't be luckier than I am tonight' was the first compliment that melted her reserve. Now, as his plane warms up for take-off, he offers her the lucky penny and she returns the compliment, 'I've had all my luck.' He pockets it with the words, 'We need just a bit more.' The final shot is a cliché – Joan in close-up, her head raised to the sight of the plane, to the height that implies both Fred's vulnerability and his dominance of space.

My title for this chapter is taken from a moment in *Broadway Melody of 1940* in which George Murphy, uncertain of his talent and ability in the face of the Astaire character's constant tuition, cries to him, 'Why do you keep changing the steps?' The six films considered here express Astaire's inventiveness, his endlessly restive innovation. The decisive break with the Astaire-Rogers cycle in *Broadway Melody of 1940* is in the move away from emotional intensity and towards a different valuation of performance, which is worked out dramatically in the narrative of the film. The break is expressed by ending the film with an image of its three principals on-stage, taking a bow at the end of an occasion of professional performance. *Second Chorus* takes this further in that the climactic show in the film is an Astaire solo dance – but with an orchestra on-stage – offered as a triumphant public performance. The minimal love scene that follows demonstrates that although the Astaire character is now an assured success in love and in his profession, the image of the couple's dancing together is no longer a way of expressing their relationship to each other and does not end the film. If the Paulette Goddard character were entirely unable to dance, *Second Chorus* would work almost as well – it would lose only one small dance number from which nothing follows.

Unsurprisingly, given the directorial presence of Mark Sandrich, *Holiday Inn* dramatises the tension between the consummate professional and the intensities of emotional commitment that marked the Astaire-Rogers cycle. In terms of feeling, Bing Crosby and Marjorie Reynolds are playing the Astaire and Rogers roles here, and Astaire is continuing the pattern of his two previous films in acting the innovative, show-saving professional (as in his suddenly having to invent the 'Say It with Firecrackers' number). He can find a context for his dance in any of the milieux that the film shows us, but only once, in 'Be Careful, It's My Heart', briefly reminds us that the dance carries the possibility of changing a partner's relationship to him. *Holiday Inn* is remarkably successful in synthesising its two governing impulses. The lovers, bound by song rather than dance, are triumphant, but so is the professional performer, who again ends up on stage, with a former partner, who has been propelled (the film seems to acknowledge this by showing Lila being gently shoved onto the stage) back into the plot for him. All this is presented within a framework which claims another kind of professionalism, reminding us that conveying emotion and grace is the work of Hollywood.

It is in the two films with Hayworth that the ideal of the professional is challenged by positioning Astaire so that the importance of his public role and public skill is questioned. What connects the apparently different plots is the idea of someone who thinks of himself as an 'important guy' being in a situation – drafted into the army, or penniless in a foreign land – in which his reputation counts for little or nothing. The challenge to his self-esteem is more easily met in *You'll Never Get Rich* – a film set in America, where even an army training base still recognises a good morale-raising show – but the impulse expressed in the solo dance is now confined to the guardhouse. It is in the guardhouse, not on the stage, that we last see Astaire.

In *You Were Never Lovelier*, Astaire's sense of his own importance is overtly embattled and he has to cast off the mantle of the show-fixing, professional dancer and redefine his dance in terms of spontaneity and emotional openness. The whole film can be read as a dialogue between Astaire's 'importance' and his 'plainness' – his being, as he puts it to Maria Acuña, 'strictly from corn'. His final seduction of her turns on things that are very different from his dance: using the imagery of armour and weaponry as fun or disguise or play and falling off a horse wearing a costume in which it is quite impossible to dance.

This sense of not being an important guy is the link between the films with Hayworth and *The Sky's the Limit*. The description of himself in *You Were Never Lovelier* – 'I'm a plain, ordinary guy from Omaha, Nebraska, just an old-fashioned everyday mid-westerner' – becomes the moment in *The Sky's the Limit* when Fred asks Joan (the subject of the conversation being celebrity photographs), 'Couldn't I be the one who never gets his name mentioned, the one they call a "friend"? You know: "Ginger Rogers and friend"?'

The Sky's the Limit has a plot which gives Fred Atwell a reason to hide the identity as a 'flying tiger' that would make him seem important and to deny his (Fred Atwell's and Fred Astaire's) other form of skill, or importance, concealing it behind a mask of facetiousness. At the end of 'A Lot In Common', when the astonished Joan asks him where he learned to dance, he replies: 'Arthur Murray' (a highly successful chain of dance studios in the 'thirties and 'forties). Part of the shift from fairy-tale to the quotidian is expressed in the move from Hayworth to Leslie – a movement from a star whose beauty is understood as extraordinary, or 'difficult', to one whose beauty is shown as an enhancement of the everyday, one who we see getting up in the morning with her hair all over her face. (Joan's other suitor, Harriman, the proprietor of *Eyeful* magazine, is surrounded even in his last sequence by images of idealised or glamorised women). Fred and Joan personify the American democratic couple, the plain serviceman and his girl, not so far from the characters who will be presented by Robert Ryan and Ginger Rogers in *Tender Comrade* a few months later. Their dance comes across, not as professional performance but as spontaneous perfection ('A Lot In Common') and private expression of emotion ('Shining Hour'), the opposite pole from the conclusion of *Broadway Melody of 1940*.

CHAPTER FIVE

ON WITH THE DANCE
THE LATER 'FORTIES

Between 1944 and 1947, Astaire made two films directed by Vincente Minnelli, *Ziegfeld Follies* (1945) and *Yolanda and the Thief* (1946), and then *Blue Skies* (Stuart Heisler, 1946), after which he announced that he was retiring. In the same period, Rogers was more prolific, with six films. Of these, I shall look at four: *Lady in the Dark* (Mitchell Leisen, 1944), *I'll Be Seeing You* (William Dieterle, 1944), *Weekend at the Waldorf* (Robert Z. Leonard, 1945) and *Magnificent Doll* (Frank Borzage, 1945). (I have been unable to see *Heartbeat*, Sam Wood, 1946, and *It Had to Be You*, Don Hartman and Rudolph Maté, 1947.) Before the two careers touched again, Astaire made *Easter Parade* (Charles Walters, 1948), which can be seen as a preliminary to the final Astaire-Rogers collaboration, *The Barkleys of Broadway* (Charles Walters, 1949).

1. ASTAIRE IN COLOUR

Tender Comrade and *The Sky's the Limit* marked a point at which the careers of Astaire and Rogers were contiguous: both films were made at RKO in black and white, and their next films would be in colour. In both cases, the fact that they were filmed in black and white is appropriate to the kinds of setting – such as a California munitions factory and a canteen for servicemen – that are being represented. The films' leading characters are contemporary figures, in both cases an American serviceman and his lover, and the fact (*Tender Comrade*) or the possibility (*The Sky's the Limit*) of the death of the serviceman touches both couples.

Settings like those of *Ziegfeld Follies* and *Yolanda and the Thief* would not be easy to find except on a Hollywood tour. They may contain references to the world in which we live, but do not represent any part of it except, of course, what is created on theatrical stages or film sets. *Ziegfeld Follies*, which Astaire began immediately after *The Sky's the Limit*, was delayed in production and released after *Yolanda and the Thief*, in January 1946; it has three main contributions by Astaire to its revue structure, 'This Heart of Mine', 'Limehouse Blues' and 'The Babbitt and the Bromide'.

'Limehouse Blues' most sharply expresses the shift of setting from the previous films. It is not set in America but in the Chinese area of east London identified by the title. It is populated by figures who represent types of the exotic – the principal players (Astaire, Lucille Bremer and Robert Lewis), inhabitants of the Chinese demi-monde, are surrounded by London bobbies and pearly Kings

Above: Astaire and Bremer dance to 'This Heart of Mine' in Ziegfeld Follies.

Left: Johnny (Astaire) and Yolanda (Lucille Bremer) in costume for the 'Dream Ballet' in Yolanda and the Thief.

and Queens. The innovation here is that the woman is socially inaccessible to the man (it is implied that Bremer is a high-class courtesan and Astaire a penniless loafer). This situation can be overturned only in the willow-pattern dream world in which the couple dance together, located as the fantasy of the dying Astaire, who has been shot as he witnesses the robbery of a Limehouse curio shop. A further change from Astaire's previous films is in the type of dance: a move from an extension of ballroom dancing towards something analogous to a stage ballet. The change of emphasis is indicated by the ballet shoes worn by Bremer as opposed to the shoes with heels in which the woman dances in nearly all of Astaire's previous musicals.

Stanley Green in *Starring Fred Astaire* (pp.274-275) gives the origin of 'Limehouse Blues' as being the 'Beggar Waltz', which was originally performed with Tilly Losch in the last stage show in which Astaire appeared with his sister Adele, *The Band Wagon* (1931). Astaire is returning here to the stage work he did before his film career began. The same is true of 'The Babbitt and the Bromide', a sketch with the same title, music and lyrics as one performed by Fred and Adele Astaire in *Funny Face* (1927). While it offers a new pairing of Astaire with Gene Kelly, it is also a deliberate reference back, past the period with Rogers, to Astaire's most important early partner.

In 'This Heart of Mine', Astaire sings to Lucille Bremer the Arthur Freed/ Harry Warren song that he had released on record in 1944. The sketch has no earlier original, and the setting is much closer to the 'thirties musicals, a high-toned society affair in which Bremer plays a princess, Astaire a jewel-thief who cons his way in, sings and dances with Bremer (here wearing heels) until, as the ball winds up, he lifts her bracelet. She now offers him her necklace, and they dance off together. The character given to Astaire is less innovative than that given to Bremer – although this is the first time he overtly plays a lover as con artist, elements of this character can be found in his earlier roles. Bremer's total openness to the man's approach and seduction signifies her innocence, her lack of any context for his behaviour. The stolen and offered jewels can easily be seen as having sexual significance expressing a transaction in which virginity is threatened but can also happily be lost. Thus, the self-contempt of the man (for abusing a virgin's trust) melts into their mutual triumph (in her gift of her sexual innocence to him).

Other writers have noticed that similar characters and plot appear at feature length in *Yolanda and the Thief*, in which the mood of guilt, or self-contempt, affecting Johnny Riggs (Astaire) is emphasised by the innocence of Yolanda Aquaviva (Bremer). The setting is a country called Patria, which for narrative purposes must nominally be accessible by train from the United States, but otherwise is a world of exotic colour and design, characterised by a mood of continual celebration (birthday, homecoming, carnival, wedding), sexual innocence and harmony with nature. Here a dream-sequence ballet is, as it was in 'Limehouse Blues', an extension of an already exotic landscape. We are prompted to see Patria as connected not with other spots on the map, but with Hollywood. Aunt Amarilla (Mildred Natwick) looks hard at the Padre (Francis Pierlot) and asks, 'Were you by any chance in *Going My Way*?'. Perhaps the

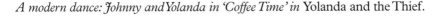

A modern dance: Johnny and Yolanda in 'Coffee Time' in Yolanda and the Thief.

Johnny (Bing Crosby), Jed (Astaire) and newcomer Mary (Joan Caulfield) in
Blue Skies.

sequence that is nearest to making a connection to an outside world, through the costumes and dance style of Astaire and Bremer, is 'Coffee Time', by far the nearest number in style to those of the previous musicals, a modern dance as opposed to a ballet. The eerie, insistently swirling pattern on the floor of the set may function here to preserve a sense of the otherness of the setting, which is not carried on this occasion by the dance itself.

Blue Skies returns to more familiar settings, opening in the theatres and night spots of New York and shifting to nightclubs in a number of American cities, but never leaving the United States. There are substantial similarities to *Holiday Inn*, the previous film to co-star Astaire and Bing Crosby. Both films contain a range of old and new Irving Berlin songs, and both plots deal with the rivalry of two evidently successful entertainers for the love of a young girl who is at the start of her career. The film was to have been directed by Mark Sandrich (who died suddenly nine days into the shooting), and the adaptation of the original story was by Allan Scott, who, among all his other connections to Astaire's and Rogers's work, had made an uncredited contribution to the script of *Holiday Inn*. However, the role of Jed Potter was apparently conceived for an actor called Paul Draper who was fired after a few days' work, and the material was doubtless reworked into its present form after the death of Sandrich and Draper's departure. This reworking may well have taken into account the fact that *Blue Skies* was thought of as Astaire's last film before his retirement, which is clear from his account of it in his autobiography (Astaire, p.282).

The starting point of *Blue Skies* seems similar to that of *Holiday Inn*. Newcomer Mary (Joan Caulfield) has to choose between Jed Potter (Astaire), who represents the lure of Broadway and a star career, and Johnny Adams (Bing Crosby), who tells her that 'a woman can be ambitious just to be a woman'. Echoing the 'White Christmas' sequence of *Holiday Inn*, the film finds a domestic setting in which Johnny can sing 'All By Myself' to Mary, and they end the song in harmony. But the difference between Johnny and Jim Hardy, the Crosby character in the earlier film, is hinted at even before he sings this number, when it becomes clear that he is selling his nightspot. Where Jim represented settling down, Johnny's creativity is locked into a compulsively repeated cycle of designing, building and selling nightclubs; the act of turning one concept for a nightclub into reality leads only to the imagining of another.

Architectural models pay an important part here, informing two crucial sequences. Visually they dominate the setting of Mary's unsuccessful proposal of marriage to Johnny in which he rebuffs her with the excuse of his lack of 'stability'. The couple do finally marry, and when, immediately after the birth of their first child, Johnny visits Mary in hospital, she is given a line about having had a baby that day, to which Johnny replies 'I've had one too', unwrapping his gift, a model of yet another nightclub.

The example of two mutually incompatible forms of gendered creativity here is part of a wider vision of the disparate energies and desires of the three principals. Mary is aware that her desire for Johnny is disastrous but beyond her ability to control or modify. When Jed asks her if she thinks Johnny is the right man for her, she shakes her head sorrowfully and replies 'No, but he's the only one'. Johnny has a sense of being the wrong man for her, knowing that he is unable to change his behaviour even as he protests his intention of doing so (which gives pathos to the assertion of 'Blue skies from now on' in the film's title song, as if one could, by singing, overturn the mutability of the weather). Jed, meanwhile, is unable to 'care very deeply for anybody'. His words describe Johnny, but they seem an accurate description of his own relationship with Mary, his awareness that his desire to marry her is oddly insubstantial, unconvincing even to himself. This ambiguous feeling evokes only a limited response in her, and although they are supposedly dance partners, we do not see them dance together after their brief initial number ('A Pretty Girl Is Like a Melody'). This void gives rise to what must be one of the bleakest passages in any of Astaire's musical films, in which, after Mary's divorce from Johnny, Jed describes his now imminent marriage to her: 'It's going to be a very small affair. I'm not even sure the bride will be there' (the background music here is a subdued rendering of 'Blue Skies').

Jed with the dancers in the lead-in to 'A Couple of Song and Dance Men' in Blue Skies.

There is a carefully played contrast with the film's minor couple, Johnny's sidekick Tony (Billy De Wolfe) and the singer Nita (Olga San Juan), whose apparent ease and warmth is an integral part of the film's vision. Their compatibility seems a matter of chance and good fortune, no more subject to their control than the unhappy relationships of the three principals. The film ends with a sequence in which Mary returns yet again, nominally to Johnny, but leaves with Jed on one arm and Johnny on the other. There is no evidence that anything between the three has changed, or could be different, and the prominence of Tony and Nita in the final minute seems to assure us that at least some stories – however accidentally – can still end on a clearly positive note.

On repeated viewing, *Blue Skies* seems an extreme film, depicting a paralysis in post-war American lives against a plethora of numbers by Irving Berlin (the poster for the film claimed 32 of them). The effect is to emphasise the sense of extremity, as if even the denseness and brilliance of the lyrics and music cannot solve the deadlock and lack of satisfaction at the centre of its plot.

In spite of any limitations that may have been imposed by Astaire's late entry into the film, his role can nonetheless be viewed as a development of his earlier work. The loss of confidence or lack of resolution in relation to the woman which was a threat in *You Were Never Lovelier* (*see* p.185) seems full-blown here: two of Astaire's three big dance numbers avoid presenting a significant couple. The first, 'Puttin' on the Ritz' is a bravura solo performance, with Astaire dancing

Jed dances 'Heat Wave' with Nita (Olga San Juan) in Blue Skies.

with images of himself, even though it occurs at exactly the point in the plot – Mary's triumph in her Broadway opening with Jed – at which a duet might have been expected. The other is the big dramatic climax of the narrative, 'Heat Wave', which Astaire dances not with Caulfield, but with Olga San Juan (with whom he has no substantial relationship in the film) as Caulfield watches from the wings. The most relaxed number is danced with another man, when Astaire and Crosby perform 'A Couple of Song and Dance Men'. Perhaps behind all of this was the idea of a final film. It is as if Astaire wished to make his exit from films as a solitary figure, rather than via a drama built around the image of a couple dancing together. The strange *Blue Skies* is an ending, marking the closing of a phase in Astaire's work. *Easter Parade* will be a radical departure.

2. ROGERS IN THE DARK: PUNISHMENT, IMPRISONMENT, YOUTH AND AGE

Lady in the Dark (Mitchell Leisen, 1944) is set in the editorial offices of *Allure* magazine, dubbed by one character 'a world of women', but in fact totally controlled by men. (No suggestion that *haute couture* clothing is chosen or purchased by women ever enters into the film – the only group to figure as consumers are 'the advertisers'.) As the editor of *Allure*, Liza Elliott (Rogers) exercises power over her staff, but she is also explicitly the person through whom a group of three men relate to this women's world. Kendall Nesbitt (Warner Baxter) represents the power of capital: he is a businessman who financially underwrote the setting up of the magazine and wants to marry Liza if he can negotiate a divorce settlement. Randy Curtis (Jon Hall) is a Hollywood star who poses for the magazine and also wishes to marry Liza; his physical presence reduces the women employees to near-idiotic (and thus comedic) concupiscence. Charlie Johnson (Ray Milland) is one of two men working for *Allure*; he wishes to replace Liza and become editor of the magazine, believing that jobs which confer power are the property of men and for a woman to have such a job is 'flying in the face of nature'. The other man working for *Allure* is photographer Russell Paxton (Misha Auer), who is coded as gay and is the only one of the four who shows no desire to assert power over Liza.

In the face of these pressures, Liza both dresses and behaves in a way that for the men of the film (particularly Johnson) defines her as mannish rather than feminine. That she is also deeply unhappy, anxious and depressed is hardly surprising, given her situation. But the film is not about that situation, or rather not directly. It overlays it, and in part conceals it, with another, psychoanalytic discourse. In other words, the possibility that Liza's feelings might be directly, or simply, produced by her current situation is ignored, and it is assumed without hesitation that the explanation for them must lie elsewhere.

The film begins with Liza submitting to the power of two more men: Dr Carlton (Edward Fielding) and his psychoanalyst colleague Dr Brooks (Barry Sullivan). (The script's opening line is of Dr Carlton giving an order to a woman.) Dr Brooks starts with a clear demonstration of power, insisting that he will accept Liza as a patient only if she submits to analysis there and then.

With the help of several dream and flashback sequences, the analyst duly comes up with an explanation for Liza's condition. We are made aware of her absolute love for her father – 'I . . . thought he was the most wonderful man in the whole world' – and the narcissism and indifference of her mother (under analysis, Liza recalls her mother flirting while she is trying to sing for her). These things having been established as the cause of Liza's condition, the analyst tells her that she has 'attempted to dominate all men'. She is advised to find a figure who will dominate her. Of the three suitors, Nesbit and Curtis abruptly prove weak at this juncture, leaving her to choose the unremitting dominance of Johnson – 'I've always had to win because I'm me', he remarks. Misha Auer closes the film by pronouncing that this is the end, the absolute end.

Through Auer, *Lady in the Dark* may perhaps register a sense of its own preposterousness, even of its deeply reactionary project, both in its presentation of women (and of men) and of its appropriation of psychoanalysis as no more

Liza (Rogers) dreams uneasily of marriage in Lady in the Dark.

than a tool to allow it to elucidate the patient's trauma in such a way that the advice can be to reimpose its conditions. This is not, incidentally, a comment on the stage show by Moss Hart, Ira Gershwin and Kurt Weill on which the film was based – the distance between the two is considerable. The stage material was rewritten by Frances Goodrich and Albert Hackett, who are given the writing credit in Leisen's film, but David Chierichetti, in his valuable book on Leisen (*Mitchell Leisen: Hollywood Director*, Photoventures Press, 1995), quotes the director in interview: 'The Hacketts got credit but their script was thrown in the waste-paper basket'. Leisen claims to have written the film himself on the basis of Moss Hart's 'original prompt copy'. Then again, the film was not released as Leisen shot it. Two numbers that had been filmed but were then cut by the producer, Buddy DeSylva, might have gone a little way to reduce the emphasis on male empowerment in the released version. These were 'Tchaikovsky', a major element of the stage success that was sung in the film by Misha Auer, and 'My Ship', an *a capella* number sung by Rogers in a high-school flashback.

Reservations about *Lady in the Dark* often seem to centre on the performance of Rogers, rather than on the film's project. The idea that Rogers was somehow not clever enough to 'understand' the film, or – outrageously – not mentally unhealthy enough for it (attitudes well presented in Chierichetti's discussion of responses to the film) seem to endorse the values of the film. The explanation that the actress is somehow psychically 'wrong' involves ignoring the disgraceful circumstances in which she is having to operate, at their clearest in the unredeemedly sexist and sadistic role of Charlie Johnson. Ray Milland, who played the part, subsequently commented that 'everybody thought *Lady in the Dark* was so wonderful at the time, but I always disliked it' (Chierichetti, p.190).

Rogers notes in her autobiography that *Lady in the Dark* was her first film in colour, and then tells us how little she liked it, a view evidently shared by almost all the Hollywood professionals involved, even though the film was a substantial commercial success. The decision to film in colour emphasised the glamour of *haute couture* and glossy magazine publishing (very different from the settings of Rogers's immediately preceding films), and the move into colour parallels that in Astaire's films with Minnelli. But the difference is that the exotic and glamorous here is always negatively conceived as troubling or threatening. This is not only true where we might obviously expect it, in her first two dreams, which are nightmares, but also in the set design of her waking world, for example in the clouded, fragmented mirror over the mantelpiece in her apartment and the oppressive bed-head in her boudoir. Even the offices of *Allure* are decorated with portentous artwork rather than, say, fashion stills – the icon next to Liza's desk, the print of Manet's *The Fifer* on the wall. The only exceptions to this atmosphere are the circus dream-sequence and Rogers's performance of 'Jenny', but this song, no longer preceded in the film by the 'Tchaikovsky' number to which it had been a response in the stage show, seems to have little to do with the narrative that surrounds it.

Rogers's other film released in 1944 was filmed in black and white and more clearly relates to her work earlier in the 'forties. *I'll Be Seeing You* (William Dieterle) is a variation on the furlough movie in which the furlough granted to the woman is from imprisonment rather than warfare – during it, she falls in love. The film ends with the couple parting to wait, not for the man's return, but for the woman's release. Rogers plays Mary Marshall, a woman who has served three years of a sentence for manslaughter, and her lover is Zachary Morgan (Joseph Cotton), a soldier who has returned from fighting as a result of 'neuro-psychiatric' disorder, in other words, shell-shock. (A similar structure is used in *Remember the Night*, which was directed by Leisen in 1940 and written by Preston Sturges. In this, the criminal woman is played by Barbara Stanwyck and the lover by Fred MacMurray. Both films have the couple make their way to a benign American family milieu away from the big city, both are set in the Christmas/New Year season, and both end with the male lover seeing the woman return to prison.)

I'll Be Seeing You resembles *Tender Comrade* in that the hero is an ordinary American soldier – Zachary is a sergeant, not an officer. The social status of the benign family here can be established by contrasting Mary's Aunt Sarah (Spring Byington) and Uncle Henry (Tom Tully) with another American family in wartime, the Hiltons in *Since You Went Away* (John Cromwell, 1944). (Both films

Mary (Rogers) and Zachary (Joseph Cotten) have Christmas dinner with Mary's uncle and aunt in I'll Be Seeing You.

were produced by David O. Selznick and made within a short time of each other.) The difference is the absence of a servant like the Hiltons' maid Fidelia (Hattie McDaniel). The Marshalls emerge as an idealised plain, small-town American couple, conscious of the narrow range of their lives and ambitions. This is expressed in an early conversation in which Sarah tells Mary that 'I accepted what I thought was second-best and made that do', as opposed to the dreams of glamour that are glossed by Mary as 'palaces and rainbows'.

The Rogers character in *I'll Be Seeing You* is now depicted as being distinctly older she has been than hitherto, and this is established by also casting a star whose age was part of her image for a contemporary audience – the seventeen-year-old Shirley Temple, in the role here of Mary's cousin (and the Marshalls' daughter) Barbara. Superficially this seems similar, say, to the casting of Kim Hunter as the newly married wife and Rogers as the slightly older woman in *Tender Comrade*. In the earlier film, however, the characters were merely at different stages of essentially similar lives – the gap between them was purely chronological. In *I'll Be Seeing You*, traumatic experience has made Mary fundamentally different from a young girl such as Barbara.

The experience is recounted in flashback by Mary to Barbara. Familiar elements of the Rogers persona are involved: the orphaned daughter who becomes a secretary/typist to a man who represents for her a privileged world. Invited by this man to what she believes is a party, Mary is a self-made Cinderella who buys her own evening gown and imagines his 'high-class friends'. That Dieterle never shows us the man's face places him as the anonymous product of Mary's fantasies of palaces and rainbows, of herself as Cinderella. In his apartment, he attempts to rape her and is accidentally killed in the ensuing struggle.

Despite the fact that she is sexually untouched and that her imprisonment is evidently unjust, Mary clearly regards herself as somehow tainted, unsure of her right to the kind of future represented by the domesticity of the Marshalls' kitchen. In the course of the film, her feeling for an ordinary American serviceman displaces fantasies of elegant apartments and rich friends. Immediately after the sequence in which the attempted rape is seen in flashback, Mary and Zachary take a lakeside walk outside town. The American nostalgia for freedom and space is associated with childhood as the couple find a tiny, model boat by the lakeside and link their fantasies to those of its owner: 'Some little kid probably owned that boat, thought it could take him all the way around the world and back.' The finding of a lost object, a battered relic of childhood, comes to symbolise the acceptance by the couple of the distance that now exists between them and the young. The film ends with Mary and Zachary celebrating their possession of each other by acting as if they were still children, throwing stones at a lamp post.

The significance of the shift represented by *I'll Be Seeing You* becomes clear in the relatively insubstantial *Weekend at the Waldorf* (Robert Z. Leonard, 1945). A point of Rogers's pre-1944 film persona had been her youth, her sense of optimism and promise, the idea of being able to start over, but her later roles deal with her age by looking back at her youth, recalling the lost or frozen promise of a time now past. The role of Mary Marshall in *I'll Be Seeing You* shows the Rogers character as having crossed the divide between youth and maturity and being able to cross back only in imagination or ritual. (Dieterle touches on this in the lakeside sequence with some business about a sign indicating a border that may not be crossed. It is literally a state line that presumably relates to the conditions of Mary's parole, but is more important for its symbolic significance than for its literal meaning in the plot.)

Rogers accepted her role in *Weekend at the Waldorf* in preference to a number of other projects at a stage in her career when she was able to capitalise on the commercial success of *Lady in the Dark*, apparently turning down the Olivia de Havilland role in *To Each His Own* (Mitchell Leisen, 1946) for it. Her role is the first of several in her later career in which she plays a major star of stage or screen, but elsewhere a much younger woman is also present, one who cannot yet claim the fulfilled ambition that is expressed in the stage of life reached by the Rogers character. Irene Malvern (Rogers) is set against Bunny Smith (Lana Turner) in *Weekend at the Waldorf*, Dinah Barkley (Rogers) against Shirlene May (Gale Robbins) in *The Barkleys of Broadway*, Beatrice Page (Rogers) against Sally Carver (Pat Crowley) in *Forever Female* (Irving Rapper, 1953) and Carlotta Marin (Rogers) against Nanny Ordway (Peggy Ann Garner) in *Black Widow* (Nunnally Johnson, 1954).

In *Weekend at the Waldorf*, the keynote of Irene's sense of herself is loss. Her life has consisted of 'school – theatre – pictures'. She complains, 'I've never lived . . . nothing has ever happened to me'. To an enquiry as to whether she is engaged, or married, or divorced, she replies with the words, 'I work'. Her sense of loneliness and fatigue is given depth by the background to the film, which is an overt reworking of *Grand Hotel* (Edmund Goulding, 1932), a point it takes care to stress. Behind Rogers's role lies that of Greta Garbo in the earlier film and more broadly the myth of one of the greatest (unmarried) stars and the price paid for making art in film.

It begins with a clear reminder of lost youth, when an invitation to attend the marriage of a childhood friend, Dr Robert Campbell (Warner Anderson) reduces Irene to tears. A series of farcical mistakes and chances now throws her together with Chip Collyer (Walter Pidgeon). When the doctor's nervous young bride-to-be (Phyllis Thaxter) calls on her, she establishes her status as the older woman (and one with no romantic interest in Dr Campbell) by producing Chip and claiming him to be her husband. This imitation of married life supplies Chip with a strategy. As the Campbell wedding ceremony takes place, Chip 'marries' Irene, slipping a ring (a cigar-band) on her finger. His miming of what it might be like to be married continues with a sequence which stresses Chip's domesticity. They quarrel, part, 'divorce' (issuing a public statement to make it clear that they were not married), encounter each other again and fall into an embrace.

Well played by Rogers and Pidgeon as amiable light comedy, *Weekend at the Waldorf* relates back to much earlier Hollywood cinema. The proposition that romance requires a kind of trickery, as if finding yourself behaving as if you were married constituted a route to actual marriage, takes us back yet again to the comedy of remarriage and (say) to *It Happened One Night*.

The Irene/Chip plot is counterpointed throughout the film with another plot strand of the *Grand Hotel* format – at no point do the two strands touch directly. This concerns the hotel stenographer Bunny Smith (Lana Turner) having to choose between romance with a young soldier Captain James Hollis (Van Johnson) and a job as 'confidential secretary' to a corrupt businessman, Martin X. Edley (Edward Arnold). This is loosely similar to narratives that had been played by Rogers earlier, with the class distinction between the two suitors inverted – Hollis is an officer and Edley a self-made man.

By the end of the film, these interleaved strands have suggested a distinction between the two women which goes beyond age. In marrying Hollis, Bunny is, conventionally enough, constructing a future, represented by a world which they have discussed – bee-keeping in Jasmine, California. (There is a sub-plot about Hollis's medical condition, which means that she can be said to have given him a new lease of life.) In marrying Chip, Irene is at least in part constructing a past; she wants to be able to behave as if she has always been married to him, using intimacy to overcome her sense of remoteness, or loss. The gesture with which the film ends expresses something of this quality, the cosy parting of an older married couple. We see Irene waving to Chip's departing plane, and this cliché of wartime romance (as at the end of *The Sky's the Limit*) is reinflected as intimate domesticity. The camera's point of view, directly outside the plane's window, abolishes the sense of distance and speed as we watch Chip lighting a cigarette with Irene's lighter.

In Frank Borzage's historical biopic, *Magnificent Doll* (1945), Rogers plays Dolly Payne, who becomes the wife of President James Madison. As in *Kitty Foyle*, the Rogers chracter has a choice between the good American democrat, James Madison (Burgess Meredith), and the glamorous but corrupt American aristocrat,

Aaron Burr (David Niven). Burr is presented negatively as a sensualist and a dandy. His attitude towards ordinary Americans is made clear in a sequence in which he claims to be accompanying Dolly to the theatre but actually takes her to an inn, where he watches voyeuristically when a fight breaks out: for him, the behaviour of the common people is just a form of theatre. Against this Madison is posed as an intellectual with a background of benign southernness rather than northern repression, who plays at, or ironises, the idea of the dandy. A sequence in which Madison and Dolly give each other presents makes clear that fashion is a kind of joke, or act, to them.

What is striking, given the increasingly negative treatment of the American aristocrat that I have traced through a number of Rogers's films, is the role of Burr after Dolly has chosen to marry Madison. Up to this point, he has been represented negatively, but it is also clear that he has considerable sexual charisma. After the marriage, this disintegrates into a kind of psychosis, in which he believes that Dolly is acting out of sexual interest in him when her motives are wholly political, as in the sequence when she comes to him alone in order to dissuade him from running for the presidency. At this point, his own political scheming is inextricably bound up with an erotic fantasy of recapturing Dolly – 'when my day comes, I'll find some way to have you at my side'. The aristocrat is beginning to degenerate into a madman.

The main narrative of *Magnificent Doll*, which begins with Dolly meeting Madison and Burr, is preceded by a short voice-over introduction and then a sixteen-minute prologue. We see the return of John Payne (Robert H. Barrat), Dolly's father, to Virginia after the revolutionary war. Giving an account of a battlefield conversion to Quakerism and a promise to a dead friend, he disposes of his plantation, moves his family to Philadelphia and arranges Dolly's marriage, totally against her will, to his friend's son, John Todd (Horace, later and better known as Stephen McNally). Borzage establishes Dolly's sense of entrapment, loss and violation by these men – 'I've missed part of my life because you and my father took it away from me' – and the intensity of John's feeling for her. We see the slow growth of Dolly's feeling for John through their sexual rapprochement and the birth of a son, but she still refuses to admit to her husband that she loves him. Philadelphia is evacuated after an outbreak of fever, which kills the child, and strikes down John, who lies dying near a small bridge at the edge of the city. We see Dolly fight her way through foliage, rushing to the bridge. She reaches him and speaks her love to his dead body – the intense back-lighting of Rogers as she crouches down helps make it the most emotional moment in the whole film.

John Payne and John Todd both believe in their inalienable right to assert power over Dolly, respectively as a father and as a passionate male lover. In the main body of the film, this attitude is represented by Burr, in sharp contrast to Madison, who specifically rejects it. (The clearest example of this comes when Dolly asks him to decide whether or not she should visit Burr in prison, and he leaves it up to her.) Given the film's political commitment to portraying Burr as villain/madman, the erotic relationship to the patriarchal, controlling (northern) male has to be expressed in the prologue, and its relevance to the main part of the film is underlined by the resemblance between the actors playing Todd and Burr. The echoes of *Kitty Foyle* – the melodrama of the birth and death of the

Visited by Dolly (Rogers) in his prison cell in Magnificent Doll, *Aaron Burr (David Niven) believes that she is still in love with him.*

son and the intensity of the emotion directed towards the child's father – no longer have a place in the main body of the film and are assigned to the prologue. Nevertheless, *Magnificent Doll* could be said to re-enact the equivocation at the heart of *Kitty Foyle*, the concern that the intensity associated with an implicitly older form of sexual order cannot be equalled by the more prosaic equivalents in a modern, democratic America, here with a further turn of the screw, in that at the moment of greatest intensity the man in the older, less democratic couple is dead.

Dolly's past life is central to the meaning of *Magnificent Doll* even though John Todd is mentioned at length only once in the main body of the film, during Dolly's Sunday morning stroll with Madison. The point of their conversation is Dolly's placing of her (finally) intense relationship with Todd in the past and anticipating marriage to a man who 'wants you to be a part of his plans, his ambitions, and his work'. (The words are Madison's but Dolly seems to accept them by noticing that Burr does not fit this description). In *Kitty Foyle*, the choice between democrat and aristocrat remains unresolved until the last few seconds of the film. In *Magnificent Doll*, it has become a progression, as an older woman marks a movement from a remembered erotic intensity to the marriage of partnership that she is about to enter.

What Rogers's films of this period have in common is the subject of confinement. In *Lady in the Dark*, Liza's entrapment is insisted on as psychic. In *I'll Be Seeing You*, there is literal imprisonment, and in *Weekend at the Waldorf*, there is the star's imprisonment by her image, her fame locking her away from ordinary life. In *Magnificent Doll*, confinement is in the film's prologue, in the shape of Dolly's enforced marriage. Each film contains the image of a woman revisiting the past in order not to repeat it, but to understand it, not to forget it entirely but to find a perspective from which it can be viewed. Both *Lady in the Dark* and *I'll Be Seeing You* turn, in their different ways, on a recollection, presented in flashback, of a specific time in the past of the Rogers character. In *Weekend at the Waldorf*, there is instead a figure from childhood, who recalls Irene Malvern's past to her. We might see her marriage to Chip as a way of addressing the sense of loss – her lost past life – that Dr Campbell represents for her.

3. EASTER PARADE (Charles Walters, 1948)

In the films made by Astaire between 1940 and 1946, there is little, if any direct allusion to the partnership of the RKO musicals, but they remain a presence, an unspoken background, largely a matter of implicit contrasts and divergences. (The reference is strongest in the dance to 'Be Careful, It's My Heart' in *Holiday Inn*. The only specific mention of former partners in these films is the use of Hayworth's and Rogers's names in the dialogue of *The Sky's the Limit*.) *Easter Parade*, on the other hand, is widely felt to refer directly to Astaire and Rogers.

The narrative opens with the breaking up of the well-established and successful dance team of Nadine Hale (Ann Miller) and Don Hewes (Astaire), because Nadine wants to appear solo. Don then employs a new partner, Hannah Brown (Judy Garland), whom he attempts to turn into a copy of Nadine. This is disastrous, but he goes on to find an entirely different and successful style of performance with her. Meanwhile Nadine has also found success. We see these achievements in Hannah's and Hewes's performance of 'A Couple of Swells' and Nadine's performance of 'Shakin' the Blues Away'. It appears – both to the audience and to the two women – that Don must now choose between Nadine and Hannah, but Hannah realises that she can simply claim Don, and she proceeds to do so.

Put at its simplest, Nadine's role stresses the dominance of dance over song and Hannah's the dominance of song over dance. Of course, both Miller and Garland sing and dance, but the balance in performance is very different. Nadine's numbers involve song, but do without it for long stretches. In 'Shakin' the Blues Away', the song functions as an introduction to Miller's solo tap, and is then given to a chorus as she continues her dance. In 'The Girl on the Magazine Cover' she dances as a man sings to her, and her final reprise of 'It Only Happens When I Dance With You' is danced and not sung. Nadine never sings without also dancing. Hannah sings solo without dancing three times, in 'I Want to Go Back to Michigan', her reprise of 'It Only Happens When I Dance With You' and 'Better Luck Next Time'. Her song numbers with Don ('I Love a Piano', 'Snooky Ookums', 'A Couple of Swells') are choreographed, but the couple's dance would be of little moment if detached from the song. Only in 'When the Midnight Choo-Choo Leaves for Alabam' ' is there any significant dance.

*'I know just the dress to wear it with.' Johnny (Peter Lawford) brings Nadine
(Ann Miller) a present in* Easter Parade. *Don (Astaire) looks on.*

Easter Parade records a progression in which the Astaire character's attachment shifts from one woman to another and from one kind of performance to another, from waltzing with Nadine at the beginning of the film to strolling with Hannah at the end. This is strikingly unusual for Astaire, though it is partly explained by the fact that Astaire had replaced the injured Gene Kelly after rehearsals had begun but before shooting. Almost invariably in his previous films, Astaire is unattached, footloose and fancy-free before he meets the single central woman, whether she is played by Rogers, Powell, Hayworth, Leslie or Bremer. If there is a second major female role, the character has no attraction for Astaire and is firmly attached to a second man, as in the double romance plots of *Roberta* or *Follow the Fleet*. A partnership does break up at the beginning of *Broadway Melody of 1940*, but it is with another man. A closer comparison might be with *Holiday Inn*, in which Lila (Virginia Dale) is Ted's existing dance partner, then the partnership breaks up, and there is another woman to whom the Astaire character is seriously attracted. But in *Holiday Inn*, nothing turns on the difference in the styles of song and dance represented by the two women. The absence of stylistic change there is expressed in the ease with which Lila is reinserted into the plot at the end of *Holiday Inn* to give Ted a partner for the final number. *Easter Parade*, then, is the first film in which the Astaire character is put in a position to make a choice between two women.

Nadine's relationship to Don is one of professional partnership, which she has, we learn, already dissolved before the film's narrative begins. Her interest in

'I think you'll do.' Don proposes to train Hannah (Judy Garland) as his new dancing partner in Easter Parade.

Johnny (Peter Lawford) seems to be mostly as a classy escort when one is needed. Elsewhere, she appears solo both on stage and off it, and walks in the Easter Parade with her Russian wolfhounds. She seems indifferent to the possibility of marriage, or perhaps sees it as damaging to her solo ambitions. Her interest in being seen as part of a couple is strictly a matter of public performance, as when she dances in the Follies with Don towards the end of the film. On the other hand, Hannah is, from her first number, 'I Want to Go Back to Michigan', strongly identified with domesticity, marriage and retreat from the city, and this is continually reflected both in her numbers and in the nature of her role in the film. (Richard Dyer's account of Garland in his *Heavenly Bodies*, Macmillan/British Film Institute, 1987, pp.141-194, suggests a number of possible ways in which this relates to Garland's screen persona in general.) It is even possible to think of *Easter Parade* as a reworking of *Holiday Inn* with the genders of the roles changed. The character associated with song and clear ambitions for the married state, Bing Crosby, is now the one played by Judy Garland. The dancing star with grand professional ambitions and an ambiguous view of marriage, Astaire, is now the character played by Ann Miller. The figure posed between them – Marjorie Reynolds in *Holiday Inn* – is now Fred Astaire.

Two apparently romantic sequences, one with Nadine and one with Hannah are built around 'It Only Happens When I Dance with You'. The first is the opening duet, set in Nadine's apartment, where she is trying to break the news of the offer that will terminate the partnership. Don responds first with romantic words and then with dance, seducing her slowly into a waltz in the cluttered room as he sings the lyric. The pivotal moment comes as he opens the doors to the terrace – the anticipation is of a release into space and speed as the dance goes into its second movement. But Nadine mimes refusal, and the dance concludes in the room. The tone of the whole number is difficult to read. Miller's performance seems successfully to combine the notes of her attraction to Don and her concealed knowledge that she has already severed their tie. Whether or not there is something of the sexual con-man about Astaire's performance, there is at the very least a possibility of reading it as a bid to manage Nadine, a piece of poised seduction to make her yield to his will. (This is certainly suggested early in the sequence by his watching her speculatively as she moves away from him, and also by the unusually forceful kiss with which the dance ends. Within a minute, he will find out that his efforts were not so much unsuccessful as pointless, that Nadine has already signed her new contract.)

The reprise of this song, this time without dance, takes place in Don's apartment, when he has invited Hannah to dinner to celebrate their new contract with Dillingham. The sequence begins with a row, when Don's professional obsessiveness (all he wants to talk about is new dance movements for their act) exhausts Hannah's patience, and she denounces him as no more than 'a pair of dancing shoes'. At the climax of the row, she shuts her eyes and challenges him to tell her what colour they are. He answers by kissing her raised mouth. However beautiful the gesture, it contains an element of trickery. As she opens her eyes in response, of course, he can answer her question. Her mood entirely changed, Hannah sits at the piano and sings, 'It Only Happens When I Dance with You'. Don sits beside her, but facing away from the piano – at first we see his serious, contemplative attitude, then the set-up changes so that we see Hannah's face as the song reaches its climax, and the back of Don's head. It is over this image that Don delivers his line 'Why didn't you tell me I was in love with you'. This is followed by the embrace (only Hannah facing the camera) with which the sequence ends.

Easter Parade seems conscious of a difficulty that is not solved by the transferring of Don's affections from Nadine to Hannah. The first sequence reminds us that however publicly successful Nadine and Don may be, their relationship has no interior, no adequate private dimension, which puzzles or disturbs Don even as he tries to manipulate Nadine. The second sequence seems not so much to rebut the first as to complement it – now emotion, intensity and interiority are all present, but concentrated in one party. The cinematography stresses Garland's quality of singing to, or for, herself (as in some of Garland's most famous numbers – 'Have Yourself a Merry Little Christmas' as well as 'Somewhere Over the Rainbow' and here 'Better Luck Next Time'). The indirect phrasing of Don's declaration of love seems nicely appropriate. Neither of the two relationships seems successful in negotiating the border between private and public faced by a couple who perform together, one trapped in public display (Don and Nadine), the other in private, one-sided intensity (Don and Hannah).

Performing behind a mask: Don and Hannah as 'A Couple of Swells'.

In Don's big production number for the Dillingham show – 'Steppin' out with My Baby' – there is a single reaction shot of Hannah watching from the wings. Garland's strangely gauche gesture of admiration might simply be a slip in acting, but it might also be deliberate, carrying the suggestion that this absolute, confident public exposure is beyond her comprehension. The act is followed by an Astaire-Garland clown number, 'A Couple of Swells', the point of which is both the intimacy of the performance (just the two principals and simple effects,

Don and dancers in 'Steppin' Out with My Baby' in Easter Parade.

as opposed to the big number that has preceded it) and the security of performing behind a kind of mask, presenting a disguised self to the gaze of the world. The number attempts to dissolve the limits of wholly private and wholly public worlds that the film explores. It contrasts with Nadine's 'The Girl on the Magazine Cover' number in the Starlight Room, in which the adorned self (represented by a variety of models), gazes out of her 'frame' at the audience.

In the closing sequence of *Easter Parade*, Hannah and Don stroll along Fifth Avenue in the parade, a couple of swells. The business of Hannah's present to Don in his apartment of a beribboned top hat has moved into the performance of 'Easter Parade', and the couple take the song with them, so to speak, as they walk out into the street. A positive reading of this might be that what is due to the public realm (the stars' self-display, the photographers, the high-fashion clothes, the idea of marriage embodied in the production of a ring) can be successfully combined with the intimate, with private knowledge or joke (the ribbon that has just been unwound from Don's hat, the business of not knowing your left from your right hand when putting on a wedding ring.) The couple are both in costume and in disguise.

It is possible to see *Easter Parade* as some kind of *film à clef*, in which Don's and Nadine's split is related to Astaire's most famous professional parting. Jane Feuer puts it directly: '*Easter Parade* alludes to Astaire's efforts to get a new partner after the break-up with Rogers' (Feuer, p.116). This would seem to equate Rogers with Nadine, but its further implications are puzzling, as the Garland role does not appear to resemble any of Astaire's partners. What is absent after the end of the Astaire-Rogers RKO films is the effort of teaching a newcomer. Rather the opposite is true – the partners mainly stay in the tradition of enhanced ballroom dance and tap, and are all wonderfully proficient. (Think of Astaire's comment about taking dancing lessons by watching Eleanor Powell in *Broadway Melody of 1940*.)

There is a connection, but it is not simply that of one narrative imitating another. Two specific references invoke the memory of Astaire and Rogers's work. The first is in the performance of 'Beautiful Faces Need Beautiful Clothes', a compendium of fluffed dance movements in which Hannah wears an ostrich feather dress that visibly sheds during the number. Commentators have been quick to pick up the reference to the problems with feathers in filming the 'Cheek to Cheek' number of *Top Hat*. The second reference is in the final Follies number, the last reprise of 'It Only Happens When I Dance With You'. Allowing for the differences between a colour and a black and white image, Nadine's dress, a white gown melting into colour below the knee, seems evocatively like Rogers's for 'The Continental' in *The Gay Divorcée*. The connection is also evident in the choreography of Nadine's dance with Don. The final pose (Astaire with both knees bent facing Miller, her facing him with her arm outstretched) which John Mueller has described as 'distinctly unromantic' (Mueller, p.284) is surely a (deliberately?) awkward attempt to assume a pose associated strongly with Astaire and Rogers in *The Gay Divorcée* and used, for example, on covers of its sheet music.

It is easy to accept that Nadine and Don represent an unsatisfactory version of Astaire and Rogers in *The Gay Divorcée*. The Follies dance, even apart from its function in the plotting of the film, is arguably wooden, and the whole narrative underlines this point. But the film is also asking us to compare Hannah and Don with Astaire and Rogers. The 'Beautiful Faces' number clearly refers us to the gag numbers in the RKO cycle, the ones built around mistakes, such as 'I'll Be Hard to Handle' in *Roberta*, or 'I'm Putting All My Eggs In One Basket' in *Follow the Fleet*, but it is as if the fun of making mistakes has somehow leaked away, leaving only the embarrassment.

The crucial point here is that the references to earlier work involve Don with both Nadine and Hannah. I suggested in discussing *Follow the Fleet* that the strength of Astaire and Rogers was their ability to achieve both intimacy and drama, represented respectively in that film by 'I'm Putting All My Eggs in One Basket' and 'Let's Face the Music and Dance'. *Easter Parade* can be read as a commentary on Astaire and Rogers in being aware that the modes that they once successfully synthesised have now separated and have to be presented by two couples, neither of which can fully embody both. (A small note of imbalance in both couples is that the teams are called by the first name of the woman and the surname of the man: Nadine and Hughes, Hannah and Hughes. But try the sound of 'Ginger and Astaire'.)

The nearest approach to synthesis in *Easter Parade*, and by common consent a high-point of it, is 'A Couple of Swells'. The style of its performance is quite unlike that of any Astaire-Rogers number and surely recalls the other crucial partnership, that of Fred and Adele Astaire. So perhaps the film, with its 1912 setting and reliance on many early Berlin songs, is less about progression than about evocation of past achievements in Astaire's career. *The Barkleys of Broadway* will apply this note of contemplation and reprise directly to the Astaire-Rogers partnership.

4. MORTALITY AND PERFORMANCE: THE BARKLEYS OF BROADWAY (Charles Walters, 1949)

The most commonly quoted aspect of the production background to *The Barkleys of Broadway* is that the film was written as a vehicle for Astaire and Judy Garland to capitalise on the success of *Easter Parade*, that Garland was too unwell to work and that Rogers replaced her during rehearsals. It seems that although the song and dance numbers were revised in the light of the casting of Rogers, the Comden and Green script received, in John Mueller's words 'only minimal alteration' (Mueller, p.288). It is possible to look at the script with Judy Garland and *Easter Parade* in mind, rather than Rogers.

An established show-business partnership in song and dance, an obvious progression from the plotting of *Easter Parade*, is haunted by a doubt on the part of the woman about the cost of her success. Formed by her association with her older husband/teacher, she has lost a sense of what she might have achieved without him. (One might recall the moment in *Easter Parade* when Astaire insensitively tells Garland: 'I told [Nadine] I could teach any girl in the world to dance as well as she could'. The quality of Garland's delivery of her reply 'And you did', takes in the degree to which she feels Astaire's words as a negative comment on her individuality.) A man of around the woman's own age now appears and offers her a chance of a different kind of career, the keynote of which is the image of a young woman both breaking away from the older generation (her parents) and astonishing it (the judges at the Paris *conservatoire*) with her intense, revelatory self-expression. This forms the climax of the play, *The Young Sarah* [Bernhardt], in which we see the woman's triumph. She discovers that her achievement is still moulded by her older partner, who has taken care to tutor her in disguise (a telephone line and a fake accent). Convinced by this proof of his love for her – and of her value – she returns to him. Woven into the material is something about the cultural status of Broadway, a suggestion that an anxiety as to the value of 'musical comedy' compared to 'the theatre' can be solved by discovering that you can be a success in both, which enables you to return to the former.

Had Astaire made the film with Garland, the disparity of age between the man and the woman, implicit but never explored in the Astaire/Garland/Lawford triangle in *Easter Parade*, could have been explicit. The woman's breaking up of the partnership would then have been a way of putting herself in the position of both acting and beginning a new career, a star being born. This could have traded on Garland's quality of offering solo performance that was able to galvanise material and transfix an audience. Perhaps it would already have been true in 1949 that whatever she might have recited to the dumbstruck judges (and the audience) in *The Young Sarah*, the unspoken reference would have been to 'Over the Rainbow'. Such speculation is worthwhile because *The Barkleys of Broadway* is clear in its purposes for only part of the time, and some aspects seem to work awkwardly, to have been wrenched out of their original context.

In the film as we have it, Astaire and Rogers are not just a married couple, but one where the marriage is not recent. Their quarrels are not revelations, but games they play. It is clear, for example, that the argument in the taxi taking them to the party thrown by Millie Belney (Billie Burke) is familiar to both of

*Above: Josh (Astaire)
and Dinah (Rogers)
in the 'Swing Trot'
number, used as a
background to the
credits sequence of*
The Barkleys of
Broadway.

*Left: marital games.
Dinah offers to let
Josh punish her.*

them in form, if not in the local detail that prompts it. The comments of their friend Ezra Miller (Oscar Levant) also tell us that their fighting is routine and well-known in their circle. The sequence in their bedroom and bathroom after they return from the party confirms that quarrelling has become a form of domesticity, of familiarity. Finally, and perhaps most importantly, the length of their history is underlined by their physicality, the ways in which these opening sequences of the film register the physical changes which mark off the Astaire and Rogers of 1949 (fifty and thirty-eight years old respectively) from the figures of a decade earlier.

This point is addressed almost before the film has begun, in the 'Swing Trot' number that is danced as a background to the credits. It is one of two numbers in the film which Rogers dances in a dress that displays her shoulders, and we see what Arlene Croce calls 'a muscular thickness in [Rogers's] back and arms . . . the body of an athlete, not of a dancer' (Croce, p.176). In one way or another, a number of writers on the film observe this change in Rogers (fewer seem to feel called on to comment on any change in Astaire). The film makes no attempt at disguise here, as if the passage of time and the concomitant physical changes were one of the first things that needed to be established.

In the sequence in the Barkleys' home, the physical business which accompanies the marital game-playing includes Dinah Barkley (Rogers) brushing out her hair and then wearing it down. In the party sequence, we have seen Dinah in a sheath dress and with her hair in a tight bun. Now we see her in deshabille, to establish the sharp contrast between her appearance for the admiring public and her relaxed look here. This is no longer just a matter of clothes, but of effort, of working on the ageing body. (The film briefly shows a commonplace image of a woman keeping her body in condition, as we hear Dinah counting the strokes as she brushes her hair.)

The conclusion of the game-playing is Dinah's request to Josh Barkley (Astaire) that he punish her for having thrown something at him by hitting her with a shoe. As she waits, eyes closed, he kisses her (an oblique borrowing from *Easter Parade*) and goes into the number which ends the sequence, 'You'd Be Hard to Replace', which is first sung by Josh and concludes with a few very simple dance moves by the couple, muffled by their cumbersome dressing gowns. No breaks occur between these activities – the pair are just moving through different kinds of fun and pleasure. This contrasts with another established couple's dance in private, Don and Nadine's 'It Only Happens When I Dance with You' at the start of *Easter Parade*. There the performance of the dance is evidently at odds with the cramped space. In 'You'd Be Hard to Replace', the dance moves suit the tiny area, accepting the domesticity of the place rather than challenging it – as natural as walking across a room or turning over in bed.

The next two numbers extend our view of this long-standing harmony. 'Bouncin' the Blues' is presented as a rehearsal number and is connected to the previous sequence by the detail of Rogers still wearing her hair down; its point is the rapport expressed in the presentation of perfectly synchronised tap (in which it can be compared to 'The Boogie Barcarolle', Astaire's first danced number with Hayworth in *You'll Never Get Rich*).

These qualities appear in public in 'My One and Only Highland Fling', the one full number that we see that is part of the Barkleys' show. As a dance it is minimal, a matter of a synchronised stroll and a little tap, but the number is a fine example of Rogers's skill in performing the business of listening to a song. Here her repeated attempt to catch the Astaire character's eye, and eventually the attempt to make him kiss her (again with her eyes closed, but this time he kisses her on the forehead) connect to the games we have seen earlier. The offended husband role adopted for the purpose of the earlier quarrelling is now turned into that of a dour Scotsman, and both are observed by Walters with a glee that springs from the underlying rapport.

Rogers's age is marked by a contrast with another, much younger woman – a recurring element of her later films. Here the possibility of being supplanted is apparently real, in that chorus girl Shirleen May (Gale Robbins) is introduced as an understudy for Dinah's role in the show. However, Shirleen has no effect on Josh and Dinah: she is an irrelevance, of no professional interest and of no sexual interest to Josh. When the couple quarrel seriously, it is not over Shirleen; her lack of importance is shown by the simple device of having Josh and Dinah repeatedly misremember her name.

The playwright Jacques Barredout (Jacques François) is a similar age to Shirleen. However, his interest in Dinah is explicitly that of a suitor and, like earlier rivals for the hand of the girl in Astaire's work, he is both foppish and not American, a characterisation that goes back to the Erik Rhodes roles in *The Gay Divorcée* and *Top Hat*. This is, though, the first time in any of Astaire's films that the rival is a much younger man, offering Dinah both the opportunity to play a young woman on stage and to associate herself by marriage with the younger generation. While this is set up in the plotting, Dinah herself is never seen to have an interest in Barredout except in his role as her director. (At the moment when she should be savouring her triumph in his play, she is checking the telegrams and flowers for word from Josh.) Through Shirleen and Barredout, we see that neither Josh nor Dinah is interested in the idea of a younger sexual partner.

They quarrel and part over her desire to play Sarah Bernhardt in Barredout's play, in which she fails until coached by Josh (who pretends to be Barredout by imitating his accent), then succeeds brilliantly. She learns that the voice on the telephone was Josh and returns to their old apartment. Explanations follow, and their behaviour returns to its previous pattern. They exchange lines about his horrified state, embrace and go into the dance that dissolves into the film's final production number, 'Manhattan Downbeat'.

Some writers on the film have argued that what we are watching is a reprise of the professional history of Astaire and Rogers. A typical account is that we are shown the partnership split up by the woman's desire for a solo career as a 'serious' actress, and that after making 'Ginger Rogers pay a ritual penance for having deserted Fred Astaire' (Feuer, p.100), the couple are reunited. My difficulty with this reading is that the kind of career represented by the figure of Sarah Bernhardt, young or old, does not immediately seem to have much to do with Rogers's work in the 1940s. A much clearer parallel to Rogers is Nadine in *Easter Parade*. Nadine's 'Shakin' the Blues Away', the sequence in *Easter Parade* structurally parallel to the performance of Barredout's play here, is closer to earlier Rogers – say, to 'The Black Bottom' in *Roxie Hart* – than anything in *The Young Sarah*. For the plot of *The Barkleys of Broadway* to be read as reprising the stars' history, one has to accept that the figure of Bernhardt operates only at a very general level, to stand for 'seriousness'.

A further puzzle is the one scene from the first night of the play that we are shown, Sarah Bernhardt's (Dinah's) audition recital to the judges at the *conservatoire*. It is offered as a moment of unambiguous triumph, both in the response of the audience in the theatre and in terms of Josh's role as her teacher/lover. But we cannot believe in it. Even if we accept that inspired performance overwhelms the judges, the decision to convey this by having Rogers declaim the Marseillaise feels like an error and is compounded by having her speak the lines in French (the other girls in the scene speak their audition pieces in English). That her accent was a problem – to my ear it has an unfortunate affinity with her fake Scottish accent from 'My One and Only Highland Fling' – is recorded by John Mueller, who comments that 'MGM studio heads considered replacing it with something in English, at least for distribution in French areas' (Mueller, p.298). (Perhaps Comden and Green knew all this. Although the plot takes Dinah's triumph seriously, there is a larger frame in which the writers invite us to share their sense of the difference between the felicities of musical comedy and their feeling that this piece of 'legitimate theatre' is pretentiously serving the myth of the discovery of female genius by men sitting in judgement.)

The importance of Bernhardt to an understanding of Astaire's and Rogers's final film together is clearer if we relate it to the meaning of the quarrel between Dinah and Josh. Carefully contained within the comic mode of the film, it is the subject of mortality. In the opening sequences, the couple play a game in which Josh acts the hypochondriac and Dinah alternately the indifferent and concerned listener. Josh half-seriously claims that he has caught a cold waiting in the snow for Dinah when she first met Barredout, then that he has concussion from a blow on the head. Such moments are part of their mild, familiar forms of amusement with each other. In the light of this, the sequence at Millie's country house, to which she has invited the principals for the weekend to celebrate the completion of Barredout's play, is pivotal. It appears to be about to repeat the

Dinah faking illness in The Barkleys of Broadway. *Josh and Ezra (Oscar Levant) are taken in.*

pattern, for again Dinah is talking to Barredout while Josh meets with bad weather, this time rain rather than snow. But now Dinah is stretched out on the sofa pretending to be ill. Comically (for us) the tables are turned as Josh is all concern, his own soaked state forgotten. It is when he discovers Barredout's note and learns that Dinah's sickness was only an act that the serious quarrel follows. The marital pastime in which the threat of illness is Josh's property has been usurped, and he has found himself responding to an acted image of illness.

A reference in the country-house sequence to *Camille* alludes to the fact that many of Bernhardt's famous leading roles – for example, those in *La Dame aux Camélias*, *Jeanne d'Arc*, *Cléopâtre*, *Hamlet* and *Théodora* – involved an extended death scene for her character. Indeed, her fame might be thought to turn on the representation of the descent into death. Implicitly what Josh is unable to face is not so much Dinah's desire to act in 'serious' drama or to play young Bernhardt, but the subject of mortality. (Youth might have been a more substantial issue had Garland played the part.) Not only has Dinah borrowed his comic role of invalid, but in contemplating playing Bernhardt she has redefined it, opening a window on to a world in which the performance of illness and death is a public spectacle, not a private game.

That the subject of mortality lies behind the couple's split and reconciliation is confirmed by the exchange which follows the revealing of Josh's deception. He moves instantly back into the role of the man who can treat his own death as a comic turn:

Josh: Why, you know that I almost walked into the East River?
Dinah: No!
Josh: I almost shot myself!
Dinah: No!
Josh: I almost jumped off that roof...
Dinah: Why my poor darling, you might have almost killed yourself!
Josh: I know!

A few moments later, Josh tells Dinah that they will have 'nothing but fun set to music', as they move into the final number. This could be thought of as putting death back where it (almost) belongs, or belongs for these musicals, as a gag, and an intuition of loss which is countered by dance.

Ideas of death and culture come together in the performance of 'classics' and involve the character of Ezra, played by the pianist Oscar Levant. Early in the film, as the first party sequence draws to a close, Josh and Dinah are asked to perform a number, but they decline, as they are already preoccupied with quarrelling over Barredout. Ezra steps into the breach. After some business in which he sits at the piano ignoring suggestions from the floor, he plays Aram Khachaturian's 'Sabre Dance'. The significance of the choice is that it sets up the idea of the performance of something currently popular, relatively contemporary in composition (the Sabre Dance, from Khachaturian's ballet *Gayane*, was composed in 1942) and firmly rooted in classical traditions. (A suggestion from one of the partygoers was George Gershwin's 'Rhapsody in Blue'.)

Ezra's second appearance at the piano is at a hospital benefit performance which he has tricked the estranged Josh and Dinah into attending. Before they go on stage, Ezra and the MGM orchestra perform something which we will pre-

Celebrating the past: Josh and Dinah reprise the Gershwins' 'They Can't Take That Away from Me' in The Barkleys of Broadway.

sumably have no difficulty in accepting as a classic, Tchaikovsky's *Piano Concerto No.1*. (We hear about six minutes of extracts, interrupted when the camera cuts away to the quarrelling couple.) This might seem a random or inessential sequence, but its purpose is to contextualise what follows.

Ezra acknowledges the applause that greets his performance with the words: 'I'm touched, the piano is touched, and [*with a glance heavenwards*] Tchaikovsky is touched'. What follows is the one number imported into the film from the 'thirties Astaire-Rogers cycle: Astaire sings and dances with Rogers to the Gershwins' 'They Can't Take That Away from Me'. Like the Tchaikovsky, this number is an established classic by a composer who is no longer living and invokes a past era. By 1949, the distance from the world of the 'thirties Astaire-Rogers musicals had been emphasised by the deaths of both George Gershwin in 1937 and Jerome Kern in 1945.

Astaire and Rogers are offering a performance which deliberately refers in several ways to the past, to the cycle at its height. The words and music are borrowed from the score of *Shall We Dance*, released a few weeks before Gershwin's sudden death at the age of thirty-eight. In the choreography, the pattern of the dance follows the drama of seduction in the great Astaire-Rogers duets. And surely the logic behind the unusual dressing of Rogers in white is to recall the world of black-and-white film. The concession to Technicolor was a changing colourwash on the backstage curtain, but the dress shows as white throughout the number, an anomaly sufficient to draw a comment from Rogers in her autobiography: 'A white dress in a color film is supposedly outlawed . . .' (Rogers, p.255).

The sequence may look back to the past, but it also acknowledges the present, reframing a number that was not danced in its original version, so exploring new possibilities for it. And there is the awareness of ageing expressed, as in

'Swing Trot', through the image of Rogers in an off-the-shoulder dress, and subtly present even in the tone of the dance itself. John Mueller, in his finely detailed description, describes it as having 'a studied awkwardness that is built in' (Mueller, p.296). Quoting the past points up the years that have passed, as evidenced by the two bodies. What distinguishes the performance is the clarity with which this is acknowledged.

'They Can't Take That Away from Me' relates to the peaks of the Astaire-Rogers cycle. The background to the number is the memory of two sequences of genius which share its preoccupation with dance and the passage of time – 'Let's Face the Music and Dance' from *Follow the Fleet* and the last section of *Shall We Dance* (plus 'Never Gonna Dance' from *Swing Time*, if the end of dance can be taken to be the end of life). The film invokes those highpoints, and in presenting to our eyes the older Astaire and Rogers, gives them added resonance.

This forms a framework for understanding *The Barkleys of Broadway*, which does not, however, need to be claimed as one of the great films of the cycle. At its centre is the idea of performance in time, of presenting material that has been and will be rendered differently, better or worse, on other occasions in the past and the future. All of this acknowledges that alongside delight and confidence (and vitality) stand error and risk (and mortality). In the films of Astaire and Rogers, we can find this inseparability sufficiently represented and properly embraced.

I will end with two further reflections on the film. The first is inspired by a pratfall gag from 'My One and Only Highland Fling', the last one in the couple's dance career together. Astaire and Rogers have sat down together on a prop stump in the pasteboard 'Scotland' set, and the lyric has become a patter of exchanged lines about previous suitors. As this ends, it rises to what might be a romantic line: Astaire sings 'I'm not having any but you' on a rising note, and stands up. This causes the stump to tilt, depositing Rogers so that she sings the first words of her chorus 'When I went out dancing . . .' from her tumbled position on the ground. It is a tiny reminder of one quality of Astaire and Rogers that goes back as far as *Flying Down to Rio*, the sense of a couple with their feet on the ground, accepting their subjection to gravity because they know how they can deploy it in the great passages of their dance.

Compare this with 'Shoes With Wings On', Astaire's only solo dance number in *The Barkleys of Broadway*, which is performed after Josh and Dinah have had their serious quarrel. The use of special effects, here the disembodied dancing shoes, follows a trend in Astaire's solos in his immediately preceding films (the concealed spring which magically returns his stick to his hand in 'Puttin' On The Ritz' in *Blue Skies*, the use of slow-motion in the solo dance section of 'Steppin' Out With My Baby' in *Easter Parade*). The contrast with the duet indicates something of the meaning of the two forms of dance. In the solo dance, imagination, aided by the technology of film, briefly frees the dancer from the human limitations of weight or time. In dance by the couple, we see our world and what it is possible to make of its spaces – in the light of such movements we can find that our earthbound nature is made acceptable, even delicious.

Equality and affection: matched costumes in 'My One and Only Highland Fling'.

BIBLIOGRAPHY

This bibliography lists books and articles that are directly referred to or quoted in the text.

Agee, James *Agee on Film: Volume One: Reviews and Comments*, Grosset & Dunlap, Universal Library Edition, New York, 1969

Altman, Rick *The American Film Musical*, Indiana University Press, Bloomington, 1987

Altman, Rick (editor) *Genre: The Musical* (BFI Readers in Film Studies Series), Routledge & Kegan Paul, London, 1981

Astaire, Fred *Steps in Time*, Da Capo Press, New York, 1981

Capra, Frank *The Name Above the Title: An Autobiography*, The Macmillan Company, New York, 1971

Carney, Raymond *American Vision: The Films of Frank Capra*, Cambridge University Press, Cambridge, 1986

Castle, Irene (as told to Bob and Wanda Duncan) *Castles in the Air*, Doubleday, New York, 1958

Castle, Irene *My Husband*, Charles Scribner's Sons, New York, 1919

Cavell, Stanley *Contesting Tears: The Hollywood Melodrama of the Unknown Woman*, University of Chicago Press, 1996

Cavell, Stanley *Pursuits of Happiness: The Hollywood Comedy of Remarriage*, Harvard University Press, Cambridge, Massachusetts, 1981

Chierichetti, David *Mitchell Leisen: Hollywood Director*, Photoventures Press, Los Angeles, 1995

Croce, Arlene *The Fred Astaire and Ginger Rogers Book*, Galahad Books, New York, 1972

Dickens, Homer *The Films of Ginger Rogers*, The Citadel Press, Secaucus, N.J., 1980

Dyer, Richard *Heavenly Bodies: Film Stars and Society*, Macmillan (BFI Cinema Series), London, 1987

Dyer, Richard 'Resistance through charisma: Rita Hayworth and Gilda' in *Women in Film Noir*, edited by E. Ann Kaplan, British Film Institute, London, 1980

Erenberg, Lewis A. *Steppin' Out: New York Nightlife and the Transformation of American Culture 1890-1930*, University of Chicago Press, 1984

Eyman, Scott *Ernst Lubitsch: Laughter in Paradise*, Simon & Schuster, New York, 1993

Feuer, Jane *The Hollywood Musical*, Macmillan (BFI Cinema Series), London, 1982

Freud, Sigmund *Civilization, Society and Religion* (Pelican Freud Library Vol. 12), Penguin Books, Harmondsworth, 1985

Frye, Northrop *Anatomy of Criticism: Four Essays*, Princeton University Press, 1971

Frye, Northrop *A Natural Perspective: The Development of Shakespearean Comedy and Romance*, Harcourt, Brace & World, Inc., New York, 1975

Green, Stanley *Starring Fred Astaire*, Dodd, Mead & Co., New York, 1973

Jasen, David A. *Tin Pan Alley*, Omnibus Press, London, 1990

Matthiessen, F. O. *The James Family*, Alfred A. Knopf, New York, 1947

Morley, Christopher *Kitty Foyle*, Grosset & Dunlap, New York, n.d. (c.1940)

Mueller, John *Astaire Dancing: The Musical Films*, Hamish Hamilton, London, 1986

Rogers, Ginger *Ginger: My Story*, Headline, London, 1991

Thomson, David *Showman: The Life of David O. Selznick*, André Deutsch, London, 1993

Warner, Marina *From the Beast to the Blonde: On Fairy Tales and Their Tellers*, Vintage, London, 1995

Wood, Robin 'Democracy and Shpontanuity: Leo McCarey and the Hollywood Tradition' in *Film Comment*, Volume 12 No.1, January/February 1976

The American Film Institute Catalog of Motion Pictures Produced in the United States was consulted in the preparation of the filmography. The relevant volumes are those for the 1930s and the 1940s, both published by the University of California Press, Berkeley, in 1993 and 1999 respectively.

FILMOGRAPHY

This filmography covers Astaire's and Rogers's work from *Flying Down to Rio* to *The Barkleys of Broadway*. I have consulted the books by Croce, Dickens, Green and Mueller, and the relevant volumes of the American Film Institute's *Catalog of Motion Pictures produced in the United States*. Full details of all of this material are given in the bibliography.

I have not included the two careers before and after the period of collaboration. These fall outside the range of this book. The most complete listing of Rogers's work outside the period I cover can be found in Dickens, and Green comprehensively covers Astaire's stage work and his later musical and non-musical films, as well as providing a discography and listing of radio and televison work.

It is difficult to establish a precise order for the films, especially at the points when Astaire and Rogers were working separately. The dates before the titles below are the copyright dates, but I have also included details of when the films were shot. Running times are also not easy to pin down, as films were cut after preview and in some cases may have been released in slightly differing versions. I have simply recorded variant running times where I have found them listed.

29 December 1933
FLYING DOWN TO RIO

RKO Radio Pictures. Shooting: 23 August - 6 October and late October - 7 November 1933. New York premiere 21 December 1933. 80/89 minutes.

Directed by Thornton Freeland. Associate Producer: Lou Brock. Executive Producer: Merian C. Cooper. Lyrics: Edward Eliscu and Gus Kahn. Music: Vincent Youmans. Screenplay: Cyril Hume, H.W. Hanemann, Erwin Gelsey, from a play by Anne Caldwell, based on a story by Lou Brock. Dance Director: Dave Gould. Assistant Dance Director: Hermes Pan. Art Directors: Van Nest Polglase, Carroll Clark. Costumes: Walter Plunkett. Musical Director: Max Steiner. Arrangements: Eddie Sharpe, Bernhard Kaun, R.H. Bassett and others. Director of Photography: J. Roy Hunt. Special Photographic Effects: Vernon Walker. Editor: Jack Kitchin. Sound Recording: P.J.Faulkner, Jr. Music Recording: Murray Spivack. Sound

Cutter: George Marsh. Miniatures: Don Jahraus. Make-up Artist: Mel Burns. Research Director: Elizabeth McGaffey. Associate Director: George Nicholls, Jr. Stills Photographer: John Miehle, Kent Fox.

With: Dolores Del Rio (Belinha de Rezende), Gene Raymond (Roger Bond), Raul Roulien (Julio Rubeiro), Ginger Rogers (Honey Hale), Fred Astaire (Fred Ayres), Blanche Friderici (Aunt Titia), Franklin Pangborn (Mr Hammerstein), Eric Blore (assistant hotel manager), Walter Walker (Sr de Rezende), Etta Moten (singer at casino), Roy D'Arcy, Maurice Black, Armand Kaliz (Greeks), Paul Porcasi (Mayor of Rio), Luis Alberni (casino manager), Clarence Muse (Haitian golfer), Betty Furness, Lucille Brown, Mary Kornman (Belinha's friends), Reginald Barlow (Alfredo), Eddie Borden, Jack Rice, Ray Cooke, Jack Good (musicians), Wallace MacDonald (pilot), Gino Corrado (messenger), Harry Semels (sign poster), Movita Castenada, Alice Gentle, Hazel Hayes (singers), Martha La Venture (dancer), Sidney Bracey (chauffeur), Harry Bowen (airport mechanic), Manuel Paris (man at aviators' club), Adrian Rosley (club manager), Alice Ardell (maid), Francisco Maran (waiter), Julian Rivero, Pedro Regas (billboard workers), Howard Wilson, Margaret Mearing, Helen Collins, Carol Tevis, Eddie Tamblyn, Rafael Alvir, Barbara Sheldon, Douglas Williams, Alma Travers, Juan Duval, Eddie Boland, The American Clippers Band (band) and The Brazilian Turunas (casino orchestra).

Musical/Dance Numbers: 'Music Makes Me' sung by Rogers. 'Orchids in the Moonlight' sung by Roulien. 'The Carioca' sung by Moten and two uncredited singers, danced by Astaire and Rogers, chorus, with the Brazilian Turunas. 'Orchids in the Moonlight' (reprise) sung by Roulien, danced by Astaire and Del Rio. 'Music Makes Me' (reprise), danced by Astaire. 'Flying Down to Rio', sung by Astaire, danced by flying chorus. Not used: 'The Guest is Always Right', 'The Streets of Rio'.

Chance at Heaven and *Rafter Romance* (both William A. Seiter, 1933) appear listed after *Flying Down to Rio* in some filmographies, but both were made and released earlier in 1933 and are therefore not included here.

26 March 1934
UPPER WORLD

Warner Brothers - Vitaphone Pictures. Shooting ended 13 January 1934. 70/74 minutes.

Directed by Roy Del Ruth. Production Supervisor: Robert Lord. Screenplay: Ben Markson, based on a story by Ben Hecht. Director of Photography: Tony Gaudio. Art Director: Anton Grot. Editor: Owen Marks. Sound Recording: Gordon M. Davis. Musical Director: Leo F. Forbstein. Costumes: Orry-Kelly. Make-up Artist: Perc Westmore. Assistant Director: Lee Katz.

With: Warren William (Alexander Stream), Mary Astor (Mrs Hettie Stream), Ginger Rogers (Lilly Linder), Theodore Newton (Rocklen), Andy Devine (Oscar, chauffeur), Dickie Moore (Tommy Stream), J. Carrol Naish (Lou Colima), Robert Barrat (Commissioner Clark), Robert Greig (Caldwell, butler), Ferdinand Gottschalk (Marcus), Willard Robertson (Captain Reynolds), Mickey Rooney (Jerry), John M. Qualen (Chris, janitor), Henry O'Neill (banker), Sidney Toler (Officer Moran), Frank Sheridan (Inspector Kellogg), Nora Cecil (housekeeper), Lester Dorr (steward), Wilfred Lucas (captain), Cliff Saum (sailor), William Jeffrey (Bradley), Edward Le Saint (Henshaw), John Elliott (Crandall), Armand Kaliz (Maurice), Milton Kibbee (pilot), Marie Astaire, Joyce Owen, Lucille Collins (chorus girls), Jay Eaton (salesman), James P. Burtis, Henry Otho (policemen), Douglas Cosgrove (Johnson), Guy Usher (Carter), Clay Clement (medical examiner), James Durkin, Monte Vandergrift, Jack Cheatham (detectives), William B. Davidson (city editor), Edwin Stanley (fingerprint expert), Howard Hickman (judge), Frank Conroy (attorney), Tom McGuire (bailiff), Bert Moorhouse (court clerk), Sidney De Grey (foreman), Harry Seymour (passerby).

On some prints the title appears as one word: *Upperworld*.

Rogers's persona as a working-class New Yorker had been firmly established by a number of her early 'thirties films. Here she is a chorus girl with whom an American businessman (William) has an affair as a result of being neglected by his wife (Astor). The film is unusual for Rogers in being decidedly dark. Her ex-boyfriend (Naish) attempts blackmail, and the Rogers character dies in an act of sacrifice, killed by a bullet meant for the businessman. The inconvenient memory of the affair is completely erased in the final reconciliation between husband and wife.

4 May 1934
FINISHING SCHOOL

RKO Radio Pictures. Shooting: 24 January - 21 February 1934. 70/73 minutes.

Directed by Wanda Tuchock and George Nicholls, Jr. Executive Producer: Merian C. Cooper. Associate Producer: Kenneth McGowan. Screenplay: Wanda Tuchock, Laird Doyle based on a story by David Hempstead. Director of Photography: J. Roy Hunt. Art Directors: Van Nest Polglase, Al D'Agostino. Editor: Arthur Schmidt. Sound Recording: John L. Cass. Musical Director: Max Steiner. Music Recording: Murray Spivack. Costumes: Walter Plunkett. Make-up Artist: Mel Burns. Still Photographer: John Miehle.

With: Frances Dee (Virginia Radcliff), Billie Burke (Mrs Radcliff), Ginger Rogers (Cecilia 'Pony' Ferris), Bruce Cabot (Ralph McFarland), John Halliday (Frank Radcliff), Beulah Bondi (Miss Van Alstyne), Sara Haden (Miss Fisher), Marjorie Lytell (Ruth Wallace), Adalyn Doyle (Madeline), Dawn O'Day [Anne Shirley] (Billie), Rose Coghlan (Miss Garland), Ann Cameron (Miss Schmidt), Claire Myers, Suzanne Thompson, Edith Vale (girls), Caroline Rankin (Miss Weber), Jack Norton (drunk), Joan Barclay (short girl), Helen Freeman (Dr. Hewitt), Irene Franklin (Aunt Jessica). With Florence Roberts, John David Horsley, Eddie Baker.

Some filmographies suggest that the film was also based on the play *These Days* by Katherine Clugston, but the AFI Catalog notes that the play is not credited by any contemporary source.

The film is an interesting precursor to *Stage Door*. The setting is a smart finishing school for girls, and Rogers is third billed as 'Her Pal', the sharp, experienced friend of 'The Girl', the refined, virginal leading lady (Dee). The Rogers role is to speak the truth about the 'genteel racketeering' that goes on in the school, and promote the love affair between Dee and her doctor suitor (Cabot). The film concludes with a clear condemnation of the snobbery of the school milieu.

15 May 1934
CHANGE OF HEART

Fox Pictures. Shooting: 23 February - early April 1934. New York premiere: 10 May 1934. 76 minutes.

Directed by John G. Blystone. Produced by Winfield Sheehan. Screenplay: Sonya Levien, James Gleason, based on the novel *Manhattan Love Song* by Kathleen Norris. Additional Dialogue: Samuel Hoffenstein. Dialogue

Director: James Gleason. Director of Photography: Hal Mohr. Set Decorator: Jack Otterson. Editor: James B. Morley. Sound Recording: Joseph Aiken. Costumes: Rita Kaufman. Musical Director: Louis De Francesco.

With: Janet Gaynor (Catherine Furness), Charles Farrell (Chris Thring), James Dunn (Mack McGowan), Ginger Rogers (Madge Rountree), Beryl Mercer (Harriet Hawkins), Gustav Von Seyffertitz (Dr Kurtzman), Fiske O'Hara (T.P. McGowan), Irene Franklin (Greta Hailstrom), Kenneth Thompson (Howard Jackson), Theodore Von Eltz (Gerald Mockby), Drue Leyton (Mrs Gerald Mockby), Nella Walker (Mrs Frieda Mockby), Shirley Temple (Shirley, girl on airplane), Barbara Barondess (Phyllis Carmichael), Jane Darwell (Mrs McGowan), Mary Carr (Mrs Rountree), Yolanda Patti (waitress), Ed Mundin (barker), Nick Foran (singer), Leonid Kinsky (guest), Frank Moran (moving man), Nell Craig (adoption assistant), Lillian Harmer (landlady), Poppy Wilde, Bess Flowers (party guests), William Norton Bailey (man in street), Mischa Auer, Jamiel Hassan (in Greenwich Village sequence).

Musical Numbers: 'So What?' (Music and lyrics by Harry Akst), 'College Stunts' (J.S. Zamecnik & Walter O'Keefe).

Now generally forgotten, Charles Farrell and Janet Gaynor were one of the most popular star couples of the late 'twenties and early 'thirties. Rogers appears here as the figure threatening their romance, in the last of the couple's twelve films together.

24 May 1934
TWENTY MILLION SWEETHEARTS

First National & Vitaphone Pictures. Shooting from 28 December 1933. 89 minutes.

Directed by Ray Enright. Production Supervisor: Sam Bischoff. Lyrics: Al Dubin. Music: Harry Warren. Screenplay: Warren Duff, Harry Sauber, based on a story by Paul Finder Moss and Jerry Wald. Dialogue Director: Stanley Logan. Director of Photography: Sid Hickox. Operating Cameraman: Wesley Anderson. Art Director: Esdras Hartley. Editor: Clarence Koster. Sound Recording: Gordon M. Davis. Unit Manager: Al Alborn. Musical Director: Leo F. Forbstein. Music Mixer: George R. Groves. Costumes: Orry-Kelly. Make-up Artist: Perc Westmore. Unit Mixer: Clare A. Riggs. Assistant Director: Gordon Hollingshead. Technical Advisor: William Ray.

With: Pat O'Brien (Rush Blake), Dick Powell (Clayton), Ginger Rogers (Peggy), The Four Mills Brothers as themselves, Ted Fio Rito and His Band as themselves, The Three Radio Rogues as themselves, Allen Jenkins (Pete), Grant Mitchell (Sharpe), Joseph Cawthorne (Brockman), Joan Wheeler (Marge), Henry O'Neill (Tappan), Johnny Arthur (secretary), The Debutantes as themselves, Muzzy Marcellino as himself, Grace Hayle (Mrs Brockman), Oscar Apfel (manager), Billy West (bellboy), Gordon [Bill] Elliott (gigolo - first man), Eddie Kane (second man), Larry McGrath (third man), Diane Borget (girl), Bob Perry (manager), Rosalie Roy (girl operator), Eddie Foster (first hillbilly), Billy Snyder (second hillbilly), Matt Brooks (third hillbilly), Morris Goldman (fourth hillbilly), Milton Kibbee (announcer), John Murray (second announcer), Sam Hayes (Peggy's announcer), Dick Winslow (page boy), Leo Forbstein (Brusiloff), Harry Seymour (announcer), Eddie Schubert (reporter), George Chandler (first reporter), Sam McDaniel (waiter), William B. Davidson (manager), George Humbert (headwaiter), Charles Halton (sound effects man), Charles Sullivan (taxi driver), Nora Cecil (lady in bed), Charles Lane (reporter).

Musical Numbers: 'Fair and Warmer', 'Out For No Good', 'What Are Your Intentions', 'I'll String Along With You' (all Dubin & Warren), 'How'm I Doing?' (Don Redman).

The plotting here is close to that of the Astaire-Rogers musicals. Rogers plays 'Radio's Sweetheart, the Cinderella Girl', and her relationship with Powell, an aspiring singer being handled by a pushy promoter (O'Brien), moves through initial antagonism to love, to a sense of complete loss when the romance appears to have collapsed, to final triumph. Significant differences – apart from the absence of dance – are the importance of the promoter figure in controlling the lovers' actions and the presentation of Powell as a heart-throb. His success on radio is accompanied by a montage of his adoring female fans.

11 October 1934
THE GAY DIVORCEE

RKO Radio Pictures. Shooting: 28 June - 13 August, retakes from 1 September 1934. 107 minutes.

Directed by Mark Sandrich. Produced by Pandro S. Berman. Lyrics: Cole Porter, Herb Magidson, Mack Gordon. Music: Cole Porter, Con Conrad, Harry Revel. Screenplay: George Marion Jr, Dorothy Yost, Edward Kaufman, from the stage musical *Gay Divorce*, book by Dwight Taylor, musical adaptation by Kenneth Webb and Samuel Hoffenstein. Dance Director: Dave Gould. Assistant Dance Director: Hermes Pan. Art Directors: Van Nest Polglase, Carroll Clark.

Costumes: Walter Plunkett. Musical Director: Max Steiner. Orchestrations: Clifford Vaughan, Maurice de Packh, Bernhard Kaun, Howard Jackson, Eddie Sharpe, Gene Rose. Director of Photography: David Abel. Special Photographic Effects: Vernon Walker. Finger Doll Chorus Dance: Frank Warde. Music Recording: Murray Spivack, P.J. Faulkner, Jr. Sound Recording: Hugh McDowell, Jr. Sound Cutter: George Marsh. Make-up Artist: Mel Burns. Research Director: Elizabeth McGaffey. Assistant Director: Argyle Nelson. Editor: William Hamilton. Production Associate: Zion Myers. Still Photographer: John Miehle.

With: Fred Astaire (Guy Holden), Ginger Rogers (Mimi Glossop), Alice Brady (Hortense Ditherwell), Edward Everett Horton (Egbert Fitzgerald), Erik Rhodes (Rodolfo Tonetti), Eric Blore (waiter), William Austin (Cyril Glossop), Betty Grable (hotel guest), Charles Coleman (Guy's valet), Lillian Miles (singer). Paul Porcasi (French headwaiter), George Davis, Alphonse inspector), Cyril Thornton (customs official), Charles Hall (call boy at dock), Art Jarrett.

Musical/Dance Numbers: 'Don't Let it Bother You' (Gordon & Revel) sung by French chorus, danced by Astaire. 'A Needle in a Haystack' (Magidson & Conrad) sung and danced by Astaire. 'Let's K-nock K-nees' (Gordon & Revel) sung by Grable and Horton, danced by Grable, Horton and hotel guests. 'Night and Day' (Porter) sung by Astaire, danced by Astaire and Rogers. 'The Continental' (Magidson & Conrad) sung by Rogers, Rhodes, Miles, danced by Astaire and Rogers, chorus.

11 January 1935
ROMANCE IN MANHATTAN

RKO Radio Pictures. Shooting: 14 September - 19 October 1934. 75/78 minutes.

Directed by Stephen Roberts. Produced by Pandro S. Berman. Screenplay: Jane Murfin, Edward Kaufman, based on a story by Norman Krasna and Don Hartman. Director of Photography: Nick Musuraca. Art Directors: Van Nest Polglase, Charles Kirk. Editor: Jack Hively. Sound Recording: John Tribby. Musical Director: Al Colombo. Miniatures: Don Jahraus. Research Director: Elizabeth McGaffey. Make-up Artist: Mel Burns. Special Photographic Effects: Vernon Walker. Assistant Director: Dewey Starkey. Still Photographer: John Miehle.

With: Francis Lederer (Karel Novak), Ginger Rogers (Sylvia Dennis), Arthur Hohl (Attorney Pander), Jimmy Butler (Frank Dennis), J. Farrell MacDonald (Officer Murphy), Helen Ware (Miss

Anthrop), Eily Malyon (Miss Evans), Oscar Apfel (judge), Lillian Harmer (landlady), Reginald Barlow (customs inspector), Donald Meek (minister), Sidney Toler (sergeant), Harold Goodwin (doctor).

Between two films set in England and France, Pandro Berman cast Rogers in a celebration of America through an exemplary narrative of the creation of an American family. A penniless immigrant from Europe (Lederer) encounters a 19-year-old chorus girl (Rogers) struggling to bring up her kid brother (Butler) in the Manhattan of the Depression. The girl feeds and shelters the hungry man – the film follows the process of turning this pair into the good American couple. The immigrant becomes the head of the family, taking over the role of wage-earner, learning to speak correct English and finally, with the help of other ex-immigrants (a group of Irish-American cops), becoming a citizen and a husband in a sequence in which the two things are telescoped together. In this structure, America, described by Lederer's character as 'so beautiful, so big, so friendly, so warm' can be thought of as a woman, who both nurtures the immigrant male and is conquered by him. The film, which ends with the marriage to Rogers, opens with shots of immigrants gazing at the Statue of Liberty. The connection between Rogers and the figure of Liberty will recur when Rogers adopts the characteristic pose of the statue in *Once Upon a Honeymoon*.

26 February 1935
ROBERTA

RKO Radio Pictures. Shooting: 26 November 1934 - 21 January 1935. 105/106 minutes.

Directed by William A. Seiter. Produced by Pandro S. Berman. Lyrics: Otto Harbach. Music: Jerome Kern. Additional Lyrics: Dorothy Fields and Jimmy McHugh. Screenplay: Jane Murfin, Sam Mintz, Allan Scott. Additional Dialogue: Glenn Tryon. Based on the stage musical *Roberta*, book by Otto Harbach, music by Jerome Kern, and the novel *Gowns by Roberta* by Alice Duer Miller. Dance Director: Fred Astaire. Assistant Dance Director: Hermes Pan. Art Directors: Van Nest Polglase, Carroll Clark. Costumes: Bernard Newman. Musical Director: Max Steiner. Orchestrations: Gene Rose, Wayne Allen. Music Recording: P.J. Faulkner, Jr. Sound Recording: John Tribby. Sound Cutter: George Marsh. Director of Photography: Edward Cronjager. Set Dressing: Thomas K. Little. Editor: William Hamilton. Assistant Director: Edward Killy. Production Associate: Zion Myers. Still Photographer: John Miehle.

With: Irene Dunne (Stephanie), Fred Astaire (Huckleberry ['Huck'] Haines), Ginger Rogers (Countess Scharwenka, *née* Lizzie Gatz), Randolph Scott (John Kent), Helen Westley (Roberta), Victor Varconi (Ladislaw), Claire Dodd (Sophie Teale), Luis Alberni (Alexander Voyda), Ferdinand Munier (Lord Henry Delves), Torben Meyer (Albert), Lucille Ball (girl in salon), Mike Tellegen, Sam Savitsky (restaurant cossacks), Adrian Rosley (professor), Bodil Rosing (Fernande), Grace Hale (lady reporter), William B. Davidson (ship's officer), Michael Visaroff (waiter), Mary Forbes (Mrs. Teale), Candy Candido, Muzzy Marcellino, Gene Sheldon, Howard Lally, Hal Borne, Charles Sharpe, Ivan Dow, William Dunn, Phil Cuthbert, Delmon Davis, William Carey, Paul McLarind (Wabash Indianians), Lucille Ball, Jane Hamilton, Margaret McChrystal, Kay Sutton, Maxine Jennings, Virginia Reid, Lorna Low, Lorraine DeSart, Wanda Perry, Diane Cook, Virginia Carroll, Betty Dumbries, Donna Roberts (mannequins), Judith Vosselli, Rita Gould.

Musical/Dance Numbers: 'Indiana' (Ballard Macdonald & James F. Hanley), sung by the Indianians. 'Let's Begin' (Harbach, revised by Fields, & Kern), sung by Astaire, Candido, danced by Astaire, Candido, Sheldon. 'Russian Song' (traditional), sung by Dunne. 'I'll Be Hard to Handle' (Bernard Dougall, rewritten by Fields, & Kern), sung by Rogers, danced by Astaire and Rogers. 'Yesterdays' (Harbach & Kern), sung by Dunne. 'I Won't Dance' (Oscar Hammerstein, lyric rewritten by Fields, & Kern), sung by Astaire and Rogers, danced by Astaire. 'Smoke Gets in Your Eyes' (Harbach & Kern), sung by Dunne. Fashion Show sequence (background: 'Don't Ask Me Not to Sing', sung by Astaire): 'Lovely to Look At' (Fields & Kern), sung by Dunne and male chorus, reprise sung and danced by Astaire and Rogers. 'I Won't Dance' (reprise), danced by Astaire and Rogers. Background: 'The Touch of Your Hand', 'You're Devastating'.

11 April 1935
STAR OF MIDNIGHT

RKO Radio Pictures. Shooting 25 January - 1 March 1935. 90 minutes.

Directed by Stephen Roberts. Produced by Pandro S. Berman. Screenplay: Howard J. Green, Anthony Veiller, Edward Kaufman, based on the novel *Star of Midnight* by Arthur Somers Roche. Director of Photography: J. Roy Hunt. Art Directors: Van Nest Polglase, Charles Kirk. Editor: Arthur Roberts. Sound Recording: John L. Cass. Musical Director: Max Steiner. Costumes: Bernard Newman. Make-up Artist:

Mel Burns. Research director: Elizabeth McGaffey. Assistant Director: James Anderson. Still Photographer: John Miehle.

With: William Powell (Clay Dalzell), Ginger Rogers (Donna Mantin), Paul Kelly (Jim Kinland), Gene Lockhart (Horatio Swayne), Ralph Morgan (Roger Classon), Leslie Fenton (Tim Winthrop), Vivien Oakland (Jerry Classon), J. Farrell MacDonald (Inspector Doremus), Russell Hopton (Tommy Tennant), Frank Reicher (Abe Ohlman), Robert Emmett O'Connor (Sergeant Cleary), Francis McDonald (gangster), Paul Hurst (Corbett), Spencer Charters (doorman), George Chandler (witness).

29 August 1935
TOP HAT

RKO Radio Pictures. Shooting: 8 April - 5 June 1935. 99/101 minutes.

Directed by Mark Sandrich. Produced by Pandro S. Berman. Lyrics and Music: Irving Berlin. Screenplay: Dwight Taylor, Allan Scott, adapted by Karl Noti from the play *The Girl Who Dared* by Alexander Farago and Aladar Laszlo. Dance Director: Hermes Pan. Art Directors: Van Nest Polglase, Carroll Clark. Costumes: Bernard Newman. Musical Director: Max Steiner. Orchestrations: Edward Powell, Maurice de Packh, Gene Rose, Eddie Sharpe, Arthur Knowlton. Director of Photography: David Abel. Special Photographic Effects: Vernon Walker. Music Recording: P.J. Faulkner, Jr. Sound Recording: Hugh McDowell, Jr. Sound Cutter: George Marsh. Set Decorator: Thomas Little. Make-up Artist: Mel Burns. Assistant Director: Argyle Nelson. Research Director: Elizabeth McGaffey. Editor: William Hamilton. Still Photographer: John Miehle.

With: Fred Astaire (Jerry Travers), Ginger Rogers (Dale Tremont), Edward Everett Horton (Horace Hardwick), Helen Broderick (Madge Hardwick), Erik Rhodes (Alberto Beddini), Eric Blore (Bates), Leonard Mudie (flower shop manager), Lucille Ball (flower shop assistant), Edgar Norton (London hotel manager), Gino Corrado (Venice hotel manager), Peter Hobbes (call boy), Frank Mills (lido waiter), Tom Ricketts (Thackeray Club waiter), Dennis O'Keefe (elevator passenger), Robert Adair (London hotel desk clerk), Frank Mills (waiter with steak), Ben Holmes, Nick Thompson, Tom Costello, John Impolite, Genaro Spagnoli, Rita Rozelle, Phyllis Coghlan, Charles Hall.

Donald Meek (curate) and Florence Roberts (curate's wife) appeared in a sequence cut after the first previews in July 1935.

Musical/Dance Numbers: 'No Strings (I'm Fancy Free)', sung and danced by Astaire. 'Isn't This a Lovely Day (To Be Caught in the Rain)', sung by Astaire, danced by Astaire and Rogers. 'Top Hat, White Tie and Tails', sung by Astaire, danced by Astaire and male chorus. 'Cheek to Cheek', sung by Astaire, danced by Astaire and Rogers. 'The Piccolino', sung by Rogers, danced by Astaire and Rogers, chorus. Unused: 'Get Thee Behind Me, Satan', 'Wild About You'.

22 November 1935
IN PERSON

RKO Radio Pictures. Shooting: from 29 July 1935. 83 minutes.

Directed by William A. Seiter. Produced by Pandro S. Berman. Screenplay: Allan Scott, based on a novel by Samuel Hopkins Adams. Music and Lyrics: Oscar Levant and Dorothy Fields. Director of Photography: Edward Cronjager. Art Directors: Van Nest Polglase, Carroll Clark. Editor: Arthur Schmidt. Sound Recording: Clem A. Portman. Musical Director: Roy Webb. Dance Director: Hermes Pan. Sound Mixer: P. J. Faulkner, Jr. Costumes: Bernard Newman. Make-up Artist: Mel Burns. Still Photographer: John Miehle.

With: Ginger Rogers (Clara Corliss, a.k.a. Clara Colfax), George Brent (Emory Muir), Alan Mowbray (Jay Holmes), Grant Mitchell (Judge Thaddeus Parks), Samuel S. Hinds (Dr Aaron Sylvester), Joan Breslau (Minna), Louis Mason (Sheriff Twing), Spencer Charters (Justice of the Peace Lunk), Lew Kelly (mountain man), Bob McKenzie (theatre manager), Lee Shumway (studio representative), William B. Davidson (Director, Bill Sumner), Tiny Jones (woman in theatre), Bud Jamison (man in elevator), George Davis (taxi driver).

Musical/Dance Numbers: 'Don't Mention Love to Me', sung by Rogers. 'Got a New Lease on Life', sung by Rogers. 'Out of Sight, Out of Mind', sung and danced by Rogers, male chorus.

It is a pity that *In Person* is now a difficult film to find, as it bears a unique relationship to the Astaire-Rogers cycle. At an early stage in its development, it was possibly conceived as an Astaire-Rogers vehicle (according to a 'Hollywood Reporter' article of November 1934 quoted in the *AFI Catalog*), and the screenplay is by the major writer of the cycle, Allan Scott. No doubt the script was rewritten to suit the final casting, and it became a commentary on Astaire and Rogers, a comedy based around the reaction of a Hollywood star to fame and to the particular stress of being one half of a star couple. Rogers plays the

Alan Mowbray, Rogers and George Brent in In Person.

star in retreat, hidden from her public by a completely impenetrable disguise. (The disguise, which includes glasses and false teeth, does indeed render Rogers unrecognisable and plain – RKO seems to have taken a decision not to release stills of her in it.) She is faced with a choice between Mowbray (who plays the Astaire role and can announce, 'I've co-starred in every picture that Carol Corliss has ever made') and Brent, who knows Hollywood only as part of the cinema audience. The narrative involves flight from the city to a country cottage, but a cottage from which it is possible to go to the cinema, as the Rogers and Brent characters do. They see Rogers in the final moments of a film called, indicatively, 'No Escape'. The Rogers character combines confidence and power (Carol Corliss the star, her talent as a singer and dancer) with retreat and collapse (the disguise, the fear of the fans), and *In Person* can be seen as an early exploration, as the cycle neared its peak, of the tensions explored in the final Astaire-Rogers films.

20 February 1936
FOLLOW THE FLEET

RKO Radio Pictures. Shooting: 31 October 1935 - 4 January 1936. 110 minutes.

Directed by Mark Sandrich. Produced by Pandro S. Berman. Lyrics and Music: Irving Berlin. Screenplay: Dwight Taylor and Allan Scott, based on the play *Shore Leave* by Hubert Osborne. Dance Director: Hermes Pan. Art Directors: Van Nest Polglase, Carroll Clark. Set Dressing: Darrell Silvera. Costumes: Bernard Newman. Musical Director: Max Steiner. Orchestrations and Arrangements: Gene Rose, Maurice de

Packh, Clarence Wheeler, Walter Scharf, Roy Webb. Director of Photography: David Abel. Special Photographic Effects: Vernon Walker. Editor: Henry Berman. Technical Advisor: US Navy Lt Cmdr Harvey Haislip. Music Recording: P.J. Faulkner, Jr. Sound Recording: Hugh McDowell, Jr. Sound Cutter: George Marsh. Miniatures: Don Jahraus. Research Director: Elizabeth McGaffey. Assistant Director: Argyle Nelson.

With: Fred Astaire ('Bake' Baker), Ginger Rogers (Sherry Martin), Randolph Scott ('Bilge' Smith), Harriet Hilliard (Connie Martin), Astrid Allwyn (Iris Manning), Ray Mayer (Dopey Williams), Harry Beresford (Captain Hickey), Addison Randall (Lt Williams), Russell Hicks (Jim Nolan), Brooks Benedict (Sullivan), Lucille Ball (Kitty Collins), Betty Grable, Joy Hodges, Jeanne Gray (singing trio), Jane Hamilton (waitress), Maxine Jennings (hostess), Herbert Rawlinson (Weber), Dorothy Fleisman, Bob Cromer (contest dancers), Kay Sutton (telephone operator), Doris Lloyd (Mrs Courtney), Huntley Gordon (English officer), James Pierce (bouncer), Gertrude Short (cashier), George Magrill (quartermaster), Thomas Brower (policeman), Frederick Blanchard (Captain Jones), William Smith (Ensign Gilbert), Allen Wood (office boy), Eric Wilton (butler), Max Wagner (marine), George Lollier (deck officer), Constance Bergen (ticket seller), Tony Martin, Frank Jenks, Frank Moran, Edward Burns, Bud Geary, Frank Mills, Frank Sully, Eddie Tamblyn, Billy Dooley (sailors), Thelma Leeds, Lita Chevret.

Musical/Dance Numbers: 'We Saw the Sea', sung by Astaire, sailors. 'Let Yourself Go', sung by Rogers with Grable, Hodges, Gray. 'Get Thee Behind Me, Satan', sung by Hilliard. 'Let Yourself Go' (reprise), danced by Astaire and Rogers, Fleisman and Cromer, chorus. 'I'd Rather Lead a Band', sung and danced by Astaire, sailors. 'Let Yourself Go (second reprise), danced by Rogers. 'But Where Are You', sung by Hilliard. 'I'm Putting All My Eggs in One Basket', sung and danced by Astaire and Rogers. 'Let's Face the Music and Dance', sung by Astaire, danced by Astaire and Rogers. Unused: 'Moonlight Maneuvers', 'With a Smile on My Face'.

27 September 1936
SWING TIME

RKO Radio Pictures. Shooting: 11 May - 31 July 1936. New York premiere: 27 August 1936. 105 minutes.

Directed by George Stevens. Produced by Pandro S. Berman. Lyrics: Dorothy Fields. Music: Jerome Kern. Screenplay: Howard Lindsay and Allan Scott, from the story *Portrait of*

John Garnett by Erwin Gelsey. Additional Scriptwriting: Dorothy Yost. Dance Director: Hermes Pan. Art Directors: Van Nest Polglase, Carroll Clark. Set Decorator: Darrell Silvera. Costumes: Bernard Newman. 'Silver Sandal' set and costumes for 'Bojangles' number: John Harkrider. Musical Director: Nathaniel Shilkret. Orchestrations: Robert Russell Bennett, Hal Borne. Director of Photography: David Abel. Editor: Henry Berman. Sound Recording: Hugh McDowell Jr. Sound Cutter: George Marsh. Make-up Artist: Mel Burns. Special Effects: Vernon Walker. Assistant Directors: Argyle Nelson, Syd Fogel. Still Photographer: John Miehle.

With: Fred Astaire (John ['Lucky'] Garnett), Ginger Rogers (Penelope ['Penny'] Carrol), Victor Moore ('Pop' Cardetti), Helen Broderick (Mabel Anderson), Eric Blore (Mr Gordon), Betty Furness (Margaret Watson), Georges Metaxa (Ricardo Romero), Landers Stevens (Judge Watson), John Harrington ('Dice' Raymond), Pierre Watkin (Al Simpson), Abe Reynolds (tailor), Gerald Hamer (drunk), Edgar Dearing (policeman), Frank Jenks (Red), Howard Hickman (first minister), Ferdinand Munier (second minister), Joey Ray (announcer), Ralph Byrd (hotel desk clerk), Floyd Shackleford (butler), Frank Mills (croupier), Charles Hall (taxi driver), Jean Perry (roulette dealer), Dale Van Sickel (diner), Olin Francis (Muggsy), Fern Emmett (Watson's maid), Jack Rice (wedding guest), Frank Hammond (railroad ticket seller) Harry Bowen, Harry Bernard (stagehands), Jack Goode, Donald Kerr, Ted O'Shea, Frank Edmunds, Bill Brand (dancers), Blanca Vischer, Sailor Vincent, Marie Osborne, Bob O'Conor.

Musical/Dance Numbers: 'It's Not in the Cards' danced by Astaire, troupe (almost entirely cut from the final print). 'Pick Yourself Up' sung by Astaire and Rogers, danced by Astaire, Rogers, Moore and Broderick. 'The Way You Look Tonight', sung by Astaire and briefly Metaxa. 'Waltz in Swing Time', danced by Astaire and Rogers. 'A Fine Romance', sung by Rogers and Astaire. 'Bojangles of Harlem', sung by night club chorus, danced by Astaire, chorus. 'Never Gonna Dance', sung by Astaire, danced by Astaire and Rogers. 'The Way You Look Tonight' and 'A Fine Romance' (reprise), sung by Astaire and Rogers.

7 May 1937
SHALL WE DANCE

RKO Radio Pictures. Shooting: 24 December 1936 - 22 March 1937. 101/108/116 minutes.

Directed by Mark Sandrich. Produced by Pandro S. Berman. Lyrics: Ira Gershwin. Music: George

Gershwin. Screenplay: Allan Scott and Ernest Pagano, based on the story *Watch Your Step* by Lee Loeb and Harold Buchman, adapted by P.J. Wolfson. Dance Directors: Hermes Pan, Harry Losee. Art Directors: Van Nest Polglase, Carroll Clark. Set Decorator: Darrell Silvera. Miss Rogers's Costumes: Irene. Musical Director: Nathaniel Shilkret. Orchestrations: Robert Russell Bennett. Music Arranger: Joseph A. Livingston. Sound Recording: Hugh McDowell, Jr. Director of Photography: David Abel. Editor: William Hamilton. Make-up Artist: Mel Burns. Special Photographic Effects: Vernon Walker. Assistant Director: Argyle Nelson. Wardrobe Mistress: Edith Clark. Still Photographer: John Miehle.

With: Fred Astaire (Peter P. Peters, alias 'Petrov'), Ginger Rogers (Linda Keene, *née* Linda Thompson), Edward Everett Horton (Jeffrey Baird), Eric Blore (Cecil Flintridge), Jerome Cowan (Arthur Miller), Ketti Gallian (Lady Denise Tarrington), William Brisbane (Jim Montgomery), Ann Shoemaker (ship passenger), Ben Alexander (bandleader), Emma Young (Tai), Pete Theodore (Linda's dancing partner), Charles Coleman (policeman), Frank Moran (process server), Sherwood Bailey (newsboy), George Magrill (room steward), Leonard Mudie (waiter on ship), Henry Mowbray (radio officer), William Burress (justice of the peace), Jack Rice (hotel desk clerk), Harry Bowen (hotel carpenter), Richard Tucker (Linda's attourney), Marek Windheim, Rolfe Sedan (ballet masters), Harriet Hoctor (herself), Charles Irwin, Jean de Briac, Norman Ainsley, Sam Wren, Pauline Garon, Vasey O'Davoren, Alphonse Martel, Helena Grant, Matty Roubert, J.M. Kerrigan, Sam Hayes, Torben Meyer, Spencer Teakle.

Musical/Dance Numbers: '(I've Got) Beginner's Luck', danced by Astaire. 'Slap That Bass', Dudley Dickerson, sung and danced by Astaire. 'Walking the Dog' (background). '(I've Got) Beginner's Luck' (reprise), sung by Astaire. 'They All Laughed', sung by Rogers, danced by Astaire and Rogers. 'Let's Call the Whole Thing Off', Astaire and Rogers, danced by Astaire and Rogers. 'They Can't Take That Away from Me' sung by Astaire, reprised as dance by Astaire and Hoctor. 'Shall We Dance', sung by Astaire, danced by Astaire and Rogers, chorus. Unused: 'Hi-Ho!', 'Wake Up, Brother, and Dance'

8 October 1937
STAGE DOOR

RKO Radio Pictures. Shooting: 7 June - 31 July 1937. 92 minutes.

Directed by Gregory La Cava. Produced by Pandro S. Berman. Screenplay: Morrie Ryskind,

Astaire and Edward Everett Horton watching Rogers sing 'They All Laughed' in Shall We Dance.

Anthony Veiller, based on the play by Edna Ferber and George S. Kaufman. Music and Lyrics: Hal Borne and Mort Greene. Director of Photography: Robert de Grasse. Art Director: Van Nest Polglase. Associate Art Director: Carroll Clark. Set Decorator: Darrell Silvera. Editor: William Hamilton. Sound Recording: John L. Cass. Musical Director: Roy Webb. Costumes: Muriel King. Jewellery: Trabert & Hoeffer, Inc., Mauboussin. Make-up Artist: Mel Burns. Assistant Director: James Anderson, Still Photographer: John Miehle.

With: Katherine Hepburn (Terry Randall), Ginger Rogers (Jean Maitland), Adolphe Menjou (Anthony Powell), Gail Patrick (Linda Shaw), Constance Collier (Catherine Luther), Andrea Leeds (Kaye Hamilton), Samuel S. Hinds (Henry Sims), Lucille Ball (Judy Canfield), Pierre Watkin (Richard Carmichael), Franklin Pangborn (Harcourt), Elizabeth Dunne (Mrs Orcutt), Phyllis Kennedy (Hattie), Grady Sutton (Hattie's boyfriend), Jack Carson (Milbank), Fred Santley (Dukenfield), William Corson (Bill), Frank Reicher (stage director), Eve Arden (Eve), Ann Miller (Annie), Jane Rhodes (Ann Braddock), Margaret Early (Mary), Jean Rouverol (Dizzy), Norma Drury (Olga Brent), Peggy O'Donnell (Susan), Harriet Brandon (Madeline), Katherine Alexander, Ralph Forbes, Mary Forbes, Huntley Gordon (cast of play), Lynton Brent (aide), Theodore Von Eltz (Elsworth), Jack Rice (playwright), Harry Strang (chauffeur), Bob Perry (baggageman), Larry Steers (theatre patron), Mary Bovard, Frances Gifford, Josephine Whittell, Ada Leonard, Mary Jane Shower, Diana Gibson, Linda Gray, Alison Craig, Adele Pearce [Pamela Blake], Lynn Gabriel (actresses), Jack Gardner (script clerk), Ben Hendricks, Jr. (waiter), Jack Gargan, Theodore Kosloff, Gerda Mora, Julie Kingdon (dancing instructors), Al Hill (taxi driver). With Byron Stevens, D'Arcy Corrigan, Philip Morris, and 'Whitey' as Eve's cat.

Musical/Dance Number: 'Put Your Heart into Your Feet and Dance', danced by Rogers and Miller.

19 November 1937
A DAMSEL IN DISTRESS

RKO Radio Pictures. Shooting: 22 July - 16 October 1937. 98/100 minutes.

Directed by George Stevens. Produced by Pandro S. Berman. Lyrics: Ira Gershwin. Music: George Gershwin. Screenplay: P.G. Wodehouse, Ernest Pagano, S.K. Lauren from the novel *A Damsel in Distress* by Wodehouse and play by Wodehouse and Ian Hay. Dance Director: Hermes Pan. Art Directors: Van Nest Polglase,

Carroll Clark. Musical Director: Victor Baravalle. Orchestrations: Robert Russell Bennett, Ray Noble, George Bassman. Director of Photography: Joseph H. August. Special Effects: Vernon Walker. Set Decorator: Darrell Silvera. Sound Recording: Earl A. Wolcott. Editor: Henry Berman. Assistant Director: Argyle Nelson.

With: Fred Astaire (Jerry Halliday), George Burns and Gracie Allen (themselves), Joan Fontaine (Lady Alyce Marshmorton), Reginald Gardiner (Keggs), Ray Noble (Reggie), Constance Collier (Lady Caroline Marshmorton), Montagu Love (Lord John Marshmorton), Harry Watson (Albert), Jan Duggan, Mary Dean, Pearl Amatore, Betty Rone (madrigal singers), Mary Gordon (cook), Frank Moran (policeman), Joe Niemeyer (cockney street dancer), Charles Bennett (barker at carnival), Jack Walklin, James Clemens, Kenneth Terrell, James Fawcett (drunks in funhouse).

Musical/Dance Numbers: 'I Can't Be Bothered Now', sung and danced by Astaire. 'The Jolly Tar and the Milkmaid', sung by Astaire and madrigal singers. 'Put Me to the Test', danced by Astaire, Burns and Allen. 'Stiff Upper Lip', sung by Allen, danced by Astaire, Burns and Allen, fairgoers. 'Things Are Looking Up', sung by Astaire,

Joan Fontaine and Astaire in A Damsel in Distress.

Peggy Conklin, Lee Bowman, Shimen Ruskin and Rogers in Having Wonderful Time.

danced by Astaire and Fontaine. 'Sing of Spring', sung by madrigal singers. 'A Foggy Day', sung by Astaire. 'Nice Work if You Can Get It', sung by madrigal singers, reprised as drum solo and dance by Astaire. 'Ah! che a voi perdoni Iddio ' (from Flotow's *Marta*), sung by Gardiner dubbed by Mario Berini.

13 May 1938
VIVACIOUS LADY

RKO Radio Pictures. Shooting: mid-April 1937 [interrupted - see below], then mid-December 1937 - 5 March 1938. 90 minutes.

Directed by George Stevens. Produced by Pandro S. Berman. Screenplay: P. J. Wolfson, Ernest Pagano, based on a story by I.A.R. Wylie. Music and Lyrics: George Jessel, Jack Meskill, Ted Shapiro. Director of Photography: Robert de Grasse. Art Directors: Van Nest Polglase, Carroll Clark. Set Decorator: Darrell Silvera. Editor: Henry Berman. Sound Recording: Hugh McDowell, Jr. Musical director: Roy Webb. Orchestrations: Robert Russell Bennett. Vocal

Arrangements: Roger Edens. Costumes: Bernard Newman, Irene. Make-up Artist: Mel Burns. Assistant Director: Argyle Nelson. Still Photographer: John Miehle.

With: Ginger Rogers (Frances Brent, a.k.a. Francey La Roche), James Stewart (Peter Morgan), James Ellison (Keith Morgan), Charles Coburn (Dr Morgan), Beulah Bondi (Mrs Morgan), Frances Mercer (Helen), Phyllis Kennedy (Jenny), Alec Craig (Joseph), Franklin Pangborn (apartment manager), Grady Sutton (Culpepper), Hattie McDaniel (maid), Jack Carson (waiter captain), Willie Best (porter), Dorothy Moore (hat check girl), Maurice Black (headwaiter), Frank M. Thomas (conductor), Spencer Charters (quarrelling husband), Maude Eburne (quarrelling wife), Jane Eberling (girl on bus), Marvin Jones (boy on bus), Bobby Barber (Italian), Ray Mayer, George Chandler (men on train), Harry Campbell, June Johnson, Kay Sutton, Phyllis Fraser, Bud Flanagan [Dennis O'Keefe], Edgar Dearing, Helena Grant, Vivian Reid, William Brisbane, Vernon Dent, Katharine Ellis, June Horne, Dorothy Johnson, Phoebe

Terbell, Robert Wilson, Stanley Blystone, Barbara Pepper.

Musical Number: 'You'll Be Reminded of Me', sung by Rogers.

The film was commenced in April 1937, but after four days James Stewart was taken ill and the shoot postponed until the December. In the interval Rogers made *Stage Door* in June and July and *Having Wonderful Time* in September, October and November.

1 July 1938
HAVING WONDERFUL TIME

RKO Radio Pictures. Shooting: 24 September - 29 November 1937. 69/71 minutes.

Directed by Alfred Santell. Produced by Pandro S. Berman. Screenplay: Arthur Kober, based on his play. Music and Lyrics: Sammy Stept, Charles Tobias, Bill Livingston. Director of Photography: Robert de Grasse. Art Directors: Van Nest Polglase, Perry Ferguson. Set Decorator: Darrell Silvera. Editor: William Hamilton. Sound Recording: John E. Tribby. Musical Director: Roy Webb. Dialogue Director: Ernest Pagano. Costumes: Renie. Wardrobe Supervisor: Edward Stevenson. Make-up Artist: Mel Burns. Special Photographic Effects: Vernon L. Walker. Assistant Director: James Anderson. Still Photographer: John Miehle.

With: Ginger Rogers (Teddy Shaw), Douglas Fairbanks, Jr (Chick Kirkland), Peggy Conklin (Fay Coleman), Lucille Ball (Miriam), Lee Bowman (Buzzy Armbruster), Eve Arden (Henrietta), Dorothea Kent (Maxine), 'Red' Skelton (Itchy Faulkner), Donald Meek (P.U. Rogers), Jack Carson (Emil Beatty), Kirk Windsor (Henry), Clarence H. Wilson (Mr G), Allan [Rocky] Lane (Mac), Grady Sutton (Gus), Shimen Ruskin (Shrimpo), Dorothy Tree (Frances), Leona Roberts (Mrs Shaw), Harlan Briggs (Mr Shaw), Inez Courtney (Emma), Juanita Quigley (Mabel), Betty Rhodes (singer), George Meeker, Ronnie Rondell (subway mashers), Elise Cavanna (office supervisor), Mary Bovard, Frances Gifford, Peggy Montgomery, [Baby] Marie Osborne, Mary Jane Irving, Wesley Barry, Dorothy Moore, Stanley Brown, Etienne Girardot, Margaret Seddon, Kay Sutton, Dorothy Day, Lynn Bailey, Tommy Watkins, Cynthia Hobard Fellows, Steve Putnam, Bill Corson, Bob Thatcher, Ben Carter, Russell Gleason, Florence Lake, Vera Gordon, Margaret McWade.

The role of Vivian, played by Ann Miller, was cut from the release print. Miller appears briefly in group shots.

Musical/Dance Numbers: 'My First Impression of You', sung by Rhodes. 'Nighty Night', background music.

2 September 1938
CAREFREE

RKO Radio Pictures. Shooting: 14-15 April 1938 [golf sequence], then 9 May - 21 July 1938. 80/83 minutes.

Directed by Mark Sandrich. Produced by Pandro S. Berman. Lyrics and Music: Irving Berlin. Screenplay: Ernest Pagano and Allan Scott, from a story by Marian Ainslee and Guy Endore, adapted by Dudley Nichols and Hagar Wilde. Dance Director: Hermes Pan. Art Directors: Van Nest Polglase, Carroll Clark. Set Decorator: Darrell Silvera. Miss Rogers's gowns: Howard Greer. Wardrobe Supervisor: Edward Stevenson. Musical Director: Victor Baravalle. Musical Arrangements: Robert Russell Bennett, Conrad Salinger, Gene Rose. Orchestrations: Robert Russell Bennett, Leonid Raab, Conrad Salinger, Max Reese. Director of Photography: Robert de Grasse. Special Photographic Effects: Vernon Walker. Sound Recording: Hugh McDowell, Jr. Editor: William Hamilton. Make-up Artist: Mel Burns. Assistant to Producer: Fred Fleck. Assistant Director: Argyle Nelson. Still Photographer: John Miehle.

With: Fred Astaire (Dr. Tony Flagg), Ginger Rogers (Amanda Cooper), Ralph Bellamy (Stephen Arden), Luella Gear (Cora Cooper), Jack Carson (Connors), Clarence Kolb (Judge Joseph Travers), Franklin Pangborn (Roland Hunter), Walter Kingsford (Dr Powers), Kay Sutton (Miss Adams), Hattie McDaniel (Amanda's maid), Paul Guilfoyle (elevator starter), Richard Lane (headwaiter), Edward Gargan (policeman), Charles Coleman (doorman), James Finlayson (golf pro.), Ray Hendricks (waiter), James Burtis (truck driver), Harold Minjur (radio announcer), Harry Bailey (sponsor), Frank Moran (cab driver), Grace Hayle, Jack Arnold, Phyllis Kennedy, William Carson, and Robert B. Mitchell and His St. Brendan's Boys.

Musical/Dance Numbers: 'Since They Turned Loch Lomond into Swing', harmonica and dance by Astaire. 'The Night is Filled with Music', played by dance orchestra. 'I Used to be Color Blind', sung by Astaire, danced by Astaire and Rogers. 'The Yam', sung by Rogers, danced by Astaire and Rogers. 'Change Partners', sung by Astaire, danced by Astaire and Rogers.

Astaire and Rogers dance in a dream sequence in Carefree.

30 March 1939
**THE STORY OF VERNON
AND IRENE CASTLE**

RKO Radio Pictures. Shooting: 10 November
1938 - 26 January 1939. 90/93 minutes.

Directed by H.C. Potter. Produced by George
Haight. Production Supervisor: Pandro S.
Berman. Screenplay: Richard Sherman, from the
book *My Husband* and the magazine article 'My
Memories of Vernon Castle' by Irene Castle,
adapted by Oscar Hammerstein II and Dorothy
Yost. Dance Director: Hermes Pan. Art
Directors: Van Nest Polglase, Perry Ferguson. Set
Decorator: Darrell Silvera. Sound Recorder:
Richard Van Hessen. Costumes: Irene Castle,
Walter Plunkett, Edward Stevenson. Musical
Director: Victor Baravalle. Orchestrations: Roy
Webb, Robert Russell Bennett, Edward Powell,
Hugo Friedhofer, David Raksin, Leonid Raab.
Director of Photography: Robert de Grasse.
Special Photographic Effects: Vernon Walker,
Douglas Travers. Assistant Director: Argyle
Nelson. Director of Additional Scenes: Leigh
Jason. Technical Adviser: Irene Castle. Editor:
William Hamilton. Make-up Artist: Mel Burns.

Still Photographer: John Miehle.

With: Fred Astaire (Vernon Castle), Ginger
Rogers (Irene Foote Castle), Edna May Oliver
(Maggie Sutton), Walter Brennan (Walter Ash),
Lew Fields (himself), Etienne Girardot (Papa
Aubel), Janet Beecher (Annie Foote), Rolfe
Sedan (Emile Aubel), Leonid Kinskey (Parisian
artist), Robert Strange (Dr Hubert Foote),
Clarence Derwent (Louis Barraya), Frances
Mercer (Claire Ford), Victor Varconi (Russian
nobleman), Donald MacBride (Fort Worth hotel
manager), Douglas Walton (student pilot), Sonny
Lamont (plump tap dancer), Roy D'Arcy (actor
in *Patria*), Bruce Mitchell (movie director), Dick
Elliott (train conductor), Marjorie Bell, Eleanor
Hansen, Ethyl Haworth, Mary Brodel (Irene's
friends), David McDonald, John Meredith (army
pilots), Tiny Jones (lady in revolving door), Fred
Sweeney (streetcar conductor), Adrienne
D'Ambricourt (French landlady), Emmett
O'Brien (dancer in drag in 'Who's Your Lady
Friend?'), Don Brodie, Bill Franey, Joe
Bordeaux, Neil Burns, Jack Perrin, Bill Paton,
'Buzz' Barton, Neal Hart, Frank O'Connor, D.
H. Turner, Max Darwyn, Leonard Mudie, Hugh

McArthur, Esther Muir, Theodore Von Eltz, George Irving, Willis Clare, Russell Hicks, Hal K. Dawson, Kay Sutton, Allen Wood, Armand Cortez, Eugene Borden, Elspeth Dudgeon, Dorothy Lovett.

Musical/Dance Numbers: 'Oh, You Beautiful Doll' (Brown & Ayer), sung by male chorus. 'Glow-Worm' (Robinson & Lincke), sung by female chorus. 'By the Beautiful Sea' (Atteridge & Carroll), sung by male chorus. 'Row, Row, Row' (Jerome & Monaco), sung by male chorus. 'Yama Yama Man' (Davis & Hoschna), sung and danced by Rogers. 'Come, Josephine in My Flying Machine' (Bryan & Fischer), sung by chorus. 'By the Light of the Silvery Moon' (Madden & Edwards), danced by Astaire. 'Cuddle Up a Little Closer, Lovely Mine' (Harbach & Hoschna), sung by chorus. 'Only When You're in My Arms' (Kalmar, Ruby & Conrad), sung by Astaire. 'Waiting for the Robert E. Lee' (Gilbert & Muir), danced by Astaire and Rogers. 'The Darktown Strutters' Ball' (Brooks), sung by Louis Mercier, dubbed by Jean Sablon. 'Too Much Mustard' (Macklin), danced by Astaire and Rogers. 'Rose Room' (Williams & Hickman), danced by Astaire and Rogers. 'Très Jolie' (Waldteufel), danced by Astaire and Rogers. 'When They were Dancing Around' (McCarthy & Monaco), danced by Astaire and Rogers. 'Little Brown Jug' (Winner), danced by Astaire and Rogers. 'Dengozo' (Nazareth), danced by Astaire and Rogers. Medley including 'The Syncopated Walk' (Berlin), 'You're Here and I'm Here' (Smith & Kern), 'Chicago' (Fisher), 'Hello, Frisco, Hello' (Buck & Hirsch), 'Way Down Yonder in New Orleans' (Creamer & Layton), 'Take Me Back to New York Town' (Sterling & Von Tilzer), danced by Astaire and

Walter Brennan, Rogers and Astaire in The Story of Vernon and Irene Castle.

Rogers and Frank Albertson in Bachelor Mother.

Rogers. 'It's a Long Way to Tipperary' (Judge & Williams), sung by male chorus. 'Hello, Hello, Who's Your Lady Friend?' (David & Lee), sung and danced by Astaire and soldiers. 'Keep the Home Fires Burning' (Ford & Novello), 'Smiles' (Callahan & Roberts), both played by orchestra. Medley including 'Destiny Waltz' (Baynes), 'Night of Gladness' (Ancliffe), 'Missouri Waltz' (Royce & Logan), danced by Astaire and Rogers. 'Over There' (Cohan), background.

6 July 1939
BACHELOR MOTHER

RKO Radio Pictures. Shooting: 6 March - 29 April 1939. 82 minutes.

Directed by Garson Kanin. Produced by B.G. DeSylva. Production Supervisor: Pandro S. Berman. Screenplay: Norman Krasna, based on a story by Felix Jackson. Director of Photography: Robert de Grasse. Art Directors: Van Nest Polglase, Carroll Clark. Set Decorator: Darrell Silvera. Editors: Henry Berman, Robert Wise. Sound Recording: Richard Van Hessen. Musical Director: Roy Webb. Dance Director: Hermes Pan. Costumes: Irene. Make-up Artist: Mel Burns. Special Photographic Effects: Vernon L. Walker. Assistant Director: Edward Killy. Still Photographer: John Miehle.

With: Ginger Rogers (Polly Parrish), David Niven (David Merlin), Charles Coburn (John B. Merlin), Frank Albertson (Freddie Miller), E.E. Clive (butler), Elbert Coplen, Jr (Johnnie, baby), Ferike Boros (Mrs Weiss), Ernest Truex (investigator), Leonard Penn (Jerome Weiss), Paul Stanton (Hargraves), Gerald Oliver-Smith (Hennessy), Leona Roberts (old lady), Dennie Moore (Mary), June Wilkins (Louise King), Frank M. Thomas (doctor), Edna Holland (matron), Irving Bacon (clerk at exchange department), Reed Hadley (dance partner),

Chester Cute (man in park), Florence Lake (woman in park), Barbara Pepper (dance-hall hostess), Horace MacMahon, Charles Hall (bouncers), Edythe Elliott, Murray Alper, Dorothy Adams, Charles Halton, Nestor Paiva, Hugh Prosser, Hal K. Dawson.

8 September 1939
FIFTH AVENUE GIRL

RKO Radio Pictures. Shooting: 20 May - 28 June, retakes 9 August 1939. 83 minutes. New York premiere: 25 August 1939.

Directed and Produced by Gregory La Cava. Screenplay: Allan Scott. Director of Photography: Robert de Grasse. Art Directors: Van Nest Polglase, Perry Ferguson. Set Decorator: Darrell Silvera. Editors: William Hamilton, Robert Wise. Sound Recording: John L. Cass. Musical Director: Robert Russell Bennett. Costumes: Howard Greer. Make-up Artist: Mel Burns. Assistant Director: Edward Killy. Still Photographer: John Miehle.

With: Ginger Rogers (Mary Gray), Walter Connolly (Timothy Borden), Verree Teasdale (Martha Borden), James Ellison (Mike Fairnsbrother), Tim Holt (Tim Borden), Kathryn Adams (Katherine Borden), Franklin Pangborn (Higgins), Ferike Boros (Olga), Louis Calhern (Dr Kessler), Theodore Van Eltz (Terwilliger), Alexander D'Arcy (maître d'hôtel), Bess Flowers (woman in nightclub), Jack Carson (sailor on bench), Robert Emmett Keane (boring seal expert), Manda Lane, Mildred Coles, Larry McGrath, Kerman Cripps, Louis King, Dick Hogan, Earl Richards, Philip Warren, Dell Henderson, Cornelius Keefe, Bob Perry, Dorothy Dilly, Lionel Pape, Max Wagner, Kenny Williams, George Rosener, Aaron Gonzalez and his Tango-Rumba Band.

Musical Number: 'Tropicana' (Aaron Gonzalez).

According to the *AFI Catalog*, an ambiguous ending in which the final shot implies that Tim is allowing Mary to walk away from the Borden house was replaced after sneak previews with the current ending, in which he carries her over the threshold.

9 February 1940
BROADWAY MELODY OF 1940

Metro-Goldwyn-Mayer. Shooting: early September - late November 1939. 100/102 minutes.

Directed by Norman Taurog. Produced by Jack Cummings. Lyrics and Music: Cole Porter.

Rogers and Walter Connolly in Fifth Avenue Girl.

Screenplay: Leon Gordon and George Oppenheimer, from a story by Jack McGowan and Dore Schary. Additional Scriptwriting: Preston Sturges, Albert Mannheimer, Walter DeLeon, Eddie Moran, Thomas Phipps, Vincent Lawrence, Sid Silvers. Dance Director: Bobby Connolly. Additional Choreography: Albertina Rasch. Art Director: Cedric Gibbons. Associate Art Director: John S. Detlie. Art Director for Musical Numbers: Merrill Pye. Set Decoration: Edward B. Willis. Costumes: Adrian, Valles. Musical Director: Alfred Newman. Additional Music: Walter Ruick, Roger Edens. Orchestrations: Edward Powell, Leo Arnaud, Charles Henderson. Additonal Musical Arrangements: George Bassman, Murray Cutter, Wally Heglin. Music Supervisor: Roger Edens. Directors of Photography: Oliver T. Marsh, Joseph Ruttenberg. Editor: Blanche Sewell. Sound Recording: Douglas Shearer.

With: Fred Astaire (Johnny Brett), Eleanor Powell (Clare Bennett, *née* Brigit Callahan), George Murphy (King Shaw), Frank Morgan (Bob Casey), Ian Hunter (Bert Matthews), Florence Rice (Amy Blake), Lynne Carver (Emmy Lou Lee), Ann Morriss (Pearl de Longe), Trixie Firschke (juggler), Douglas McPhail (masked singer), Charlotte Arren (audition singer), Johnny Broderick (audition accompanist), Herman Bing (silhouette artist), Jack Mulhall (theatre manager), Barbara Jo Allen (receptionist), Irving Bacon (soda jerk), Joseph Crehan (dance hall manager), James Flavin (dance hall worker), Joe Yule (unemployed actor), Hal K. Dawson (press agent), Gladys Blake (dance hall bride), George Chandler (dance hall groom), William Tannen (Emmy Lou's friend), Chic Collins (sailor at dance hall), Hal LeSeur (Morgan's chauffeur), Libby Taylor

(Clare's maid), Blair Wolstencroft (unicyclist), E. Alyn Warren (stage doorman), Mary Field (second dance hall bride), Carmen D'Antonio (soprano in 'Begin the Beguine'), The Music Maids (singing quartet in 'Begin the Beguine').

Musical/Dance Numbers: 'Please Don't Monkey With Broadway', sung and danced by Astaire and Murphy. 'I Am the Captain', sung and danced by Powell, sailors. 'Between You and Me', sung by Murphy, danced by Powell and Murphy. 'I've Got My Eyes on You', sung and danced by Astaire. 'Jukebox Dance', danced by Astaire and Powell. 'I Concentrate on You', sung by McPhail, danced by Astaire and Powell. 'Begin the Beguine', sung by The Music Maids and Carmen D'Antonio, dubbed by Lois Hodnett, danced by Astaire and Powell, chorus. 'I've Got My Eyes on You' (reprise), sung by chorus, danced by Astaire, Powell, Murphy. Unused: 'I Happen to be in Love', 'I'm So in Love with You'.

22 March 1940
PRIMROSE PATH

RKO Radio Pictures. Shooting: from early November 1939. 93 minutes.

Directed and produced by Gregory La Cava. Screenplay: Allan Scott, Gregory La Cava, based on the play *The Primrose Path* by Robert Buckner and Walter Hart, and the novel *February Hill* by Victoria Lincoln. Director of Photography: Joseph H. August. Art Directors: Van Nest Polglase, Carroll Clark. Set Decorator: Darrell Silvera. Editor: William Hamilton. Sound Recording: John L. Cass. Musical Director: Werner R. Heymann. Costumes: Renie. Make-up Artist: Mel Burns. Special Photographic Effects: Vernon L. Walker. Assistant Director: Edward Killy. Still Photographer: John Miehle.

With: Ginger Rogers (Ellie May Adams), Joel McCrea (Ed Wallace), Marjorie Rambeau (Mamie Adams), Henry Travers (Gramp), Miles Mander (Homer Adams), Queenie Vassar (Grandma), Joan Carroll (Honeybell), Vivienne Osborne (Thelma), Carmen Morales (Carmelita), Gene Morgan (Hawkins), Lorin Raker, Charles Lane, Mara Alexander, Herbert Corthell, Charles Williams, Larry McGrath, Jack Gardner, Nestor Paiva, Jacqueline Dalya, Lawrence Gleason, Jr., Ray Cooke.

23 August 1940
LUCKY PARTNERS

RKO Radio Pictures. Shooting: 6 April - 6 July 1940. 99/102 minutes.

Directed by Lewis Milestone. Produced by George Haight. Executive Producer: Harry

Edington. Screenplay: Allan Scott, John Van Druten, based on the film *Bonne Chance* (Fernand Rivers, 1935), written by and starring Sacha Guitry. Director of Photography: Robert de Grasse. Art Directors: Van Nest Polglase, Carroll Clark. Set Decorator: Darrell Silvera. Editor: Henry Berman. Sound Recording: John E. Tribby. Musical director: Dimitri Tiomkin. Costumes: Irene. Make-up Artist: Mel Burns. Special Photographic Effects: Vernon L. Walker. Assistant Director: Argyle Nelson. Property Man: Gene Rossi. Still Photographer: John Miehle.

With: Ronald Colman (Paul Knight Somerset, a.k.a. David Grant), Ginger Rogers (Jean Newton), Spring Byington (Aunt Lucy), Jack Carson (Freddie Harper), Cecelia Loftus (Alice Sylvester), Billy Gilbert (Charles), Hugh O'Connell (clerk at Niagara hotel), Brandon Tynan (Alvah Sylvester), Harry Davenport (judge), Leon Belasco (Nick no.1), Edward Conrad (Nick no.2), Olin Howard (tourist), Benny Rubin (first spieler), Tom Dugan (second spieler), Walter Kingsford (Wendell), Otto Hoffman (clerk), Helen Lynd (Ethel), Lucille Gleason (Ethel's mother), Alex Malesh (art dealer), Dorothy Adams (maid in apartment), Billy Benedict (bellboy), Frank Mills (bus driver), Dorothy Vernon (woman on bus), Allen Wood, Murray Alper, Dick Hogan (bellboys), Fern Emmett (maid at hotel), Bruce Hale (bridegroom), Jane Patten (bride), Max Wagner (waiter), Tommy Mack (Joseph), Al Hill (motorcycle cop), George Watts (plainclothes cop), Edgar Dearing (desk sergeant), Grady Sutton (reporter), Robert Dudley (bailiff), Charles Halton (newspaperman), Harlan Briggs (mayor), Nora Cecil (clubwoman), Lloyd Ingraham (chamber of commerce representative), Gayne Whitman (voice of announcer).

27 December 1940
KITTY FOYLE

RKO Radio Pictures. Shooting: 26 August - 26 October 1940. 105/107 minutes.

Directed by Sam Wood. Produced by David Hempstead. Executive Producer: Harry E. Edington. Screenplay: Dalton Trumbo, based on the novel *Kitty Foyle* by Christopher Morley. Additional Dialogue: Donald Ogden Stewart. Director of Photography: Robert de Grasse. Special Photographic Effects: Vernon L. Walker. Art Directors: Van Nest Polglase, Mark-Lee Kirk. Set Decorator: Darrell Silvera. Editor: Henry Berman. Sound Recording: John L. Cass. Musical Director: Roy Webb. Costumes: Renie.

Solo dominance: Astaire conducts and dances in Second Chorus.

Make-up Artist: Mel Burns. Assistant Director: Argyle Nelson. Still Photographer: John Miehle.

With: Ginger Rogers (Kitty Foyle), Dennis Morgan (Wyn Strafford), James Craig (Mark), Eduardo Cianelli (Giono), Ernest Cossart (Pop, Kitty's father), Gladys Cooper (Mrs Strafford), Odette Myrtil (Delphine Detaille), Mary Treen (Pat), Katharine Stevens (Molly), Walter Kingsford (Mr. Kennett), Cecil Cunningham (grandmother), Nella Walker (Aunt Jessica), Edward Fielding (Uncle Edgar), Kay Linaker (Wyn's wife), Richard Nichols (Wyn's son), Florence Bates (customer), Heather Angel (woman in prologue), Tyler Brooke (man in prologue), Frank Milan (Parry), Charles Quigley (Bill), Harriette Brandon (Miss Bala), Howard Entwistle (butler), Billy Elmer (Neway), Walter Sande (trumpeter), Ray Teal (saxophonist), Joey Ray (drummer), Mel Ruick (violinist), Doodles Weaver (pianist), Theodore Von Eltz (hotel clerk), Max Davidson (flower man), Charles Miller (doctor), Mary Gordon (charwoman), Mimi Doyle (Jane), Hilda Plowright (nurse), Gino Corrado (guest at Giono's), Hattie Noel, Spencer Charters, Julie Carter, Jane Patten, Renee Haal, Mary Currier, Patricia Maier, Brooks Benedict, Tom Quinn.

Musical Numbers: 'I'll See You in My Dreams' (Isham Jones), 'Happy Days are Here Again' (Milton Ager & Jack Yellen), 'Want a Girl?' (composer not known).

3 January 1941
SECOND CHORUS

Paramount Pictures, released by Astor Pictures. Shooting: late July - early September 1940. 83 minutes.

Directed by H.C. Potter. Produced by Boris Morros. Lyrics: Johnny Mercer. Music: Artie Shaw, Bernard Hanighen, Hal Bourne. Additional Music: Maceo Pinkard, Victor Young, Johnny Green. Screenplay: Elaine Ryan and Ian McClellan Hunter, from a story by Frank Cavett. Additional Scriptwriting: Johnny Mercer. Dance Director: Hermes Pan. Art Director: Boris Leven. Set Decoration: Howard Bristol. Wardrobe: Helen Taylor. Musical Director: Ed Paul. Orchestrations: Ed Paul, Artie Shaw, Gregory Stone, Johnny Guarnieri. Director of Photography: Theodore Sparkuhl. Editor: Jack Dennis. Assistant Editor: Fred Feitshans. Sound Recording: William Wilmarth. Associate Producer: Robert Stillman. Associate Director: Frank Cavett. Assistant Director: Edward Montagne. Production Manager: Joe Nadel.

With: Fred Astaire (Danny O'Neill), Paulette Goddard (Ellen Miller), Artie Shaw as himself, Burgess Meredith (Hank Taylor), Charles Butterworth (J. Lester Chisholm), Frank Melton (Ellen's friend), Jimmy Conlin (Mr. Dunn), Dan Brodie (hotel clerk).

Astaire's trumpet-playing was dubbed by Bobby Hackett, Meredith's by Billy Butterfield.

Musical/Dance Numbers: 'I Ain't Hep to that Step but I'll Dig It' (Mercer & Bourne), sung by

Astaire, danced by Astaire and Goddard. 'Sweet Sue' (Will Harris & Victor Young), played by Hackett and Butterfield, orchestra. 'Love of My Life' (Mercer & Shaw), sung by Astaire with the Shaw orchestra. 'I'm Yours' (E.Y. Harburg & Johnny Green), played by Hackett and Butterfield with the Shaw orchestra. 'Concerto for Clarinet (Swing Concerto)', played by the Shaw orchestra. 'Poor Mr Chisholm (Hoe Down the Bayou)' (Mercer & Hanighen), sung by Astaire, reprised as dance by Astaire with the Shaw orchestra.

Stills exist of 'Me and the Ghost Upstairs' (Mercer & Hanighen), a number with Astaire and Hermes Pan. The number may have been fully shot but was not used.

17 July 1941
TOM, DICK AND HARRY

RKO Radio Pictures. Shooting: mid-February - 9 May 1941. 86 minutes.

Directed by Garson Kanin. Produced by Robert Sisk. Screenplay: Paul Jarrico. Director of Photography: Merritt Gerstad. Art Directors: Van Nest Polglase, Mark-Lee Kirk. Set Decorator: Darrell Silvera. Editor: John Sturges. Sound Recording: Earl L. Wolcott. Musical Director: Roy Webb. Costumes: Renie. Make-up Artist: Mel Burns. Special Photographic Effects: Vernon L. Walker. Assistant Director: Fred A. Flock. Still Photographer: John Miehle.

With: Ginger Rogers (Janie), George Murphy (Tom), Alan Marshal (Dick Hamilton), Burgess Meredith (Harry), Joe Cunningham (Pop), Jane Seymour (Ma), Lenore Lonergan (Babs), Vicki Lester (Paula), Phil Silvers (ice cream salesman), Betty Breckenridge (Gertrude), Sid Skolsky (announcer), Edna Holland (Miss Schlom), Gus Glassmire (music store proprietor), Netta Packer (sales clerk), Sarah Edwards (Mrs Burton), Ellen Lowe (matron), William Halligan (Mr Burton), Joe Bernard (judge), Gertrude Short (bridge playing matron), Edward Colebrook (stalled car driver), Gayle Mellott (Brenda), Dorothy Lloyd (gypsy oracle), Berry Kroeger (boy lead), Lurene Tuttle (girl lead), Knox Manning (radio announcer), William Alland (newsreel announcer), Jack Briggs (boy), Jane Patten, Theodore Ramsey.

Musical Number: 'Tom Collins' (Gene Rose & Roy Webb).

25 September 1941
YOU'LL NEVER GET RICH

Columbia Pictures. Shooting: 20 May - 24 July 1941. 88 minutes.

Directed by Sidney Lanfield. Produced by Samuel Bischoff. Lyrics and Music: Cole Porter. Additional Music: Charles Bradshaw, Nico Grigor. Screenplay: Michael Fessier and Ernest Pagano. Dance Director: Robert Alton. Art Director: Lionel Banks. Costumes: Irene. Musical Director: Morris Stoloff. Assistant Musical Director: Paul Mertz. Musical Arrangements: Carmen Dragon, Leo Arnaud, Paul Mertz. Orchestrations: Leo Shuken. Director of Photography: Philip Tannura. Editor: Otto Meyer. Music Recording: P. J. Faulkner. Assistant Editor: Gene Anderson. Technical Advisor: Jack Voglin.

With: Fred Astaire (Robert Curtis), Rita Hayworth (Sheila Winthrop), Robert Benchley (Martin Courtland), John Hubbard (Tom Barton), Osa Massen (Sonya), Frieda Inescort (Julia Courtland), Guinn Williams (Kewpie Blain), Donald MacBride (top sergeant), Cliff Nazzaro (Swivel Tongue), Ann Shoemaker (Mrs Barton), Marjorie Gateson (Aunt Louise), Boyd Davis (Colonel Shiller), Robert McWade (army doctor), Martha Tilton (singer), Emmett Vogan (Martin's chauffeur), Jack Rice (jewellery salesman), Robert Homans (Joe), Sunnie O'Dea (Marge, chorus girl), Lester Dorr (newspaper photographer), Tim Ryan (policeman), Edward McWade (army doctor), Harry Burns (foreigner at Grand Central), Hal K. Dawson (information clerk), Monty Collins (man in barracks), Jack O'Malley (sentry), Harold Goodwin (Captain Williams), Paul Phillips (Captain Nolan), Eddie Coke (chauffeur), Frank Wayne, Tony Hughes (prisoners), Frank Sully, Garry Owen (Robert's guards), Harry Strang (orderly), Forrest Prince (dancer in 'Wedding Cake Walk'), Frank Ferguson (justice of the peace), Larry Williams, James Millican (soldiers), The Delta Rhythm Boys [Rudolph Hunter, John Porter, Lucius Brooks, Leon Buck] (guardhouse inmates). Jazz group: Chico Hamilton (drums), Buddy Colette (clarinet), A. Grant (guitar), Joe Comfort (jug), Red Mack (trumpet).

Musical/Dance Numbers: 'The Boogie Barcarolle' danced by Astaire and Hayworth, chorus. 'Dream Dancing', played by orchestra. 'Shootin' the Works for Uncle Sam', sung by Astaire, chorus, danced by Astaire, chorus. 'Since I Kissed my Baby Goodbye', sung by Delta Rhythm Boys, danced by Astaire. 'A-stairable Rag (March Milastaire)', danced by Astaire, with jazz group. 'So Near and Yet So Far', sung by Astaire, danced by Astaire and Hayworth. 'Wedding Cake Walk', sung by Tilton, danced by Astaire, Hayworth, chorus.

20 February 1942
ROXIE HART

20th Century-Fox Pictures. Shooting: late October - early December 1941, retakes 2 Jan 1942. 72/75 minutes.

Directed by William A. Wellman. Produced by Nunnally Johnson. Screenplay: Nunnally Johnson, based on the play *Chicago* by Maurine Watkins. Director of Photography: Leon Shamroy. Art Directors: Richard Day, Wiard B. Ihnen. Set Decorator: Thomas Little. Editor: James B. Clark. Sound Recording: Alfred Bruzlin, Roger Heman. Musical Director: Alfred Newman. Costumes: Gwen Wakeling. Dance Director: Hermes Pan. Make-up Artist: Guy Pearce. Assistant Director: Ad Schaumer.

With: Ginger Rogers (Roxie Hart), Adolphe Menjou (Billy Flynn), George Montgomery (Homer Howard), Lynne Overman (Jake Callahan), Nigel Bruce (E. Clay Benham), Phil Silvers (Babe), Sara Allgood (Mrs Morton, matron), William Frawley (O'Malley), Spring Byington (Mary Sunshine), Ted North (Stuart Chapman), Helene Reynolds (Velma Wall), George Chandler (Amos Hart), Charles D. Brown (Charles E. Murdock), Morris Ankrum (Martin S. Harrison, District Attorney), George Lessey (judge), Iris Adrian ('Two-Gun' Gertie), Milton Parsons (announcer), Billy Wayne (court clerk), Charles Williams (photographer), Leon Belasco (waiter), Lee Shumway (policeman), Larry Lawson, Harry Carter (reporters), Pat O'Malley (policeman), Bob Perry (prisoner's bailiff), Jeff Corey (orderly), Phillip Morris (policeman), Jack Norton (producer), Leonard Kibrick (newsboy), Frank Orth, Alec Craig, Edward Clark (idlers at bar), Frank Darien (Finnegan), Jim Pearce (policeman), Arthur Aylesworth (Mr Wadsworth), Margaret Seddon (Mrs. Wadsworth), Stanley Blystone (policeman), Mary Treen (secretary).

Musical/Dance Numbers: 'Chicago (That Toddling Town)' (Fred Fisher), background to credits. 'Here Am I Broken Hearted' (B.G. DeSylva, Lew Brown & Ray Henderson), sung by Montgomery. 'Black Bottom' (Ray Henderson), danced by Rogers and cast in jail sequence, 'Grab It by the Horn and Hit It while It's Hot' (composer unknown), danced by Rogers.

12 June 1942
HOLIDAY INN

Paramount Pictures. Shooting: 28 November 1941 - 30 January 1942. 100 minutes. New York premiere, 4 August 1942.

Directed and Produced by Mark Sandrich. Music and lyrics: Irving Berlin. Screenplay: Claude Binyon, adapted by Elmer Rice from an idea by Irving Berlin. Dance Director: Danny Dare. Assistant Dance Director: Babe Pierce. Art Directors: Hans Dreier, Roland Anderson. Costumes: Edith Head. Musical Director: Robert Emmett Dolan. Assistant Musical Director: Arthur Franklin. Vocal Arrangements: Joseph H. Lilley. Additional Arrangements: Paul Wetstein, Gilbert Grau, Herbert Spencer, Walter Scharf. Make-up Artist: Wally Westmore. Sound Recording: Earl Hayman, John Cope. Director of Photography: David Abel. Editor: Ellsworth Hoagland. Assistant Director: Charles C. Coleman, Jr.

With: Bing Crosby (Jim Hardy), Fred Astaire (Ted Hanover), Marjorie Reynolds (Linda Mason) [singing dubbed by Martha Mears], Virginia Dale (Lila Dixon), Walter Abel (Danny Reed), Louise Beavers (Mamie), Marek Windheim (headwaiter), Irving Bacon (Gus), Jacques Vanaire (assistant headwaiter), Judith Gibson (cigarette girl), Shelby Bacon (Vanderbilt), Joan Arnold (Daphne), John Gallaudet (Parker), James Bell (Dunbar, film director), Leon Belasco (flower shop owner), Harry Barris (band leader), Robert Homans (studio doorman), Bud Jamison (santa claus), Kitty Kelly (drunken woman), Bob Crosby's Bob Cats (band at Holday Inn).

Musical/Dance Numbers: 'I'll Capture Your Heart Singing', sung by Crosby, Astaire, Dale. 'Lazy', sung by Crosby. 'You're Easy to Dance With', sung by Astaire, male chorus, danced by Astaire and Dale. 'White Christmas', sung by Crosby, Reynolds. 'Happy Holiday', sung by Crosby, Reynolds, chorus. 'Holiday Inn', sung by Crosby, Reynolds. 'Let's Start the New Year Right', sung by Crosby. 'Abraham', sung by Crosby, Beavers, Reynolds, chorus. 'Be Careful, It's My Heart', sung by Crosby, danced by Astaire and Reynolds. 'I Can't Tell a Lie', sung by Astaire, danced by Astaire and Reynolds, with the Bob Cats. 'Easter Parade', sung by Crosby. 'Let's Say It with Firecrackers', sung by chorus, danced by Astaire. 'Song of Freedom', sung by Crosby, chorus. 'I've Got Plenty to Be Thankful For', sung by Crosby. Background: 'Oh, How I Hate to Get Up in the Morning'. Unused: 'It's a Great Country'.

16 October 1942
THE MAJOR AND THE MINOR

Paramount Pictures. Shooting: 13 March - early May 1942. 100 minutes.

Directed by Billy Wilder. Produced by Arthur Hornblow, Jr. Screenplay: Charles Brackett, Billy

Wilder, based on the play *Connie Goes Home* by Edward Childs Carpenter, based on the story *Sunny Goes Home* by Fannie Kilbourne. Director of Photography: Leo Tover. Art Directors: Hans Dreier, Roland Anderson. Editor: Doane Harrison. Sound Recording: Harold Lewis, Don Johnson. Musical Director: Robert Emmett Dolan. Costumes: Edith Head. Make-up Artist: Wally Westmore. Assistant Director: C.C. Coleman.

With: Ginger Rogers (Susan Applegate), Ray Milland (Major Kirby), Rita Johnson (Pamela Hill), Robert Benchley (Mr Osborne), Diana Lynn (Lucy Hill), Edward Fielding (Colonel Hill), Frankie Thomas (Cadet Osborne), Raymond Roe (Cadet Wigton), Charles Smith (Cadet Korner), Larry Nunn (Cadet Babcock), Billy Dawson (Cadet Miller), Lela Rogers (Mrs Applegate), Aldrich Bowker (Rev. Doyle), Boyd Irwin (Major Griscom), Byron Shores (Captain Durand), Richard Kiske (Will Duffy), Norma Varden (Mrs Osborne), Gretl Sherk (Mrs Schackleford), Stanley Desmond (Shumaker), Will Wright (first ticket agent), William Newell (second ticket agent), Freddie Mercer (boy in railroad station), Carlotta Jelm (girl in railroad station), Tom McGuire (news vendor), George Andersen (man with 'Esquire'), Stanley Andrews (first conductor), Emory Parnell (second conductor), Guy Wilkerson (farm truck driver), Milt Kibbee (station agent), Archie Twitchell (sergeant), Alice Keating (nurse), Ralph Gilliam, Dick Chandlee, Buster Nichols, Stephen Kirchner, Kenneth Grant, Billy Clauson, John Bogden, Bradley Hail, Billy O'Kelly, Jack Lindquist, David McKim, Jim Pilcher, Don Wilmot (cadets), Billy Ray (Cadet Somerville), Marie Blake (Bertha), Mary Field (mother in railroad station), Dell Henderson (doorman), Ed Peil, Sr (stationmaster), Ken Lundy (elevator boy), Tom Dugan (deadbeat), Dickie Jones, Billy Cook, Ethel Clayton, Gloria Williams, Lynda Grey.

19 October 1942
YOU WERE NEVER LOVELIER

Columbia Pictures. Shooting: 2 June - 7 August 1942. 98 minutes.

Directed by William A. Seiter. Produced by Louis F. Edelman. Lyrics: Johnny Mercer. Music: Jerome Kern. Additional Music: Raphael Hernandez, Noro Morales, J. Camacho, Gilbert Valdes, Franz Liszt. Screenplay: Michael Fessier, Ernest Pagano and Delmer Daves, from a story by Carlos Oliveri and Sixto Pondal Rios. Dance Director: Val Raset. Art Director: Lionel Banks. Associate Art Director: Ralph Sternad. Set

Decoration: Frank Tuttle. Costumes: Irene. Musical Director: Leigh Harline. Assistant Musical Director: Paul Mertz. Orchestrations: Leigh Harline, Conrad Salinger, Lyle 'Spud' Murphy. Director of Photography: Ted Tetzlaff. Editor: William Lyon. Sound Recording: P. J. Faulkner. Assistant Director: Norman Deming.

With: Fred Astaire (Robert Davis), Rita Hayworth (Maria Acuña) [singing dubbed by Nan Wynn], Adolphe Menjou (Eduardo Acuña), Xavier Cugat (himself), Leslie Brooks (Cecy Acuña), Adele Mara (Lita Acuña), Isabel Elsom (Maria Castro), Gus Schilling (Fernando), Barbara Brown (Delfina Acuña), Douglas Leavitt (Juan Castro), Catherine Craig (Julia Acuña), Kathleen Howard (grandmother Acuña), Mary Field (maid), Larry Parks (Tony), Stanley Brown (Roddy), Lina Romay, Miguelito Valdes (singers).

Musical/Dance Numbers: 'Chiu, Chiu' (Niconar Molinare), sung by Romay, chorus, Cugat orchestra. 'Dearly Beloved', sung by Astaire, Cugat orchestra, reprised and danced by Hayworth. 'Audition Dance', danced by Astaire with Cugat orchestra. 'I'm Old Fashioned', sung by Hayworth, danced by Astaire and Hayworth. 'Shorty George', sung by Astaire with Cugat orchestra, danced by Astaire and Hayworth. 'Wedding in the Spring', sung by Romay with Cugat orchestra. 'You Were Never Lovelier', sung by Astaire, reprised as brief dance by Astaire and Hayworth. 'These Orchids', sung by delivery boys. Unused: 'On the Beam'. A longer dance version of 'You Were Never Lovelier' with Astaire and Hayworth was filmed but not used.

30 October 1942.
TALES OF MANHATTAN

20th Century-Fox Pictures. Shooting: 22 October 1941 - 5 February 1942. 118 minutes in total, Rogers's episode 25 minutes.

Directed by Julien Duvivier. Produced by Boris Morros and S.P. Eagle. Screenplay: Ben Hecht, Ferenc Molnar, Donald Ogden Stewart, Samuel Hoffenstein, Alan Campbell, Ladislaus Fodor, L. Vadnai, L. Gorog, Lamar Trotti, Henry Blankfort. Director of Photography: Joseph Walker. Art Directors: Richard Day, Boris Leven. Set Decorator: Thomas Little. Editor: Robert Bischoff. Sound Recording: W.D. Flick, Roger Heman. Musical Director: Edward Paul. Musical Score: Sol Kaplan. Vocal Arrangements: Hall Johnson. Orchestrators: Charles Bradshaw, Hugo Friedhofer, Clarence Wheeler. Costumes: Dolly Tree, Bernard Newman, Gwen Wakeling, Irene. Make-up Artist: Guy Pearce. Assistant Director: Robert Stillman. Unit Manager: J.H. Vadel.

With (episode starring Rogers only): Ginger Rogers (Diane), Henry Fonda (George), Gail Patrick (Ellen), Cesar Romero (Harry), Roland Young (Edgar), Marion Martin (Miss 'Squirrel' Grey), Eugene Palette (Luther).

Tales of Manhattan was shot as six episodes, linked only by the device of following the history of a single garment, a man's dress tailcoat. One episode, starring W.C. Fields, Phil Silvers and Margaret Dumont, was deleted after shooting – the other four episodes starred Charles Boyer, Rita Hayworth, Charles Laughton, Edward G. Robinson, Paul Robeson, Ethel Waters and Eddie 'Rochester' Anderson.

The *donnée* of the Rogers episode is that her character has never truly noticed the Fonda character, the friend of her two-timing fiancé. Believing that he has received a passionate letter from another girl, she sees him in a new light. The climax of the sketch, as the couple drift from quoting the letter into declarations of their love for each other, is perhaps as near as scriptwriting and performance can come to offering the equivalent of a danced duet in words.

4 November 1942
ONCE UPON A HONEYMOON

RKO Radio Pictures. Shooting: 8 June - 21 August, additional scenes 2 - 29 September 1942. 116 minutes.

Directed and produced by Leo McCarey. Screenplay: Sheridan Gibney, based on a story by Leo McCarey, Sheridan Gibney. Director of Photography: George Barnes. Art Directors: Albert S. D'Agostino, Al Herman. Set Decorators: Darrell Silvera, Claude E. Carpenter. Editor: Theron Warth. Sound Recording: Steve Dunn. Musical Director: Robert Emmett Dolan. Costumes: Miss Leslie. Make-up Artist: Mel Burns. Montage: Douglas Travers. Special Photographic Effects: Vernon L. Walker. Assistant Directors: Harry Scott, James Anderson. Still Photographer: John Miehle.

With: Ginger Rogers (Katie O'Hara), Cary Grant (Pat O'Toole), Walter Slezak (Baron Von Luber), Albert Dekker (Gaston Leblanc), Albert Basserman (General Borelski), Ferike Boros (Elsa), John Banner (Kleinoch), Harry Shannon (Ed Cumberland), Natasha Lytess (Anna), Hans Conreid (Schneider, tailor), Alex Malesh (waiter), Walter Byron, Otto Reichow (guards), Peter Seal (Polish orderly), Hans Wollenberger (waiter), Walter Stahl, Russell Gaige (guests of Von Luber), Dina Smirnova (traveller, Warsaw), George Irving (American consul), William Vaughn (German colonel), Dell Henderson (American attache), Carl Ekberg (Hitler), Fred Niblo (ship's captain), Oscar Lorraine (ship's steward), Bert Roach (bartender), Emory Parnell (quisling), Boyd Davis (Chamberlin), Claudine De Luc (hotel proprietor), Rudolph Myzed, Felix Bosch, Joseph Kamaryt, Leda Nicova.

21 August 1943
THE SKY'S THE LIMIT

RKO Radio Pictures. Shooting: 13 January - early March 1943. 89 minutes.

Directed by Edward H. Griffith. Produced by David Hempstead. Lyrics: Johnny Mercer. Music: Harold Arlen. Additional Music: Freddie Slack. Screenplay: Frenk Fenton and Lynn Root from their story *A Handful of Heaven*, derived from the story *On Special Service* by William T. Ryder. Additional Scriptwriting: S. K. Lauren. Dance Director: Fred Astaire. Art Directors: Albert S. D'Agostino, Carroll Clark. Set Decoration: Darrell Silvera, Claude Carpenter. Costumes: Renie. Musical Director: Leigh Harline. Orchestrations: Leigh Harline, Roy Webb, Phil Green, Phil Moore, Sid Cutner, Maurice de Packh, Jack Virgil, Gilbert Grau. Sound Recording: Richard Van Hessen. Sound Pre-recording: James G. Stewart. Director of Photography: Russell Metty. Special Photographic Effects: Vernon Walker. Associate Producer: Sherman Todd. Assistant Director: Ruby Rosenberg. Technical Advisor: Robert T. Smith. Editor: Roland Gross.

With: Fred Astaire (Fred Atwell, a.k.a. Fred Burton), Joan Leslie (Joan Manion) [singing dubbed by Sally Sweetland], Robert Benchley (Phil Harriman), Robert Ryan (Reg Fenton), Elizabeth Patterson (Mrs Fisher), Marjorie Gateson (canteen hostess), Eric Blore (Jackson), Clarence Kolb (Harvey J. Sloan), Richard Davies (Dick Merlin), Paul Hurst (longshoreman), Ed McNamara (Mac, bartender), Olin Howlin ('4F' man driving car), Joseph Kim (Chinese official), Amelita Ward (southern girl in motorcade), Neil Hamilton (navy officer on train), Frank Melton (second navy officer), Peter Lawford (USAF commander), Clarence Muse (doorman at Colonial Club), Ferris Taylor (Mr Kiefer, short order cook), Dorothy Kelly (Harriman's secretary), Al Hill (sergeant at canteen door), Larry Rio (dancing soldier at canteen), Norma Drury (Mrs Leo Roskowski), Vic Potel (first bartender), Joe Bernard (second bartender), Al Murphy (third bartender), The Freddie Slack Orchestra (The Colonial Club Orchestra).

Musical/Dance Numbers: 'My Shining Hour', sung by Leslie with the Slack Orchestra. reprised by Astaire, and as dance by Astaire and Leslie. 'A

Lot in Common With You', sung and danced by Astaire and Leslie. 'One for My Baby (and One More for the Road)' sung by Astaire, danced by Astaire. Background: 'Three Little Words' (Kalmar & Ruby), 'Can't Get Out of this Mood' (Loesser & McHugh), 'I Get the Neck of the Chicken' (Loesser & McHugh). Unused: 'Hangin' on to You'. Two numbers were filmed but cut from the film before general release: 'Harvey the Victory Garden Man', sung by Ella Mae Morse, and an Astaire solo known as 'Trestle Dance'. See Mueller, p.237.

19 December 1943
TENDER COMRADE

RKO Radio Pictures. Shooting: 13 August - 27 October 1943, retakes 12 December, 7-9, 20 January 1944. 102 minutes.

Directed by Edward Dmytryk. Produced by David Hempstead. Associate Producer: Sherman Todd. Screenplay: Dalton Trumbo, based on his own story. Director of Photography: Russell Metty. Art Directors: Al D'Agostino, Carroll Clark. Set Decorators: Darrell Silvera, Al Fields. Editor: Roland Gross. Sound Recording: Roy Meadows. Musical Score: Leigh Harline. Musical Director: C. Bakaleinikoff. Orchestrations: Maurice de Packh. Miss Rogers's Costumes: Edith Head. Gowns: Renie. Make-up Artist: Mel Burns. Special Effects: Vernon L. Walker. Assistant Director: Harry Scott. Still Photographer: John Miehle.

With: Ginger Rogers (Jo Jones), Robert Ryan (Chris Jones), Ruth Hussey (Barbara), Patricia Collinge (Helen Stacey), Mady Christians (Manya), Kim Hunter (Doris), Jane Darwell (Mrs Henderson, woman on station platform), Mary Forbes (Jo's mother), Richard Martin (Mike), Richard Gaines (Waldo), Patti Brill (Western Union girl), Euline Martin (baby), Edward Fielding (doctor), Claire Whitney (nurse), Donald Davis, Robert Anderson (boys).

9 February 1944
LADY IN THE DARK

Paramount Pictures. Shooting: 9 December 1942 - 20 March 1943, retakes 23-24 March, 16 April 1943. 100 minutes. New York premiere: 22 February 1944.

Directed and produced by Mitchell Leisen. Associate Producer: Richard Blumenthal. Executive Producer: B. G. DeSylva. Screenplay: Frances Goodrich, Albert Hackett, based on the play *Lady in the Dark* by Moss Hart. Music and Lyrics: Ira Gershwin, Kurt Weill, others as below. Director of Photography: Ray Rennahan. Art Directors: Hans Dreier, Raoul Pene du Bois. Set Decorator: Ray Moyer. Editor: Alma Macrorie. Sound Recording: Earl Hayman, Walter Oberst. Musical Director: Robert Emmett Dolan. Music Associate: Arthur Franklin. Orchestrator: Robert Russell Bennett. Vocal Arrangements: Joseph J. Lilley. Costumes: Raoul Pene du Bois, Madame Karinska. Modern Gowns: Edith Head. Dance Director: Billy Daniels. Make-up Artist: Wally Westmore. Special Photographic Effects: Gordon Jennings, Paul Lerpae, Farciot Edouart. Assistant Directors: Chico Alonso, Richard McWhorter. Colour Consultant: Natalie Kalmus. Associate Colour Consultant: Morgan Padelford. Still Photographer: G. E. Richardson. Colour: Technicolor.

With: Ginger Rogers (Liza Elliott), Ray Milland (Charley Johnson), Warner Baxter (Kendall Nesbitt), Jon Hall (Randy Curtis), Barry Sullivan (Dr Brooks), Mischa Auer (Russell Paxton), Phyllis Brooks (Allison Dubois), Mary Phillips (Maggie Grant), Edward Fielding (Dr Carlton), Frances Robinson (girl with Randy), Don Loper (Adams), Mary Parker (Miss Parker), Catherine Craig (Miss Foster), Marietta Canty (Martha), Virginia Farmer (Miss Edwards), Fay Helm (Miss Bowers), Gail Russell (Barbara), Marian Hall (Miss Stevens), Kay Linaker (Liza's mother), Harvey Stephens (Liza's father), Billy Daniels (office boy), Georgia Backus (Miss Sullivan), Rand Brooks (Ben), Pepito Perez (clown), Charles Smith (Barbara's boyfriend), Mary MacLaren (librarian), Paul McVey (Jack Goddard), Paul Pierce, George Mayon (speciality dancers), George Calliga (captain of waiters), Jan Buckingham (Miss Shawn), Jack Mulhall (photographer), Hillary Brooke (Miss Barr), Miriam Franklin (dancer), Dorothy Granger (autograph hunter), Charles Coleman (butler), Lester Sharpe (pianist), Bobby Beers (Charley as a boy), Phyllis M. Brooks (Barbara at seven), Marjean Neville (Liza at five and seven), Charles Bates (David), Audrey Young, Louise LaPlanche (office girls), Murray Alper (taxi driver), Billy Dawson (boy at circus), Priscilla Lyon (girl at circus), Buz Buckley (freckle-faced boy), Herbert Corthell (senator), Tristram Coffin, Dennis Moore, Jack Luden.

Musical/Dance Numbers: 'Girl of the Moment' (Gershwin & Weill), sung by Rogers and chorus. 'Suddenly It's Spring' (Johnny Burke & James Van Heusen), danced by Rogers and Don Loper, sung by chorus. 'Jenny' (Gershwin & Weill), sung by Rogers and chorus. 'My Ship' (Gershwin & Weill), briefly sung by Stephens and Neville.

23 December 1944
I'LL BE SEEING YOU

A Vanguard Production for Selznick International Pictures. Released through United Artists. Shooting: late March - 29 May 1944. 83/85 minutes.

Directed by William Dieterle. Produced by Dore Schary. Screenplay: Marion Parsonnet, based on the radio play *Double Furlough* by Charles Martin. Director of Photography: Tony Gaudio. Art Director: Mark-Lee Kirk. Set Decorators: Earl B. Wooden, Emile Kuri. Editor: William H. Ziegler. Editorial Supervisor: Hal C. Kern. Musical Director: Daniele Amfitheatrof. Costumes: Edith Head. Make-up Artist: William Riddle. Assistant Director: Lowell J. Farrell. Production Assistant: Lou Lusty.

With: Ginger Rogers (Mary Marshall), Joseph Cotten (Zachary Morgan), Shirley Temple (Barbara Marshall), Spring Byington (Mrs Marshall), Tom Tully (Mr Marshall), Chill Wills (Swanson), Dare Harris [John Derek](Lt. Bruce), Kenny Bowers (sailor on train), Stanley Ridges (warden), Walter Baldwin (vendor), Dorothy Stone (saleslady).

Musical Number: (credits and background) 'I'll Be Seeing You' (Irving Kahal & Sammy Fain).

After the principal photography of the film was complete, George Cukor directed some further close-ups of Shirley Temple at the request of David O. Selznick (*see* Thomson, p. 421).

12 July 1945
WEEKEND AT THE WALDORF

Metro-Goldwyn-Mayer. Shooting: 9 November 1944 - early February 1945. 128/130 minutes.

Directed by Robert Z. Leonard. Produced by Arthur Hornblow, Jr. Screenplay: Sam and Bella Spewack, based on the play *Grand Hotel* by Vicki Baum, adapted by Guy Bolton. Director of Photography: Robert Planck. Art Directors: Cedric Gibbons, Daniel B. Cathcart. Set Decorators: Edwin B. Willis, Jack Bonar. Editor: Robert J. Kern. Dance Director: Charles Walters. Sound Recording: Douglas Shearer. Musical Director: Johnny Green. Underscoring: Sidney Cutner. Orchestrations: Sidney Cutner, Ted Duncan, Leo Shuken. Choral Arrangement: Kay Thompson. Costumes: Irene, Marion Herwood Keyes. Make-up Artist: Jack Dawn. Hair Stylist: Sydney Guilaroff. Special Effects: Warren Newcombe. Assistant director: Bill Lewis. Technical Advisor: Ted Saucier.

With: Ginger Rogers (Irene Malvern), Lana Turner (Bunny Smith), Walter Pidgeon (Chip Collyer), Van Johnson (Capt. James Hollis), Robert Benchley (Randy Morton), Edward Arnold (Martin X. Edley), Constance Collier (Mme Jaleska), Leon Ames (Henry Burton), Warner Anderson (Dr Campbell), Phyllis Thaxter (Cynthia Drew), Keenan Wynn (Oliver Webson), Porter Hall (Stevens), Samuel S. Hinds (Mr Jessup), George Zucco (Bey of Aribajan), Xavier Cugat (himself), Lina Romay (Juanita), Bob Graham (himself), Michael Kirby (Lt. John Rand), Cora Sue Collins (Jane Rand), Rosemary De Camp (Anna), Jacqueline De Wit (Kate Douglas), Frank Puglia (Emile), Charles Wilson (Hi Johns), Irving Bacon (Sam Skelly), Miles Mander (British secretary), Nana Bryant (Mrs H. Davenport Drew), Russell Hicks (McPherson), Ludmilla Pitoeff (Irma), Naomi Childers (night maid), Moroni Olsen (house detective Blake), William Halligan (Chief Jennings), John Wengraf (Alix), William Hall (Cassidy, doorman), Rex Evans (pianist), Wyndham Standing (literary type), Harry Barris (Anna's boyfriend), Byron Foulger (barber), Gladden James (assistant manager), Carli Elinor (orchestra leader), Dick Crockett (bell captain), William Tannen (photographer), Mel Schubert, Jack Luden, Hal K. Dawson (clerks), Gertrude Short (telephone operator), Mary Icide (elevator girl), Helen McLeod (elevator operator), Dorothy Christy (cashier), Gloria Findlay (Turkish coffee girl), Bess Flowers (guest).

Musical Numbers: 'Guadalajara' (Sammy Fain & Ted Koehler), sung by Romay with Cugat and orchestra, chorus. 'And There You Are' (Pepe Guizar), sung by Graham with Cugat and orchestra.

15 November 1945
YOLANDA AND THE THIEF

Metro-Goldwyn-Mayer. Shooting: 15 January - mid-May 1945. 108 minutes. New York premiere: 22 November 1945.

Directed by Vincente Minnelli. Produced by Arthur Freed. Lyrics: Arthur Freed. Music: Harry Warren. Screenplay: Irving Brecher, from a story by Jacques Thery and Ludwig Bemelmans. Additional Scriptwriting: George Wells, Robert Nathan, Joseph Schrank. Associate Producer: Roger Edens. Dance Director: Eugene Loring. Art Directors: Cedric Gibbons, Jack Martin Smith. Set Decorator: Edwin B. Willis. Associate Set Decorator: Richard Pefferle. Make-up Artist: Jack Dawn. Costumes: Irene. Musical Director: Lennie Hayton. Orchestrations: Conrad Salinger, Wally Heglin, Lennie Hayton. Additional

Orchestrations: Robert Franklyn, Ted Duncan.
Director of Photography: Charles Rosher. Colour
Consultant: Natalie Kalmus. Associate Colour
Consultant: Henri Jaffa. Special Effects: A.
Arnold Gillespie, Warren Newcombe. Sound
Recording: Douglas Shearer. Editor: George
White. Colour: Technicolor.

With: Fred Astaire (Johnny Riggs), Lucille
Bremer (Yolanda Aquaviva) [singing dubbed by
Trudy Erwin], Frank Morgan (Victor 'Junior'
Trout), Mildred Natwick (Amarilla Aquaviva),
Mary Nash (duenna), Leon Ames (Mr Candle),
Ludwig Stoessel (schoolteacher), Jane Green
(mother superior), Remo Buffano (puppeteer),
Francis Pierlot (padre), Leon Belasco (taxi
driver), Charles La Torre (police chief), Richard
Visaroff (major domo), Ghislaine Perreau (child
at breakfast table), Marek Windheim (waiter on
train), Danna McGraw (Conchita), Oscar
Lorraine (Mr Banillo).

Musical/Dance Numbers: 'This is a Day for
Love', sung by schoolchildren. 'Angel', sung by
Bremer. 'Dream Ballet', danced by Astaire and
Bremer, dancers, including 'Will You Marry
Me?', sung by Bremer, chorus. 'Yolanda', sung
and danced by Astaire. 'Coffee Time', sung by
chorus, danced by Astaire, Bremer, inhabitants of
Patria.

15 January 1946
ZIEGFELD FOLLIES

Metro-Goldwyn-Mayer. Shooting: 10-18 April
1944; additonal scenes and retakes 22 December
1944, 26 January - 6 February 1945. 110 minutes.
Roadshow (Boston) premiere: August 20, 1945.
New York premiere: 22 March 1946.

Directed by Vincente Minnelli (also Norman
Taurog, George Sidney, Merrill Pye, Robert
Lewis, Lemuel Ayers, Roy Del Ruth). Produced
by Arthur Freed. Lyrics: Ralph Freed, Earl
Brent, Piave, Arthur Freed, Ralph Blane, Douglas
Furber, Charles Ingle, Kay Thompson, Ira
Gershwin. Music: Roger Edens, Giuseppe Verdi,
Harry Warren, Hugh Martin, Philip Braham,
Charles Ingle, George Gershwin. Sketches: Pete
Barry, Harry Tugend, George White, David
Freeman, Roger Edens, Kay Thompson. Dance
Director: Robert Alton (also Eugene Loring,
Charles Walters, Roy Del Ruth). Art Directors:
Cedric Gibbons, Merrill Pye, Jack Martin Smith.
Costumes: Helen Rose, Irene. Musical Director:
Lennie Hayton. Orchestrations: Conrad Salinger,
Wally Heglin. Musical Adaptation: Roger Edens.
Additional Arrangements: Ted Duncan, Calvin
Jackson, Paul Marquardt. Vocal Arrangements:
Kay Thompson. Directors of Photography:
George Folsey, Charles Rosher, Ray June.

Astaire and Gene Kelly in Ziegfeld Follies.

Photography of Puppet Sequence: William
Ferrari. Colour Consultant: Natalie Kalmus.
Associate Colour Consultant: Henri Jaffa.
Settings: Merrill Pye, Jack Martin Smith, Harry
McAfee, Edward Carfagno, Lemuel Ayers, Irene
Sharaff. Statuary: Tony Duquette. Make-up
Artist: Jack Dawn. Hairstylist: Sydney Guilaroff.
Sound Recording: Douglas Shearer. Editor:
Albert Akst. Colour: Technicolor.

With: Fred Astaire, Esther Williams, James
Melton, Marian Bell, Victor Moore, Lena Horne,
Gene Kelly, Kathryn Grayson (themselves),
William Powell (Florenz Ziegfeld), Bunin's
puppets (Ziegfeld stars), Cyd Charisse (ballet
dancer), Lucille Ball (woman with whip), Virginia
O'Brien (singer), Keenan Wynn (telephone
caller), Robert Lewis, Peter Lawford and others
(voices on telephone), Audrey Totter (voice of
telephone operator), Grady Sutton (Texan), Kay
Williams (woman), Edward Arnold (Moore's
lawyer), Joseph Crehan (judge), William B.
Davidson (high court judge), Harry Hayden
(warden), Ray Teal, Eddie Dunn, Garry Owen
(policemen), Sam Flint (flunky), Charles
Coleman (major-domo), Feodor Chaliapin
(lieutenant), Lucille Bremer (princess), Count
Stefanelli (duke), Naomi Childers (duchess),
Helen Boice (countess), Fred Astaire (impostor),
Robert Wayne (retired dyspeptic), Fanny Brice
(Norma), Arthur Walsh (telegraph boy), Hume
Cronyn (Monty), William Frawley (Mr Martin,
landlord), Red Skelton (J. Newton Numbskull),
Harriet Lee (singer), Fred Astaire (Tai Long),
Eugene Loring (head of costermonger family),

Lucille Bremer (Moy Ling), Robert Lewis (Chinese man), George Hill, Jack Deery (policemen), Rex Evans (butler), Judy Garland (great lady).

Musical/Dance Numbers: 'Ziegfeld Days' medley including 'It's Delightful to Be Married', 'Sunny', 'I'm an Indian', 'If You Knew Suzie'. 'Here's to the Girls' (R. Freed & Edens), sung by Astaire, male chorus, danced by Charisse, chorus. 'Bring On the Wonderful Men' (Brent & Edens), sung by O'Brien. 'Libiamo ne' lieti calici' (Piave & Verdi), sung by Melton and Bell, chorus. 'This Heart of Mine' (A. Freed & Warren), sung by Astaire, chorus, dance by Astaire and Bremer. 'Love' (Blane & Martin), sung by Horne. 'Limehouse Blues' (Furber & Braham), sung by Lee, danced by Astaire and Bremer. 'Wot Cher' (Ingle), sung by busker chorus. 'Madame Crematon' (Thompson & Edens), sung and danced by Garland, reporters. 'The Babbitt and the Bromide' (I. Gershwin & G. Gershwin), sung and danced by Astaire and Kelly. 'There's Beauty Everywhere' (A. Freed & Warren), sung by Grayson. The following numbers/sketches were cut: 'If Swing Goes, I Go Too', 'The Pied Piper', 'A Cowboy's Life', 'Liza', 'Baby Snooks and the Burglar', 'Death and Taxes', 'We'll Meet Again in Honolulu', the greater part of 'There's Beauty Everywhere' (*see* Mueller, pp.250-251).

10 May 1946
HEARTBEAT

RKO Radio Pictures. Shooting: 11 July - late September 1945. 100/102 minutes. New York premiere: 10 May, 1946.

Directed by Sam Wood. Produced by Robert Hakim and Raymond Hakim. Screenplay: Hans Wilhelm, Max Kolpe, Michel Duran, adaptation by Morris Ryskind, based on the film *Battement de Coeur* (Henri Decoin, 1939). Additional Dialogue: Roland Leigh. Director of Photography: Joseph Valentine. Art Director: Lionel Banks. Set Decorator: George Sawley. Editor: Roland Gross. Sound Recording: John Tribby. Musical Score: Paul Misraki. Musical Director: C. Bakaleinikoff. Costumes: Howard Greer. Make-up Artist: Mel Burns. Assistant Director: John Sherwood. Still Photographer: John Miehle.

With: Ginger Rogers (Arlette), Jean-Pierre Aumont (Pierre), Adolphe Menjou (ambassador), Basil Rathbone (Prof. Aristide), Eduardo Ciannelli (Baron Dvorak), Mikhail Rasumny (Yves Cadubert), Melville Cooper (Roland Medeville), Mona Maris (ambassador's wife), Henry Stephenson (minister), Eddie Hayden (fat thief).

Musical Number: 'Can You Guess' (Paul Misraki & Ervin Drake).

9 December 1946
MAGNIFICENT DOLL

A Hallmark Production for Universal-International Pictures. Shooting: late May - early August 1946. 95 minutes.

Directed by Frank Borzage. Produced by Jack H. Skirball and Bruce Manning. Screenplay: Irving Stone, based on a story by Stone. Director of Photography: Joseph Valentine. Art Supervisor: Jack Otterson. Art Director: Alexander Golitzen. Set Decorators: Russell A. Gausman, Ted Offenbecker. Editor: Ted J. Kent. Sound Recording: Charles Felstead. Sound Technician: Robert Pritchard. Musical Director: H. J. Salter. Orchestrations: David Tamkin. Costumes: Travis Banton, Vera West. Make-up Artist: Jack P. Pierce. Hair Stylists: Carmen Dirigo, Anna Malin. Hats: Lilly Dache. Assistant Director: John F. Sherwood. Production Manager: Arthur Siteman. Set Continuity: Adele Cannon.

With: Ginger Rogers (Dolly Payne), David Niven (Aaron Burr), Burgess Meredith (James Madison), Horace [Stephen] McNally (John Todd), Peggy Wood (Mrs Payne), Frances Williams (Amy), Robert H. Barrat (Mr Payne), Grandon Rhodes (Thomas Jefferson), Henri Letondal (Count D'Arignon), Joe Forte (Senator Ainsworth), Erville Alderson (Darcy), George Barrows (Jedson), Francis McDonald (Jenks, barber), Emmett Vogan (Mr Gallentine), Arthur Space (Alexander Hamilton), Joseph Crehan (Williams), Byron Foulger (servant), Larry Blake (Charles), Pierre Watkin (Harper), John Sheehan (janitor), John Hamilton (Mr Witherspoon), George Carleton (Howard), Harlan Tucker (Ralston), Vivien Oakland (Mrs Witherspoon), Al Hill (man), Olaf Hytten (Blennerhassett), Lee Phelps (Hatch), Joe King (jailor), Brandon Hurst (Brown), Harlan Briggs (Quinn), Larry Steers (Lafayette).

27 December 1946
BLUE SKIES

Paramount Pictures. Shooting: 16 July - late September 1945. 104 minutes. New York premiere: 17 October 1946.

Directed by Stuart Heisler. Produced by Sol C. Siegel. Music and lyrics: Irving Berlin. Screenplay: Arthur Sheekman, adapted by Allan Scott from an idea by Irving Berlin. Dance Director: Hermes Pan. Assistant Dance Director: David Robel. Art Directors: Hans Dreier, Hal

Pereira. Set Decoration: Sam Comer, Maurice Goodman. Costumes: Edith Head, Waldo Angelo. Costume Execution: Karinska. Musical Director: Robert Emmett Dolan. Associate Musical Director: Troy Sanders. Musical Arrangements: Mason Van Cleave, Hugo Frey, Charles Bradshaw, Ralph Hallenbeck, Matty Matlock, Sidney Fine. Vocal Arrangments: Joseph J. Lilley. Directors of Photography: Charles Lang, Jr, William Snyder. Colour Consultant: Natalie Kalmus. Associate Colour Consultant: Robert Brower. Special Photographic effects: Gordon Jennings, Paul K. Lerpae. Process Photography: Farciot Edouart. Make-up Artist: Wally Westmore. Sound Recording: Hugo Grenzbach, John Cope. Editor: LeRoy Stone. Colour: Technicolor.

With: Bing Crosby (Johnny Adams), Fred Astaire (Jed Potter), Joan Caulfield (Mary Adams, neé O'Hara) [singing dubbed by Betty Russell], Billy De Wolfe (Tony), Olga San Juan (Nita Nova), Jimmy Conlin (Jeffrey, Jed's valet), Cliff Nazarro (Cliff, pianist), Frank Faylen (Mack, stage manager), Jack Norton (drunk), Will Wright (Detroit stage manager), Victoria Horne (Martha, nanny), Karolyn Grimes (Mary Elizabeth Adams), Roy Gordon (Charles Dillingham), John M. Sullivan (Junior), Charles La Torre (Mr Rakopolis), John Kelly (tough guy), Frances Morris (hospital nurse), Vicki Jasmund, Norma Creiger, Joanne Lybrook, Louise Saraydar (quartet at 'Top Hat').

Musical/Dance Numbers: 'A Pretty Girl is Like a Melody', sung by male chorus, danced by Astaire. 'I've Got My Captain Working for Me Now', sung by Crosby and De Wolfe. 'You'd Be Surprised', sung by San Juan. 'All By Myself', sung by Crosby. 'Serenade to an Old Fashioned Girl', sung by Caulfield, male quartet. 'Puttin' On the Ritz', sung and danced by Astaire. '(I'll See You In) C-U-B-A', sung by Crosby and San Juan. 'A Couple of Song and Dance Men', sung by Crosby and Astaire with Nazarro, piano. 'You Keep Coming Back Like a Song', sung by Crosby, male chorus. 'Always', sung by chorus. 'Blue Skies', sung by Crosby. 'The Little Things in Life', sung by Crosby. 'Not for All the Rice in China', sung by Crosby. 'Russian Lullaby', sung by Crosby. 'Everybody Step', sung by Crosby, danced by chorus. 'How Deep is the Ocean?', sung by female chorus, Crosby. '(Running Around in Circles) Getting Nowhere', sung by Crosby. 'Heat Wave', sung by San Juan, chorus, danced by Astaire and San Juan, chorus. 'Any Bonds Today', sung by Crosby. 'This is the Army, Mr Jones', sung by Crosby. 'White Christmas', sung by Crosby. 'You Keep Coming Back Like a Song' and 'Blue Skies' (simultaneous reprise), sung by Crosby, Caulfield. Background: 'Tell Me, Little Gypsy', 'Nobody Knows', 'Mandy', 'Some

Sunny Day', 'When You Walked Out', 'Because I Love You', 'How Many Times?', 'Lazy', 'The Song is Ended'.

25 November 1947
IT HAD TO BE YOU

Columbia Pictures. Shooting: 6 May - 15 July 1947. 98 minutes.

Directed by Don Hartman and Rudolph Maté. Produced by Don Hartman. Assistant Producer: Norman Deming. Screenplay: Norman Panama, Melvin Frank, based on a story by Don Hartman, Allen Boretz. Additional Dialogue: Fred Sears. Directors of Photography: Rudolph Maté, Vincent Farrar. Art Directors: Stephen Goosson, Rudolph Sternad. Set Decorators: Wilbur Menefee, William Kiernan. Editor: Gene Havlick. Camera Operator: Irving Klein. Sound Recording: Jack Haynes. Musical Score: Heinz Roemheld. Musical Director: W.M. Stoloff. Orchestrations: Herschel Burke Gilbert. Costumes: Jean Louis. Hairstylist: Helen Hunt. Make-up Artist: Clay Campbell. Jewellery: Lackritz. Assistant Director: Sam Nelson. Still Photographer: Lippman.

With: Ginger Rogers (Victoria Stafford), Cornel Wilde ('George' Johnny Blaine), Percy Waram (Mr Stafford), Spring Byington (Mrs Stafford), Ron Randell (Oliver H.P. Harrington), Thurston Hall (Mr Harrington), Charles Evans (Dr Parkinson), William Bevan (Evans), Frank Orth (conductor Brown), Harry Hays Morgan (George Benson), Douglas Wood (Mr Kimberly), Mary Forbes (Mrs Kimberly), Anna Q. Nilsson (saleslady), Gerald Fielding (Peabody), Nancy Saunders (model), Douglas D. Coppin (boyfriend), Virginia Hunter (maid of honour), Michael Towne (first fireman), Fred Sears (second fireman), Paul Campbell (radio announcer), Mary Patterson (Victoria aged three), Judy Nugent (Victoria aged five), Carol Nugent (Victoria aged six), Jerry Hunt (Indian boy), Dudley Dickerson (porter), Ralph Peters (first cab driver), Garry Owen (second cab driver), Harlan Warde (Atherton), Myron Healy (Standish), Jack Rice (floorwalker), Vera Lewis (Mrs Brown), George Chandler, Vernon Dent.

26 May 1948
EASTER PARADE

Metro-Goldwyn-Mayer. Shooting: 19 November 1947 - mid-February 1948. 103 minutes.

Directed by Charles Walters. Produced by Arthur Freed. Music and lyrics: Irving Berlin. Screenplay, Sidney Sheldon, Frances Goodrich and Albert Hackett, based on an original story by Goodrich and Hackett. Additional Scriptwriting: Guy Bolton. Associate Producer: Roger Edens. Dance Director: Robert Alton. Art Directors: Cedric Gibbons, Jack Martin Smith. Set Decoration: Edwin B. Willis. Associate Set Decoration: Arthur Krams. Costumes: Irene, Valles. Hairstylist: Sydney Guilaroff. Make-up Artist: Jack Dawn. Musical Director: Johnny Green. Associate Musical Director: Roger Edens. Orchestrations: Conrad Salinger, Mason Van Cleave, Robert Franklin, Paul Marquardt, Sidney Cutner, Leo Arnaud. Vocal Arrangements: Robert Tucker. Director of Photography: Harry Stradling. Colour Consultant: Natalie Kalmus. Associate Colour Consultant: Henri Jaffa. Special Photographic Effects: Warren Newcombe. Sound Recording: Douglas Shearer. Editor: Albert Akst. Colour: Technicolor.

With: Judy Garland (Hannah Brown), Fred Astaire (Don Hewes), Peter Lawford (Jonathan Harrow, III), Ann Miller (Nadine Hale), Jules Munshin (Francois), Clinton Sundberg (Mike, bartender), Richard Beavers (singer), Jeni LeGon (Essie, Nadine's maid), Dick Simmons (Al, Ziegfeld stage manager), Jimmy Bates (boy in toy store), Jimmy Dodd (cab driver), Robert Emmett O'Connor (policeman), Wilson Wood (Marty, rehearsal pianist), Nolan Leary (drugstore clerk), Howard Mitchell, Bob Jellison (drugstore customers), Peter Chong (Sam, Don's valet), Benay Venuta (woman at bar), Helen Heigh (shopkeeper), Margaret Bert (florist), Fern Eggen (salesgirl in drum number), Albert Pollet (waiter), Angie Poulis (peddler with umbrella), Sig Frohlich (callboy at roof garden), Harry Fox (hotel desk clerk), Ralph Sanford (hotel detective), Pat Jackson, Dee Turnell, Bobbie Priest (speciality dancers in 'Steppin' Out With my Baby'), Hector and His Pals (dog act), Lynn and Jean Romer, Elaine Sterling, Lola Albright, Pat Walker, Pat Vaniver, Marjorie Jackson, Gail Langford, Shirley Ballard, Joi Lansing, Ruth Hall (cover girls in 'The Girl on the Magazine Cover' number).

Musical/Dance Numbers: 'Happy Easter', sung by Astaire, hat models, New Yorkers. 'Drum Crazy', sung and danced by Astaire. 'It Only Happens When I Dance with You', sung by Astaire, danced by Astaire and Miller. 'Everybody's Doin' It', danced by nightclub chorus, Garland. 'I Want to Go Back to Michigan', sung by Garland. 'Beautiful Faces Need Beautiful Clothes', danced by Astaire and Garland. 'A Fella With an Umbrella', sung by Lawford and Garland. 'I Love a Piano', sung by Garland, danced by Astaire and Garland. 'Snooky Ookums', sung by Astaire and Garland. 'Ragtime Violin', sung by Astaire, danced by

Astaire and Garland. 'When the Midnight Choo-Choo Leaves for Alabam' ', sung and danced by Astaire and Garland. 'Shakin' the Blues Away', sung by Miller, chorus, danced by Miller. 'It Only Happens When I Dance With You' (reprise), sung by Garland. 'Steppin' Out with my Baby', sung by Astaire, chorus, danced by Astaire, with speciality dancers, chorus. 'A Couple of Swells', sung by Astaire and Garland. 'The Girl on the Magazine Cover', sung by Beavers, with cover girls, Miller, chorus. 'Better Luck Next Time', sung by Garland. 'Easter Parade', sung by Garland and Astaire, chorus. Background: 'At the Devil's Ball', 'This is the Life', 'Along Came Ruth', 'Call Me Up Some Rainy Afternoon'. The Garland solo number 'Mr Monotony' was filmed but not used. It was included in the MGM fiftieth anniversary film, *That's Entertainment!* (Jack Haley, Jr, 1974).

15 March 1949
THE BARKLEYS OF BROADWAY

Metro-Goldwyn-Mayer. Shooting: mid-July - late October 1948. Colour: Technicolor. 109 minutes. New York premiere: 4 May 1949.

Directed by Charles Walters. Produced by Arthur Freed. Lyrics: Ira Gershwin. Music: Harry Warren. Screenplay: Betty Comden and Adolph Green. Additional Scriptwriting: Sidney Sheldon. Associate Producer: Roger Edens. Dance Directors: Robert Alton, Hermes Pan. Art Directors: Cedric Gibbons, Edward Carfagno. Set Decoration: Edwin B. Willis. Associate Set Decorator: Arthur Krams. Costumes: Irene, Valles. Musical Director: Lennie Hayton. Additional Conducting: Adolph Deutsch. Musical Arrangements: Conrad Salinger, Leo Arnaud, Paul Marquardt, Wally Heglin, Robert Franklin. Orchestrations: Wally Heglin, Robert Franklin, Lennie Hayton, Conrad Salinger. Vocal Arrangements: Robert Tucker. Director of Photography: Harry Stradling. Cameraman: Sammy Leavitt. Animation ['Dancing Shoes' Effects]: Irving G. Reis. Sound Recording: Douglas Shearer. Make-up Artist: Jack Dawn. Hairstylist: Sydney Guilaroff. Special Effects: Warren Newcombe. Assistant Director: Wallace Worsley. Colour Consultant: Natalie Kalmus. Associate Colour Consultant: Henri Jaffa. Editor: Albert Akst. Colour: Technicolor.

With: Fred Astaire (Josh Barkley), Ginger Rogers (Dinah Barkley), Oscar Levant (Ezra Miller), Billie Burke (Millie Belney), Jacques Francois (Jacques Pierre Barredout), Gale Robbins (Shirleen May), Clinton Sundberg (Bert Felsher), Inez Cooper (Pamela Driscoll), Carol Brewster (Gloria Amboy), Wilson Wood (Larry,

Rogers, Astaire and Gale Robbins in The Barkleys of Broadway.

press agent), Joyce Mathews (Genevieve), Roberta Johnson (Henrietta), Lorraine Crawford (Cleo Fernby), Margaret Bert (Mary, Dinah's maid), Frank Ferguson (Perkins, writer for 'Look' magazine), George Boyce, John Albright, Butch Terrell (photographers for 'Look' magazine), Les Clark (dancer in 'Shoes with Wings On'), Hans Conreid (Ladislaus Ladi), Jean Andren (first woman), Laura Treadwell (second woman), Allen Wood (taxi driver), Forbes Murray, Bess Flowers, Lois Austin, Betty Blythe (guests in theatre lobby), Bill Tannen (theatre doorman), Mahlon Hamilton (apartment doorman), Dee Turnell (blonde at cast party), Reginald Simpson (husband at cast party), Sherry Hall (chauffeur), Nolan Leary (stage doorman), Jack Rice (ticket man), Roger Moore (first man), Wilbur Mack, Larry Steers, Lillian West (guests), Bob Purcell (announcer at benefit concert), Claire Carleton (Marie). At rehearsal of *Young Sarah*: Joe Granby (Duke de Morny), Esther Sommers (Sarah Bernhardt's mother), Helen Eby-Rock (Sarah Bernhardt's aunt). At

performance of *Young Sarah*: George Zucco (judge), Mary Jo Ellis (Clementine Villard), Mimi Doyle (reader of speech from *Macbeth*).

Musical/Dance Numbers: 'Swing Trot', danced by Astaire and Rogers. *Sabre Dance* (Khatchaturian), played by Levant on piano. 'You'd Be Hard to Replace', sung by Astaire. 'Bouncin' the Blues', dance by Astaire and Rogers. 'My One and Only Highland Fling', sung and danced by Astaire and Rogers. 'A Weekend in the Country', sung by Astaire, Rogers, Levant. 'Shoes With Wings On', sung and danced by Astaire. Excerpt from *Piano Concerto in B-flat minor* (Tchaikovsky), played by Levant on piano, orchestra. 'They Can't Take That Away from Me' (I. Gershwin & G. Gershwin), sung by Astaire, danced by Astaire and Rogers. 'Manhattan Downbeat', sung by Astaire, chorus, dance by Astaire and Rogers, chorus. Background: 'Angel' (Freed & Warren), 'This Heart of Mine' (Freed & Warren). Unused: 'The Courtship of Elmer and Ella', 'Natchez on the Mississippi'.

ACKNOWLEDGEMENTS

First of all, I must thank those colleagues responsible for organising my teaching schedules and departmental duties in English and in Film and Television Studies at Warwick University during the period in which this book was written: Jeremy Treglown, Ginette Vincendeau and Helen Taylor. Their friendly assistance is the basis on which this book rests.

I owe scholarly debts to Michael Walker for his help with the filmography, to Richard Maltby for his comments on the manuscript, and to those who responded to early versions of parts of the material when it was presented as papers at Kings College London and Reading University. I am also grateful to Charles Silver and his staff at the Museum of Modern Art, New York, who gave me access to otherwise obscure films, and to the Warwick University Humanities Research Centre for funding this.

The reader of the book has also greatly benefited from the scholarship and commitment of my editors, Ian Cameron and Jill Hollis, and I thank them for pointing the way to many useful revisions, and for the clarity that they have introduced.

To Michael James I owe a unique debt for his unstintingly generous loan of precious materials from his comprehensive collection of images of Astaire and Rogers.

My final words are reserved for those who have cheered me on – and cheered me up – in this period of writing, and provided wise counsel in its difficult moments. They are Clive Bush, Jean Gallafent and V.F. Perkins, and I cannot thank them enough.

Edward Gallafent

November 2000

INDEX OF FILMS